MACROECONOMICS

Truths and Myths

**Brian K. Strow and
Claudia W. Strow**

Third Edition

Kendall Hunt
publishing company

Cover image courtesy Craig White

Kendall Hunt
publishing company

www.kendallhunt.com
Send all inquiries to:
4050 Westmark Drive
Dubuque, IA 52004-1840

Dedication

To Tucker, Colette, Oliver, and Thatcher

Brief Contents

Contents

Preface

When our oldest son lost his first tooth, he was very excited. Others in his school had lost teeth and had been rewarded with money. He came to us with his tooth in hand and asked with bright eyes, "Is the Tooth Fairy real?" After dodging the issue a bit and finally asking if he really wanted to know the truth, we responded that the Tooth Fairy was not real. His little face became totally dejected. We told him not to worry, that we would still place money under his pillow in the middle of the night. He responded, in a still very dejected manner, "Yes, but if the Tooth Fairy was real, our family would have more money. Since it isn't, our family isn't any richer; you have just taken money from you and given it to me."

Our son was only five years old at the time of that exchange, and he already knew the difference between wealth creation and income transfers. He also knew that Santa Claus, The Easter Bunny, The Tooth Fairy, and The Great Pumpkin didn't exist. Free stuff isn't just delivered to houses via sleighs and baskets. Wealth has to be created, and it can be destroyed. The purpose of this textbook is to teach students to be able to separate macroeconomic truths from myths.

Popular macroeconomic myths include, but are not limited to, the belief in macro-economic equilibrium, infallibility of aggregate data, collective decision making, under-consumption, spending multipliers, and long run economic death. Abstractly believing in myths doesn't have to hurt anyone, but if the belief in myths causes people to take harmful actions, we have a problem.

We find Don Quixote to be so fundamentally annoying not because he has mistaken beliefs, but because he actively harms innocent people based upon his mistaken beliefs. Don Quixote's apprentices account for the vast majority of macroeconomics professors in existence. The macroeconomic textbooks they write are not only full of myths, they are actively harmful. They create a false world of macroeconomic equilibrium in order to suggest solutions that are internally logical to their model, but inherently false to reality.

The Don Quixotes love to assume that there is some type of macroeconomic equilibrium that sits around just waiting for "shocks" to knock it out of equilibrium. The world is full of shocks, and even more surprises. Every day is a shock to some economic actor. No shop keeper knows exactly how many customers she'll have the next day. No consumer knows exactly what they will buy over the next year.

The truth is that individuals make decisions based on their perceived rational self-interest. They face uncertainty about the future and hold imperfect information about the world around them today. They act, and react, to the actions of others. People are responsive beings. Disequilibrium is the norm rather than the aberration. Prices of products constantly change. People move from one job to the next. Product lines get added and deleted. The economy is in motion, and will continue to stay in motion, as it is constantly battered by a myriad of forces reacting against each other.

Purveyors of macroeconomic equilibrium are often one and the same as those who advocate intervention in the economy to bring it back to equilibrium. They act as if not only is there equilibrium, but that they know where it is and how to get there. No one knows exactly how many ice cream cones the US needs to produce tomorrow. No one can know the "appropriate" amount of ice cream cone production for today let alone for tomorrow. The US economy makes a lot more than just ice cream cones.

There is no appropriate level of consumer spending. Therefore, there can never be over or under consumption. There is no set percentage of an economy that needs to be devoted to investment. Therefore there is never any over or under investment. What can exist are bad consumption and investment decisions due to imperfect information about the future. Policies that aim to increase consumption, investment, government spending, or exports in the short run are not only based on belief in fictitious equilibriums, they do damage to long run economic growth by misallocating resources.

Calls for economic stimulus packages are often advocated by politicians with short time horizons and ulterior motives. People engage in actions that they believe to be in their rational self interest. Unless someone out there knows how many ice cream cones the economy is supposed to be making, the appropriate price to sell them at, and who gets the cones, we should leave it up to the dairy farmer to determine his milk output, the ice cream company to determine their ice cream output, and the individual ice cream consumers to determine how much ice cream is "appropriately" consumed.

We're willing to bet that individuals wouldn't put themselves into $22.1 trillion of debt to buy ice cream. That kind of economic damage can only be done by someone mistakenly trying to fix that which was not broken, thereby breaking it in the process. How many people must the macroeconomic Don Quixotes hurt before they are held accountable?

The first part of this text is dedicated to the truths of long term economic growth. It attempts to explain why some countries are wealthier than others and how all economies can grow. The latter part of the book is dedicated to examining business cycles and government intervention therein. Students need to understand the Keynesian framework and its underlying assumptions to be able to assess its merit/lack thereof.

Students won't be required to believe in Santa Claus, but they need to understand that other people do. They need to be able to communicate with myth believers on their level. The inclusion in this text of myths such as macroeconomic equilibrium should in no way be misread as meaning that the authors believe in them. Rather, the boogey man is defined and exposed so that students will know not to be afraid of him in their sleep.

Finally, in this text we seek to weave the study of economic history, the history of economic thought, political economy, public finance, and public choice into the our examination of introductory macroeconomics. In this way we hope to improve students understanding of how and why government policies have affected wealth creation over time.

Chapter 1

Macroeconomics: An Overview

Economics is a social science that examines people's choices in a world of unlimited wants and scarce resources. Without always realizing it, individuals engage in economic decision making on a regular basis. For instance, when a student decides his or her major, chooses to apply for a job, makes decisions about how many hours to study each night, or decides to purchase the online textbook instead of the paper copy of the book, he or she is choosing how to use scarce resources to satisfy unlimited wants. Economics assumes that individuals purposefully engage in actions in search of happiness for themselves and those they care about. The study of economics further examines the intended and unintended consequences of the actions taken by individuals, businesses, and governments. While **microeconomics** examines the choices individual entities make, **macroeconomics** considers the economy as a whole to see how these choices work to create or destroy wealth over time within and between countries around the world.

Wealth Creation and Destruction

At any given point in time, there are only so many **resources** (natural resources, labor, capital, technology, and entrepreneurship) that can be used to create wealth. **Natural resources** are the material sources of wealth that exist in a natural state, including the land upon which production occurs. **Labor** refers to the time humans spend producing. **Capital** is a long lasting tool used for production. **Human capital** is the education, skill set, experience, and knowledge that people have. **Physical Capital** refers to forms of capital that are not human, such as a machine or factory. **Technology** specifically describes innovations that increase the usefulness of capital or electronic forms of capital. New technology is one possible product of entrepreneurship. **Entrepreneurship** refers to combining resources in a new or innovative way or risk taking. Entrepreneurship includes inventing new products or product lines, improving the quality of existing products, increasing the efficiency of existing production and distribution, engaging in arbitrage or risk taking, and connecting sellers with buyers or connecting financiers with producers.

© wavebreakmedia/Shutterstock.com

Each of these resources is scarce. **Scarcity** exists when something is limited. If you are a college student, you may find yourself with lots of free time. On the other hand, you may be working and going to school full-time and may have very little free time. Either way, I would imagine most college students feel that time is scarce. Even if they have a lot of free time, they still would like to have more time in the day. As your time is limited, you must make decisions about how to allocate it. Will you go out tonight with friends or stay in and study? Will you study one subject in great detail or will you study for several classes in less detail? Just as you decide how to allocate your scarce time, society must make choices as to how to allocate scarce resources as it determines what to produce, how to produce it, and for whom to produce.

Unlike energy, wealth can be created or destroyed. An increase in the production of output is referred to as **economic growth**. In 1651, Thomas Hobbes described the natural state of mankind as being "solitary, poor, nasty, brutish, and short."[1] For most of human history, life expectancy at birth remained under 40 years of age and most people's major economic concerns revolved around oft-rotting food, simple clothing, make-shift shelter, and herbal "remedies."

---

[1] Thomas Hobbes. *The Leviathan*

Then along came the industrial revolution, whose roots, according to Deirdre McCloskey, were in the bourgeois revolution, which started in Holland and moved to Britain and its offshoots.[2] This cultural revolution changed people's attitudes regarding the morality of wealth creation. Active pursuit of wealth creation went from being viewed as immoral to being viewed as a way to improve the standard of living. As a result, life in the industrial world is no longer defined according to Hobbesian lamentation. As shown in Table 1.1 and Figure 1.1, most of the world's wealth has been created in a relatively short period of time.

* Note that per capita income is the average income per person. The world per capita income is found by dividing the world's income by the world's population.

TABLE 1.1[3]			
Year	World Per Capita Income (1990 dollars)	World Population (In Millions)	World Income (Billions of $1990)
0	$425	250	$106
1000	$420	273	$115
1500	$545	431	$235
1820	$675	1067	$1,067
1995	$5,188	5,671	$29,423

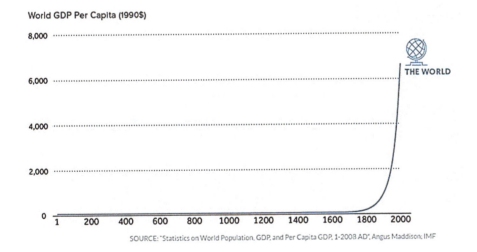

Figure 1.1

[2] McCloskey, Deirdre (2011). *Bourgeois Dignity: Why Economics Can't Explain the Modern World.* University of Chicago Press

[3] Angus Maddison, "Statistics on world population, GDP and per capita GDP, 1–2008 AD." (2010): 9–266.

Victoria Falls in Zambia
and Zimbabwe

Unfortunately wealth destruction exists as well. Choices that result in wars, most notably civil wars, can lead to rapid wealth destruction. Choices that create unpredictable economic rules of the game can also make countries poorer. Countries that have difficulty defining and enforcing property rights have difficulty creating wealth. A **property right** is the legal authority to use or consume an item as the owner sees fit. Zimbabwe was once the bread basket of Africa. Now, due largely to poor decisions made by its government, Zimbabwe is one of the poorest places on earth.

The year 1776 marked an important year for the study of macroeconomics in the context of the United States, as two major things happened in that year. The United States declared independence from Great Britain just a few months after Adam Smith published his book, *An Inquiry into the Nature and Causes of the Wealth of Nations.*[4] Smith wanted to understand why some countries become wealthier than others.

A lot has changed in the US economy since 1776. Table 1.2 illustrates that GDP per capita (average output per person) in the United States increased almost sixty-fold between 1650 and 2016. By 2019, the US was producing over $21 trillion worth of goods and services per year. As Table 1.3 shows, this makes the US economy the largest economy in the world. But is it the best?

TABLE 1.2[5]	
Year	**US Per Capita Income (1990 dollars)**
1650	$563
1720	$863
1775	$1,181
1830	$1,483
1885	$3,135
1940	$7,094
1995	$24,712
2016	$33,259

[4] Adam Smith. *An Inquiry into the Nature and Causes of The Wealth of Nations.* Edwin Cannan, ed. London: Methuen Co., Ltd. 1904.

[5] Maddison Project Database, version 2018 by Jutta Bolt, Robert Inklaar, Herman de Jong and Jan Luiten van Zanden

Source "World Economic Outlook Database". International Monetary Fund. 1 October 2018

TABLE 1.3[6]	2018 TOP 10 COUNTRIES BY NOMINAL GDP (OUTPUT) IN BILLIONS OF US DOLLARS				
Rank	**Country**	**GDP**	**Rank**	**Country**	**GDP**
1	United States	$20,513	6	France	$2,795
2	China	$13,457	7	India	$2,690
3	Japan	$5,071	8	Italy	$2,087
4	Germany	$4,029	9	Brazil	$1,909
5	United Kingdom	$2,809	10	Canada	$1,734

Determining Which Economy Is "Best"

The term "best" is a normative term. **Normative economics** refers to value laden economic analysis, or analysis based on an opinion. Like beauty, "best" is in the eye of the beholder. Still, an individual's determination of "best" is likely to be grounded in positive facts. Positive facts are statements that can be proven or disproven. **Positive economics** refers to economic analysis that is testable and fact based. If the "best" economy produces the most output per person, then the US does not have the "best" economy, Luxembourg does (see Table 1.4). If the "best" economy is one that produces the most wealth, then the US economy, being the world's largest, is the best.

Still, "best" might refer to factors other than production. If the "best" economy simply is the one that produces the most goods, slavery might be seen by some as "best" if it produces more output than a free society. If the "best"

TABLE 1.4	2017 PER CAPITA NOMINAL GDP IN US DOLLARS				
Rank	**Country**	**GDP per person**	**Rank**	**Country**	**GDP per person**
1	Luxembourg	$105,863	6	Qatar	$61,024
2	Switzerland	$80,637	7	United States	$59,792
3	Norway	$75,389	8	Singapore	$57,713
4	Iceland	$70,248	9	Denmark	$56,630
5	Ireland	$68,710	10	Australia	$55,692

[6] US Bureau of Economic Analysis, 2018

Hong Kong

economy is the one that provides the most economic freedom for individuals, then Hong Kong has the "best" (most free market) economy according to the Heritage Foundation (see Table 1.5).

Does wellbeing depend solely on money or freedom? Denmark tops the list of the happiest countries in the world. The government of Bhutan is so concerned with happiness that their national goal is to maximize gross national happiness rather than gross national product. Which, if any, of these countries is "best"? Which, if any, of these countries would you prefer to live in?

The goal of this book is not to instruct students as to which is the "best" economy in the world, because the answer to which is "best" depends on the values of the readers. Rather, through use of positive facts, readers are encouraged to determine for themselves what the "best" economy looks like and learn the appropriate policies for a "better" economy as they define it.

TABLE 1.5[7]	2018 INDEX OF ECONOMIC FREEDOM, WORLD RANKINGS		
Rank	**Country**	**Rank**	**Country**
1	Hong Kong	6	Ireland
2	Singapore	7	Estonia
3	New Zealand	8	United Kingdom
4	Switzerland	9	Canada
5	Australia	10	United Arab Emirates
.			
.			
.			
171	Djibouti	176	Eritrea
172	Algeria	177	Republic of Congo
173	Bolivia	178	Cuba
174	Zimbabwe	179	Venezuela
175	Equitorial Guinea	180	North Korea

[7] 2018 Heritage Foundation Index of Economic Freedom World Rankings

Nevertheless, most people think of wealth creation as a good thing. Most people would rather have more and better food than less food or worse quality food. Most people would rather live in a house than be homeless. Most people would prefer to wear clothes and have access to life-enhancing and extending health care than be naked or without access to health care. Wealth cannot be consumed until it is created. As a result, one reason to study macroeconomics is out of a desire to understand how countries can create wealth over time to make the world a place where an increasingly large number of people have a larger number of their needs and wants met.

Who Plans for Whom?

In a **free market economy**, individuals make decisions about what to produce, how to produce, and who gets the output. In a **command economy**, the government makes these decisions for its people. In reality, every country has some level of government intervention in their economy. **Mixed economies** occur when individuals make some economic decisions and governments make others. The US economy, then, is best described as a mixed economy. Most adult individuals in the United States choose which breakfast cereal they consume, and they choose whether or not to consume breakfast cereal at all. On the other hand, most state and local governments have decided to produce and require elementary education. Some economic decisions are made by individuals for their own benefit, while others are made by governments for the perceived benefit of their citizenry.

As noted in Table 1.5, Hong Kong and Singapore have the most free market economies in the world while North Korea, Venezuela, and Cuba have the most centralized command economies. The United States was ranked the 18th freest economy in the 2018 Heritage Foundation rankings of economic freedom. As such, citizens of the United States are accustomed to making more of their own economic choices than are citizens in most of the rest of the world. However, over the last decade, the United States has declined in its economic freedom ranking as various levels of government in the United States have started to make more economic decisions. The Affordable Health Care Act is an example where the US federal government has decided to make economic decisions regarding health insurance for millions of Americans.

The question of who should control economic decision-making and economic planning has been most distinctly addressed in the history of economic thought by Friedrich Von Hayek and Lord John Maynard Keynes. The former was of the belief that decision making and planning is best done by individuals who better know their own tastes and preferences, while the latter believed that government experts, through the collection of macroeconomic data, could better direct the economy in such a way as to meet the goals of society. Figure 1.2

GDP per Capita (Purchasing Power Parity)

Each circle represents a nation in the *Index of Economic Freedom*

Correlation: 0.647

Overall Score in the *2018 Index of Economic Freedom*

**Figure 1.2
ECONOMIC
FREEDOM AND
STANDARD OF
LIVING**

illustrates the strong positive correlation between individual decision-making (economic freedom) and economic prosperity. Figure 1.2 shows that this is true for countries in every continent.

The study of macroeconomics is full of tradeoffs for society. Sometimes society faces tradeoffs between lower unemployment and lower inflation, between short term economic stability and long term economic growth, or between lower income inequality and economic growth. It's not enough to say that unemployment is "bad." The real question becomes "what does society have to give up in order to lower unemployment today. Will inflation increase as a result? Will future unemployment increase? Will liberty decrease?"

This is where macroeconomics runs into the problem of aggregation. What may be a good idea for one consumer or businessperson may be a bad idea for another. If there is a glut of unrented condos in Las Vegas, but a shortage of new homes in Austin, should the federal government encourage across the board construction of new residential units? Should government data crunchers be pleased when government policies increase the glut of unsold Las Vegas condos?

Individuals make decisions based not only on what they know, but also on what they think will happen in the future. Unfortunately, no one has perfect information about the future. In part, that is because the future is determined not just by one individual's actions, but also by the decisions of others. If everyone else jumps off of a bridge, you still do not have to. Nevertheless, others jumping off the bridge may impact you if you are an ambulance driver, a doctor, or a performance artist in need of a flash mob.

If consumers, as a whole, decrease their savings rate and increase their consumption rates while you do the opposite, are you helped or hurt? It depends. In a market economy, their extra borrowing will give you an even greater return on your savings. If, however, the large number of borrowers turns to the government to bail them out of debt, then the government could ask the minority savers to foot the bill through higher taxes or a decrease in the value of their savings (as more money is printed).

Business people have to make choices about what to produce, how to produce it, and how to price their products. They too must work with imperfect information. Surely, yacht builders need to ponder the direction of the economy before they expand their businesses. If the economy is doing well, yacht sales should prosper. If the economy goes into recession, the demand for luxury items, like yachts, might fall.

It is not always obvious how the decisions of others will impact one's future decisions. As a result, people often make mistakes when planning for their futures or the futures of their businesses. The question is not one of whether or not dynamic planning needs to take place in an organized society. The question, as put forth by Friedrich Von Hayek, becomes "who plans for whom?"

What's Ahead

The first part of this text focuses on addressing the same question examined by Adam Smith: why are some countries richer than others? The study of the origins of countries' wealth in Smith's time was known as political economy. It was so named because government intervention in the economy, or lack thereof, has a profound impact on the growth rate of economies. For that matter, our notion of "an economy" is often that of a nation-state's economy. Since data is collected at national levels, economies tend to be defined by political borders where the subjects therein live and work within the institutional rules of the game set up by their respective government.

Governments can, and do, change over time. Politicians can be voted out of office; Monarchs can be beheaded; dictators can be overthrown. When campaigning for the US presidency in 1992, Bill Clinton's famous political tagline was "It's the economy, stupid." Politics, and therefore government institutions, shape and are shaped by macroeconomic conditions.

Macroeconomics, as a discipline, came out of The Great Depression. People wanted to understand not just long term economic trends in an economy, but also why economic growth does not happen every year at the same pace. Throughout history, the economy has experienced **business cycles**, or alternating periods of economic growth and economic contraction (see Figure 1.3).

Along with changing growth rates come the Scylla and Charybdis[8] (rock and a hard place) of price and employment instability. When average price levels increase, that is **inflation**. When they decrease, that is **deflation**. Volatile prices and **unemployment** tend to dominate short term political considerations. Unemployed workers translate into unhappy voters. People hurt by inflation (such as that of the late 1970's) and deflation (such as that of the late 1800's) often turn their anger to politicians as well. The middle portion of the text explores short term fluctuations in the economy. This portion of the text begins by defining and clarifying the economic problems of slowed growth, unstable prices, and unemployment.

In the 1930's, John Maynard Keynes wrote, *The General Theory*[9] which focused on short term fluctuations in the economy. It is from this book that modern macroeconomics became a discipline that tried to explain, and smooth out, short term economic fluctuations. Keynes' economic analysis was confined to the short run economy because he said, "…in the long run, we are all dead."[10]

The two Keynesian macroeconomic interventions intended to reduce economic volatility are fiscal and monetary policy. **Fiscal policy** involves changing the level of taxes and government spending to minimize economic fluctuations. In the United States, fiscal policy is largely handled by Congress and the President—though state and local governments sometimes conduct fiscal policy actions as well. **Monetary policy** involves increasing or decreasing the money supply to minimize economic fluctuations. In the US, monetary policy is handled by the central bank known as **The Federal Reserve**.

---

[8] A reference from Homer's *Odyssey* where Odysseus must choose to sail between two monsters.

[9] John Maynard Keynes, *The General Theory of Employment, Interest, and Money,* 1936.

[10] Ibid.

The text then examines how Keynesian fiscal and monetary policies are sometimes used in an effort to smooth out these macroeconomic conditions, but come with both short and long term tradeoffs. As such, the advantages and disadvantages of using fiscal and monetary policy are discussed.

In the end, the US economy is not an economic island. Its uses of fiscal and monetary policy impact, and are impacted by, the global economy. It is therefore important to study the US economy in an international context in order to advocate economic policies consistent with reality. The text concludes by examining the economy in an international context.

Ideas matter. By studying how countries become wealthier, or poorer, over time, students can become better advocates of government policies designed to meet their objectives. By studying short term economic fluctuations, students also can learn about the pros and cons of adopting short term economic "fixes" to the economy. Why study macroeconomics? For the same reason people study anything: to better understand and improve the world. The goal of this macroeconomics text is to make people of all ideologies better decision makers by helping them to better understand macroeconomic truths and myths.

Figure 1.3
CHANGES IN REAL GDP BY QUARTER 1947 TO 2018

Key Terms

Business cycles	Federal Reserve	Microeconomics	Property right
Capital	Fiscal policy	Mixed economy	Resources
Command economy	Free market economy	Monetary policy	Scarcity
Deflation	Human capital	Natural resources	Technology
Economic growth	Inflation	Normative economics	Unemployment
Economics	Labor	Physical Capital	
Entrepreneurship	Macroeconomics	Positive economics	

Questions for Review

1. What is economics? How does the study of macroeconomics differ from that of microeconomics?

2. In your opinion, what type of economy is "best"? What values would you use to determine best?

3. Who is in charge of fiscal policy in the United States? Who is in charge of monetary policy in the United States?

4. Which is more important to you: understanding policies that create long run economic growth or understanding policies that minimize short run economic volatility? Why? Which mattered more to Keynes? To Hayak?

5. Which of the following examples would be considered a macroeconomic topic and which would be considered a microeconomic topic?

   a. An increase in the growth rate of overall output in the United States

   b. The unemployment rate of nurses in Canada

   c. The overall unemployment rate of the United States labor force

   d. The rising price of college tuition over the last decade in the United States

   e. An increase in the overall average price level in the United States

   f. A decrease in the demand for American produced automobiles

6. Classify each of the following statements as either a normative or positive statement

   a. Capital gains taxes should be lowered to increase economic growth.

   b. If capital gains taxes are lowered, economic growth will increase.

   c. The current rate of unemployment is too high.

   d. The current rate of unemployment is 7.5%.

   e. Consumption has fallen in the US over the last decade.

   f. The US government should remove tariffs on sugar from other countries.

7. As noted in this chapter, the United States has a mixed economy. List examples of decisions that are made by individuals in the United States. List examples of economic decisions that are made by the government in the United States.

8. Is economic freedom positively or negatively correlated with per capita income? Why do you think this case?

Chapter 2

Production

"Happiness is not in the mere possession of money; it lies in the joy of achievement, in the thrill of creative effort."

— *Franklin D. Roosevelt*

At a minimum, humans need food, water, and shelter from the elements in order to survive. A diverse diet, clean water, element-resisting clothing and shelter, and access to quality health care can further increase life expectancy. Aside from these material necessities of life, people desire other goods and services. People enjoy food that tastes good, beverages that fizzle with stimulant or relaxant effects, shelter that provides heat in the winter and air conditioning in the summer, cholesterol medicine to undo the effects of double-bacon cheeseburgers, and access to education and entertainment from books, multi-media, and travel.

The chief economic problem is that, at any given time, resources are scarce. An apple, once eaten by Eve, cannot also be eaten by Adam. The challenge for the world's economy is to produce enough wealth each year to meet the needs and some of the wants of its inhabitants. With roughly seven billion people in the world, there are lots of needs and wants. Nevertheless, never before in world history have so many people had their needs and wants met. This is the result of wealth creation.

As the world's population grows, more wealth must be created annually in order to meet the needs and wants of a larger population. Furthermore, as people's needs and desires become increasingly met, they begin to expect even more wants to be met in the future. Unrealized expectations of future wealth tends to breed discontentment. Therefore, economic growth is important.

Does this mean that people *ought* to make their happiness dependent upon material consumption? Money can't buy you love, but starving to death is also a drag. It turns out that people like to consume at least as much as those around them. Even in the Ten Commandments, there were religious rules that frowned upon covetousness. The desire to "keep up with the Joneses" causes people to desire ever more economic growth and wealth.

One task of macroeconomics is to determine if a country's economy is doing a better or worse job of meeting the needs and desires of the people who live in that country. This isn't a perfect science. The United States has over 300 million inhabitants, so it is unrealistic that the government would be able to exactly know how much wealth was produced in any given year. In lieu of the exact answer, governments create proxy data that gives keen, but imperfect, insight into wealth creation. In this chapter, we examine the most commonly reported measurements for production, outline imperfections with these measurements, and examine some of the highest and lowest producing countries according to these measurements. We then introduce an application that illustrates the trad-eoffs we experience when producing.

Measuring Production

The most popular global measurement of wealth creation is **Gross Domestic Product** (GDP). GDP is the total market value of all final goods and services produced within a given country in a given year. It is typically measured on a **quarterly** (3 month) basis. If GDP estimates are higher from one quarter to the next, the economy is considered to be growing. If GDP estimates are lower from one quarter to the next, the economy is considered to be in a **contraction**. A **recession** is a prolonged period of overall economic contraction typically lasting at least two consecutive quarters. Official dating of US recessions is handled by the **Business Cycle Dating Committee** at the National Bureau of Economic

Research. According to the NBER, they define a recession as "a significant decline in economic activity spread across the economy, lasting more than a few months, normally visible in real GDP, real income, employment, industrial production, and wholesale-retail sales."[1]

GDP measures production, not consumption or happiness. The idea is to count the value of all final goods produced within a given quarter. If an orange is grown in Florida, shipped to Michigan, and sold at a grocery store to a consumer during one economic quarter, then there are a number of productive steps that need to be accounted for. An orange farmer picked an orange, a trucker transported the orange, and the grocer housed, displayed, and advertised the orange. The final sales price of the orange is then counted in GDP. That sales price takes into account all of the factors that went into getting the orange to the shelf. If an orange grows in a grove and nobody picks it, ships it, or markets it, then GDP won't go up.

© Africa Studio, 2012, under license Shutterstock, Inc.

A technical problem arises when a good (such as an orange) is produced at one farm and then is transformed into a different good (orange juice) at a different plant. In this case the orange is an **intermediate good**. Intermediate goods are goods that go into the production of a final product, and they cannot be counted in GDP without resulting in a double counting of output. In this way, a new orange sold for direct consumption in the produce aisle has to be counted as a final product, whereas one that is used to produce a future product is not. Thus, determining GDP is not as easy as just counting oranges that come off of the farm.

What if the orange is produced at the end of a quarter and placed into a jar of marmalade at the beginning of the next quarter? Since GDP attempts to measure production that occurs in each quarter, the orange needs to count as having been produced in the previous quarter, and its value must be subtracted from the final sales price of the marmalade that is finished and sold in the second quarter. In this case, the orange is referred to as **inventory**. Inventory is production that has occurred, but with which no final sale, and therefore no sales receipt, has occurred.

What if the orange is grown in Mexico, but put into juice that is otherwise made in Ohio? US GDP only is supposed to count production that happens within the physical borders of the United States. Therefore, the value of the orange must be counted as it enters the US and subtracted from the final sale price of the juice in order to determine how much GDP increased from the production of the juice.

---

[1] Public Information Office, National Bureau of Economic Research, Inc., 1050 Massachusetts Avenue, Cambridge MA 02138.

If an American juice company produces the whole juice in Mexico and sells it in Peru, US GDP won't increase at all. Conversely, if a foreign juice company produces juice in Ohio, the value of this juice is counted in US GDP. **Gross National Product** (GNP) measures the total market value of all final goods and services produced by a country's companies in a given year. GNP is not commonly used as a measure of an economy's health. A country's companies could shut down all of their domestic plants and move their jobs overseas, which may increase US GNP, but it would hurt US GDP. GDP does a better job than GNP of accounting for output derived from a country's resources.

The **Bureau of Economic Analysis** (BEA) is in charge of calculating GDP. They do so by employing the expenditure approach. They count up the demand for all final goods and services in the economy and break them into five categories: **consumption** (C), **investment** (I), **government spending** (G), and **exports** (X)-**imports** (M). Note that exports-imports is called **Net Exports**.

© Joy Brown, 2012, under license Shutterstock, Inc.

© Ferenc Cegledi, 2012, under license Shutterstock, Inc.

GDP = C + I + G + X − M

If a final good or service (other than new residential construction) is purchased by a consumer, then that purchase is counted as consumption. Consumption is the largest category of GDP.

For example, the purchase of a new car and the bill from a doctor's visit are each consumption expenditures counted in GDP. The BEA tracks retail receipts and employment data to determine the levels of consumption in the US economy. If a consumer buys a used car for $5,000 from the used car lot, GDP does not go up by $5,000. The production of that car was counted when it was first produced. If the car dealership paid $3,000 to obtain the car and then resold it for $5,000 then used car dealer services are said to have been provided, and GDP would increase by $2,000.

The investment category includes the purchase of new capital, equipment, and software by businesses and governments, changes in inventory of unsold products, and the purchase of new homes by consumers. If a winery grows grapes and makes wine in a given year but places the wine bottles in their cellar to age, inventory levels increase by the cost of production, as does GDP for the year in which production took place. When the bottle is sold a year later for $40, consumption data will show an increase in GDP of $40, but investment data will show a decrease in inventory (say the $15 it took to produce the wine), and GDP on net will go up by $25 in the new year.

Government spending, for GDP purposes, is not the same as a government's budget. The only portions of the government's budget that gets counted in GDP are payments for final goods or services. If a teacher is paid by a government to teach for $40,000 a year, then GDP increases by that amount. If your grandmother is paid $24,000 a year in Social Security payments, those payments are not counted in GDP. Your grandmother, the lovely person that she may or may not be, does not produce a good or perform a service in exchange for her check, and GDP is a measure of production. Should your grandmother be paid by the USO to sing and dance for American troops, her salary would be included in GDP. Approximately two thirds of the US federal government's budget is made up of **transfer payments**. Transfer payments just take money from Peter to give it to Paul. They are not counted in GDP.

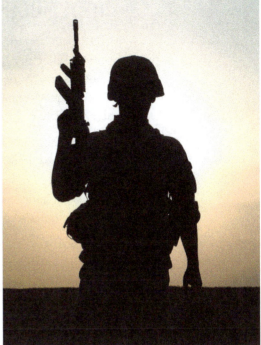

When the government pays people to provide national defense, it is considered to be a service and is counted as government spending, even if the military serviceperson is physically stationed outside of the physical boundaries of the US. In such a way, US GDP rose in WWII, as the US government funded the war effort around the globe. In this case, while US employees and capital are being employed, the "within a country" definition is less precise. Public safety, however, is being consumed by people inside of the country.

Net exports count exports (X) minus imports (M). An **export** is something that is produced domestically but sold abroad. An **import** is something that is produced abroad but purchased domestically. If you buy a banana at the local grocery store, the odds are strong that that banana was not grown in the United States, yet a sales receipt for say, $1, would be generated. Consumption increases in GDP by $1. However, when that banana hit the US border, it had a value of less than a dollar (the cost of growing it and shipping it to the US), say 75 cents. By subtracting the 75 cents worth of production that happened overseas, net GDP only increases by the remaining 25 cents.

Imperfections with GDP

GDP is an imperfect measure of production and an even more imperfect measure of wellbeing. As a measure of production, it fails to account for non-market activities, unreported incomes, and activities that transpire on the black market. If these are systematically repeated errors, then changes in GDP are still a reliable estimate of whether the economy is producing more or less than before.

Non-market transactions are transactions that do not generate sales receipts or wage data. If you mow your own grass, GDP does not go up. If you hire a lawn service and pay them $25 to mow the same grass, GDP increases by $25. Hiring out household chores (that would otherwise have been done by members of the household) does not increase production, but it does increase GDP.

From babysitting to unreported server tips, economic production often goes unreported. When was the last time you held a yard sale and reported any of the income you earned as retail services to the IRS? International GDP estimates may be difficult to compare depending on the percentage of each economy done outside the watchful eye of government accountants.

Some producers explicitly avoid informing the federal government of their production. These producers operate in the **black market**. Drug lords and organized criminals do not tend to report their production to the government because the products they are producing are illegal. From drugs to gambling to prostitution, economic production occurs, but does not make it into GDP estimates. In this way, illegal drug producing countries' GDPs may grossly underestimate how much production is really happening in their economy.

Given that the US economy produces over $21 trillion worth of goods and services in a year, it is safe to assume that not everything gets counted. In fact, quarterly GDP estimates are just that. In the month following the end of a quarter, the BEA releases its advanced estimate of quarterly GDP, using data it has collected thus far regarding economic activity in that quarter. The next month, they revise the preliminary estimate as they collect more data. The second, and last, revision comes with the final report two months after the initial estimate. Even then, the final estimate is made from survey data rather than actually adding up trillions of dollars of transactions.

GDP has larger problems serving as a measure of wellbeing. In order to account more broadly for changes in wellbeing, changes in GDP would need to be considered along with changes in leisure, environmental quality, personal health, natural disasters, wars, capital depreciation, liberty, population, income inequality, and price levels.

GDP per capita measures the average output per person. As such, it is a better measurement of people's available resources.

GDP PER CAPITA = GDP ÷ POPULATION

Yet, it too is an imperfect measurement of wellbeing. For instance, the US has a higher level of per capita GDP than France, but the French work fewer weeks per year than their American counterparts. Output per hour worked in France is actually higher than in the US. The per capita GDP of Qatar may lead the world but it may tell us very little about how the average person in Qatar is doing if there is a high level of income inequality.

GDP and GDP per capita also fail to report the level of environmental damage being produced in a given year. A country can boost its GDP by logging all of its trees, but The Lorax[2] will be happy to point out why that might harm people's long term quality of life. GDP may increase if a country dumps its toxins into rivers, but doing so will likely lower the health and wellbeing of those who rely on rivers and lakes for food or tourism.

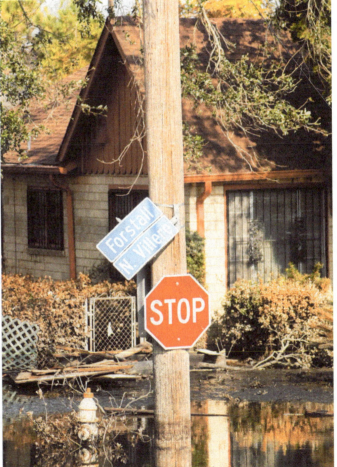

Likewise, GDP does not include a measurement of liberty. For instance, GDP in the southern US fell dramatically after emancipation. Freed slaves worked fewer hours and in more pleasant working environments following emancipation. Yet, few would say that emancipation was a bad thing, despite GDP decreasing. Much like slavery, a military draft can increase GDP by forcing people to do work for which they did not volunteer. To assume that an increase in GDP during a war draft is "good" is to prefer output over liberty.

GDP also often increases due to natural disasters. If a hurricane destroys a city and the city is rebuilt, the rebuilding of the city is included in GDP, but people aren't any better off than before the flood. The broken window fallacy[3] is to assume that breaking people's windows in order to give jobs to window repairmen is a source of wealth creation. Wars often fall into this category.

Hurricane Katrina rebuilding efforts increased GDP, but the hurricane did not make society better off.

---

[2] Seuss, Dr. Lorax. New York, Random House [1971]

[3] The fallacy noted by Frederic Bastiat in his 1850 essay "That Which is Seen and That Which is Unseen"

Inflation causes Nominal GDP to increase, just by increasing the prices for which goods are sold. **Nominal GDP** is GDP in today's prices. In order to more accurately measure if the economy produced more or less output from one time period to the next, we should examine **Real GDP** (RGDP), which is nominal GDP controlling for changes in prices. Therefore, when the BEA releases its economic growth numbers each quarter, they do so by reporting changes in RGDP.

$$\text{REAL GDP} = \frac{\text{NOMINAL GDP}}{\text{(GDP DEFLATOR)}} \times 100,$$

where the GDP deflator is a measure of price changes relative to a base year of comparison. In other words, Real GDP transforms GDP into the prices of another year (the base year).

While GDP is not a perfect indicator of production or wellbeing, a change in per capita RGDP is helpful for understanding if an economy is doing a better or worse job of producing the wealth necessary to meet the needs and desires of its citizens.

International Comparisons of GDP Per Capita

Table 2.1 compares GDP per capita between countries in 2017 US dollars. As some countries grow faster than others, their ranking in Table 2.1 continues to change on a yearly basis. Faster economic growth rates move an economy up, while slower or negative growth rates move a country's rank further down.

The **rule of 72** can help explain why seemingly small changes in GDP growth rates can impact people's quality of life over time. By dividing 72 by annual growth rate in GDP, we can find how many years it will take at that growth rate for GDP to double. For instance, an economy with a 3% annual growth rate will find that its GDP will double over 24 years compared to the 36 years needed by an economy with a 2% annual growth rate. This one percentage point change in growth can determine whether GDP after 72 years will have risen 8 fold (with a 3% annual rate of growth) or just 4 fold (with a 2% annual rate of growth).

When it comes to meeting the basic needs of humans, economic growth is most crucial in the world's poorest countries. We now turn our attention to examining tradeoffs individuals, businesses, governments, and society make when deciding what to produce.

TABLE 2.1	2017 PER CAPITA GDP IN US $[4]				
Rank	**Country**	**US $**	**Rank**	**Country**	**US $**
1	Luxembourg	$105,863	162	Ethiopia	$873
2	Switzerland	$80,637	163	Nepal	$834
—	Macau	$77,111	164	Benin	$830
3	Norway	$75,389	165	Tajikistan	$824
4	Iceland	$70,248	166	Mali	$811
5	Ireland	$68,710	167	Chad	$810
6	Qatar	$61,024	168	Guinea-Bissau	$794
7	United States	$59,792	169	Comoros	$788
8	Singapore	$57,713	170	Haiti	$784
9	Denmark	$56,630	171	Rwanda	$772
10	Australia	$55,692	172	Guinea	$749
11	Sweden	$52,925	173	Liberia	$729
12	Netherlands	$48,555	174	Uganda	$699
13	San Marino	$47,595	175	Burkina Faso	$664
14	Austria	$47,347	176	Togo	$611
—	Hong Kong	$46,080	177	Afghanistan	$588
15	Finland	$45,927	178	Yemen	$551
16	Canada	$45,094	179	Sierra Leone	$491
17	Germany	$44,769	180	Gambia, The	$480
18	Belgium	$43,488	181	Democratic Republic of the Congo	$478
19	New Zealand	$41,572	182	Madagascar	$448
20	Israel	$40,272	183	Niger	$440
21	France	$39,932	184	Mozambique	$429
22	United Kingdom	$39,800	185	Central African Republic	$387
23	Japan	$38,448	186	Malawi	$324
24	United Arab Emirates	$37,732	187	Burundi	$312
25	Italy	$31,996	188	South Sudan	$228

[4] Source: World Economic Outlook Database, October 2018, International Monetary Fund. Accessed on 10 October 2018.

Opportunity Cost

Individuals make decisions every day. If you are a college student, you probably must decide what, if anything, to eat for breakfast, whether or not to attend class, what to major in, whether or not to work while in school, and many many more decisions. Businesses decide what to produce, how much to charge for their product, and which resources to use in the production of that output. Governments decide how much to tax, who to tax, and how to spend those tax revenues (or borrowed funds). While most college students want to earn a good grade in macroeconomics, few if any of them will spend 168 hours a week studying for the one class. Studying is not free. It is not that students face a bill from their instructor every time they open up their text; it is that time is scarce and so tradeoffs have to be made. The remainder of this chapter examines the tradeoffs made in decision making and introduces a tool to help in the understanding of production tradeoffs.

So what does it cost to study an extra hour of macroeconomics? The true cost is known as opportunity cost. **Opportunity cost** is the next best forgone alternative. It is the concept that illustrates that nothing in life is free. Because everything has a cost, people compare costs and benefits in order to make choices. Suppose the gas station gives out "free" gas. Why is it not really free? What else could you be doing with your time besides waiting in line at the pump? If you miss out on the chance to meet a friend for coffee, then that is your opportunity cost of getting the "free" gas. Much like Isaac Newton's 3rd law of motion, every action has an equal and opposite reaction. In the physical universe, actions cause reactions. Choices have consequences, both intended and unintended.

In order for consumers to maximize their happiness, or for business persons to their profit, or even for governments to maximize the wellbeing of their constituents, they must follow the **golden rule of economics**. Rational happiness or profit maximization occurs when people engage in an action as long as the **marginal benefit** of that action is equal to or greater than the **marginal cost** of that action—including all relevant opportunity costs. The marginal benefit is the added benefit from undertaking an action, while the marginal cost is the added cost.

To know simply that the marginal benefit of an action is greater than zero does not provide enough information to determine if it is a good idea. It's like a one-handed clap, or a pair of one-sided scissors. Rational decisions must take the marginal cost of an action into

Even reading a library book is not free.

account as well. Looking only at marginal costs in a vacuum is as equally illogical as only looking at marginal benefits. Do high speed trains have a marginal benefit to society? Yes. Do those marginal benefits exceed their marginal costs in low population density areas? Not likely.

"Who wants more federal education spending?" Again, the answer is not that straightforward. How will the money be used to help education? Will it build buildings, provide texts, or pay teachers or administrators more? If the government increases education spending, what will it be replacing? Will it lower health care or defense spending? Will it reduce consumption or investment if taxes are raised to pay for the spending?

Opportunity costs occur both in the present and the future, but never in the past. Costs incurred in the past that can't be undone are known as **sunk costs**. They are irrelevant to the rational decision making process.

What is the opportunity cost of continuing to read this chapter? Hint: it is not the price you paid for the book, because that is a sunk cost. Instead, the opportunity cost is whatever action you are giving up by reading this book. Perhaps this is forgone time sleeping, watching television, or working out. Note the opportunity cost is not all of those activities, but just your next best option which you forgo by reading the book. Also note that even if you have checked out this book for "free" at the library, reading it is certainly not free. (Nevertheless, we believe the marginal benefit of reading the book likely exceeds the marginal cost, so please continue on…).

Another example of the irrelevance of sunk cost can be found in the decision of the US federal government along with local government to bury I-95 under Boston. This project became known as "The Big Dig." Initial estimates predicted that such a project would cost $2.5 billion dollars. The calculations of the marginal benefits of this project were greater than that, so construction began. Information was not perfect and the final price tag ended up near $18 billion, much larger than the estimated marginal benefit of the project. In a world of perfect information, politicians would have had a much harder time selling the idea of the Big Dig to voters at a cost of $18 billion.

What if the estimated marginal benefit of the completed project was $10 billion? Surely, at the time of the first cost estimate, this seemed like a worthwhile project. The marginal benefit exceeded the marginal cost. When the costs hit $10 billion why didn't they stop the project? If there is no marginal benefit to a partially built highway, then the marginal benefit of finishing the project was still $10 billion. The marginal cost is only the cost going forward. The original $10 billion worth of expenses were a sunk cost. If they had stopped the project at spending $10 billion for no benefit—they would have lost $10 billion. If they believed that the marginal cost of completion was less than $10 billion, say $8 billion, then they would have spent a total of $18 billion to get $10 billion worth of benefit. Losing $8 billion isn't great, but it is better than losing $10 billion. Failure to ignore sunk costs causes people to make irrational decisions. Thus, decision making should focus on opportunity cost and not sunk cost.

Production Possibilities and Economic Growth

One way opportunity cost can be compared is using a **production possibilities frontier** (PPF for short). A PPF is a graphical representation of all currently obtainable production options. The slope of the PPF represents the opportunity cost of production.

Assume a simplified economy in the fictitious country of Kent. Kent can produce only two goods: beer and cheese. Table 2.2 represents Kent's **production schedule**, the different production combinations available to them at a specific point in time if they fully utilize all of their existing resources and technology. Also assume that all of Kent's resources are useful for both beer and cheese production. As the country of Kent chooses (through either individual choice or government mandate) to produce more cheese, they must forgo the production of some beer. This is the opportunity cost they face for cheese production, forgone output of beer. In this case, every time Kent increases the production of cheese by 50 blocks, they forgo the production of 200 kegs of beer. To find their opportunity cost of producing 1 block of cheese, one can set up the following ratio and solve for x:

$$\frac{50 \text{ blocks}}{200 \text{ kegs}} = \frac{1 \text{ block}}{x \text{ kegs}}.$$

The opportunity cost of 1 block of cheese is 4 kegs of beer.

TABLE 2.2	KENT'S PRODUCTION SCHEDULE	
	Beer (kegs)	**Cheese (blocks)**
A	800	0
B	600	50
C	400	100
D	200	150
E	0	200

Figure 2.1a **KENT'S PRODUCTION POSSIBILITIES FRONTIER**

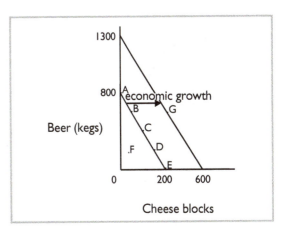

Figure 2.1b **KENT'S PRODUCTION POSSIBILITIES FRONTIER FOLLOWING ECONOMIC GROWTH**

Figure 2.1a plots the points from Kent's production schedule to form Kent's PPF. Kent can choose to produce anywhere on or inside (to the bottom left) of the PPF. If they are producing at a point like point F, inside of the PPF, they are not currently using all of their resources for production and so are producing in a manner that is **productively inefficient**. Perhaps some Kentians are unemployed. By employing them, Kent could increase the production of both beer and cheese.

If Kent is currently producing on its PPF, as in on points B or C, Kent is using all of its available resources for production and is said to be **productively efficient**. While points B and C are equally efficient from a production standpoint, there is nothing to say that they bring the same level of happiness to the citizens of Kent. Point G is currently outside of Kent's PPF. Point G is **unobtainable** with current resources and technology but could be produced in the future with the help of economic growth. See Figure 2.1b.

Economic growth, represented by an expansion of a country's PPF, can happen in the form of extensive or intensive economic growth. Extensive economic growth occurs when more resources become available to a country. Increased immigration may increase the size of the labor force. New machines, tools, or factories could be built. New natural resources could be found. An increase in resources available for production increase the possible

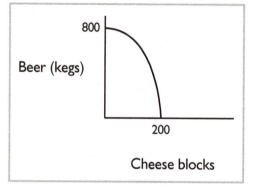

Figure 2.2   **A PRODUCTION POSSIBILITIES FRONTIER WITH SPECIALIZED RESOURCES**

production bundles available to a society, but it does not guarantee that those new bundles are actually achieved. Intensive economic growth occurs when existing resources are used to produce more output. An increase in output per unit of input represents an increase in productivity. New technology, faster computers, and more skilled workers are just a few of the ways that productivity can be enhanced.

Notice that in Figures 2.1a and 2.1b, the PPF is a straight line and opportunity cost (represented by the slope of the PPF) is constant at -4 kegs of beer per block of cheese produced. In reality, not all resources are equally good at producing everything. Some land is more fertile than other land. Some workers, like surgeons or electricians, have specialized knowledge in their field of work. California dairy producers went so far as to claim that, "Great cheese comes from happy cows. Happy cows come from California." Can a surgeon milk a cow? They probably can. Is their opportunity cost of milking a cow higher than a trained dairy worker? Yes.

Resources of all kinds are **specialized**. This means that the PPF for a country would never be a straight line, even if they only produced two goods. A curved PPF such Figure 2.2 illustrates the **law of increasing opportunity cost** due to specialization. When resources are specialized (concentrated in one area) and a country increases the production of one product, its opportunity cost of production increases. More and more resources have to be diverted from what they are good at producing to increase the production of something they are less able to produce. Specialization and trade allow a country to increase the productivity of their resources and consume at a point beyond their own PPF.

In the next chapter, we shall examine the wealth creating benefit of trade, explore the mechanisms for restricting trade, scrutinize arguments in favor of enacting such restrictions, and outline their counterarguments.

Key Terms

Black market

Bureau of Economic Analysis

Business Cycle Dating Committee

Consumption

Contraction

Exports

GDP per capita

Golden rule of economics

Government spending

Gross Domestic Product

Gross National Product

Imports

Intermediate good

Inventory

Investment

Law of increasing opportunity cost

Marginal benefit

Marginal cost

Microeconomics

Nominal GDP

Non-market transactions

Production Possibilities Frontier

Production schedule

Productively efficient

Productively inefficient

Quarterly

Real GDP

Recession

Rule of 72

Specialized

Specialization

Sunk cost

Transfer payments

Unobtainable

Questions for Review

1. What gets counted in GDP? How does it differ from GNP?

2. What are five of the ten poorest countries in the world as measured by per capita GDP?

3. In the year 2021 in the country of Macroland,
   Consumption = $15,000
   Investment = $6,000
   Exports = $10,000
   Imports = $4,000 and
   Government expenditures = $2,000.

   a. What is nominal GDP?

   b. If the GDP deflator =200 with the year 2000 as the base year, then what is RGDP?

   c. If the population of Macroland is 10, what is the RGDP per capita?

4.

	1992	2000
Nominal GDP (in trillions)	4	6
GDP deflator	100	170

a. By how much did Real GDP change between 1992 and 2000?

b. Did the economy grow between 1992 and 2000 according to these numbers?

5. Why is economic growth important?

6. How many years will it take GDP to double if the GDP growth rate is 1.5%?

7. Determine which of the following would be counted in US GDP and if so, in which category (C, I, G, X, or M).

a. the purchase of American made corn by a consumer in Canada

b. the production of a Toyota at a plant in Kentucky

c. the purchase of a new home in Oregon

d. the payment of $300 to welfare recipient

e. marijuana is grown and sold in Kentucky

f. I pay a teenager cash to mow my lawn

g. I hire a professional lawncare company such as lawn doctor to care for my lawn.

h. the purchase of 100 new shares of stock in Apple

i. Ford produces 100,000 trucks this year in Tennessee that are not sold this year.

j. the government spends 1 million dollars on school lunches

k. you purchase a used iPhone off of eBay

l. you pay T-mobile $100 a month for cell phone service

8. a. Why is GDP not a perfect measure of production? Why is Real GDP per capita not a perfect measure of wellbeing?

b. Give an example of how one of these imperfections may affect comparisons across time or between countries.

9. Why do you think GDP per capita varies so dramatically across countries?

10. Suppose that Real GDP in 2020 is 18 trillion dollars (using 2015 as the base year). The Nominal GDP in 2020 is 22 trillion dollars. What must the GDP deflator be?

11. If the population of Isle of Hope is 30 persons and the GDP is 2,100,000, then what is the GDP per capita?

12. a. What is opportunity cost?

    b. What is a sunk cost? Give Examples.

13. a. The country of Kent has 10 workers. Kent produces only two goods— diamond rings and alarm clocks. Suppose each worker can either make 12 rings or 4 clocks in one year (no workers are specialized). Draw the annual production possibilities frontier for Kent. Include labels and intercepts.

    b. Does the law of increasing opportunity costs hold true for Kent?

    c. Suppose that the workers in Kent gained new clock technology such that they can now produce 8 clocks in a given year, but they can still only make 12 rings. Draw the new PPF.

14. a. Given the production schedule below, what is the opportunity cost of producing 1 table?

	Cabinets	Tables
A	0	40
B	5	38
C	10	30
D	15	20
E	20	0

    b. Graph the PPF for this country.

    c. What is the opportunity cost of producing one box between points A and B?

    d. What is the opportunity cost of producing one box between points D and E?

    e. Does this PPF illustrate increasing opportunity costs?

    f. Graph point F at the combination of 20 tables and 25 cabinets. What term describes this point? What needs to happen in order for the country to consume at this point?

    g. Graph the point G at 3 cabinets and 10 tables. What term describes this point? What must be happening if the country is producing here?

15. Not So Curious George's Production Possibilities Frontier for one day:

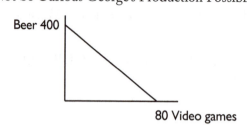

Beer 400

80 Video games

a. What is Not So Curious George's opportunity cost of producing 1 video game?

b. If Not So Curious George wanted to produce only 20 video games, how many beers could he produce in the same day?

16. Kenny gets a $20 bill in the mail from his grandpa for his birthday. He is trying to decide how to spend the $20 and has made a list of his top four choices, given in the order of preference. His first choice is to spend on a nice meal out. His second choice is to buy a t-shirt for $20. His third preference is to save the $20 for an emergency. Lastly, his fourth choice is to spend the $20 on a movie and concessions. What is the opportunity cost of going out to dinner?

Chapter

3

Specialization and Trade

"Anything you can do, I can do better. I can do anything better than you…. Can you bake a pie? No. Neither can I."

— "Anything You Can Do", Oklahoma

© Zurijeta, 2012, under license Shutterstock, Inc.

As discussed in the initial chapters, economic growth can be extremely beneficial for society in that it increases the average standard of living. Most of us like to consume far beyond what we can produce on our own. In fact, we like to consume far beyond what the United States could produce on its own.

If you examine your closets, pantries, cars, and even medicine bottles you will find that a large number of items within them were produced outside the United States. This chapter focuses on trade. In particular, it examines the most common arguments given for restricting trade along with their counter arguments. This chapter also introduces a numerical comparison of the benefits of trade. In doing so, the chapter illustrates how free trade is wealth generating.

Why Trade?

For a moment consider all of the items you have used today. Perhaps you brushed your teeth with toothpaste, cooked a tomato and cheese omelet on a stove, dressed in a sweater and jeans and tennis shoes, drove in a car to work, etc. Imagine now if you had to produce every item you consumed today. It would not be possible for us to consume at our current standard of living if we had to produce everything ourselves. Similarly, individuals who live alone on a specific piece of land and don't trade with other people live very poor existences. Their land, fixed in some particular climate, will be good at producing some things but not others. The tropical rainforest of Honduras is good for growing bananas, but not wheat. The fertile fields of Illinois are good for growing corn, but not for growing oranges. Self-sufficient farmers, therefore, lack variety in their diet. A lack of dietary variety leads to a shorter life expectancy than a diversified, balanced diet.

Life on the isolated American frontier of the 1800's involved canning of fruits and vegetables for winter, less variety of food than we see today, and frequent starvation. Less than 40% of homestead entries in Montana were completed in the 1800's. That is, even when the government was giving away free land, people couldn't generate enough wealth from the land to avoid starvation.

At the time of the American Revolution, roughly 80% of Americans were farmers. Now, fewer than 2% of Americans are farmers. This has been the result of increased use of capital, technology, education, and trade. Without trade, all of our days would be consumed worrying about where our next meal would come from. With trade, the biggest food question for many Americans seems to be, "Where do we go out to eat tonight?" And, even as the local food movement has seen a recent growth in popularity, trade still plays an important role. Those striving to eat locally can consume more if they trade with other farmers than if they consume only what they themselves can produce.

The first argument for why we should engage in trade is that voluntary trade creates wealth. When two people voluntarily agree to an exchange of goods or services, they are doing so because each values the **marginal benefit** of the other's offer to be higher than the **marginal cost** of what they have to give up. Trade creates wealth by allowing goods and services to flow from where they have a lower marginal value to where they have a higher marginal value.

A baker may like cake, but even Marie Antoinette would concede that there is only so much cake a guy can eat. Therefore, he often values the production of a new cake less than the butcher who is cake-less. By trading meat for cake, both the butcher and the baker can improve their wellbeing by giving up something of little marginal value in exchange for something of a higher marginal value to them.

Furthermore, since the baker is **specialized** at baking, the ability to trade for meat frees up his time to focus on what he produces well. By focusing on his baking, the baker specializes according to his specific skills. As resources are allowed to move from areas of production where they are ill suited to areas of production where they excel, more production is allowed to occur. This specialization and **division of labor** was a chief source of wealth creation noted in Adam Smith's *Wealth of Nations* in 1776.

The second argument in favor of trade, then, is that different resources are specialized in the production of different goods and services. In order for a Canadian to gain access to a banana, they must trade with a country whose climate is conducive to banana production. While Canada doesn't produce bananas, they do produce oil from the Alberta oil sands. The US imports more oil from Canada than from any other country in the world.

Coffee beans grow best in high altitudes such as is found in Columbia and Kenya. Cashmere comes from silk worms in Kashmir. Diamonds often come from the Southern Horn of Africa. Utility (army) knives overwhelmingly come from Switzerland. Many oriental rugs come from Pakistan. Increased trade offers greater access to a larger diversity of products.

Trade also allows countries to take advantage of economies of scale. **Economies of scale** refer to a reduction in the average costs of production that occurs as larger quantities are produced. Some products are too large for every country to make. There are only two jumbo jet producers in the world, Boeing and Airbus. Yet, many airlines in different countries want to be able to acquire jumbo jets. The scale of production of jumbo jets precludes small economies from entering the market for their production. If Air Jamaica wants a plane, they will need to trade with a country outside of the Caribbean. In fact, there are no core industries that a country must have to gain wealth. The key to wealth creation lies within every country using the unique resources and skills that exist within each country to specialize and trade with other countries.

Free trade creates wealth. Trade is not a **zero sum game**. It is **positive sum**. Since World War II, the single biggest catalyst for worldwide economic growth has been increased international trade. China used to be the richest country in the world. Then they built a great wall around themselves, isolated themselves, and became one of the poorest countries in the world. Since the early 1990's China has decided to be part of the international economy and their annual growth rate has averaged near 10%.

Transaction costs (transportation costs, cultural differences, government regulations, and currency exchanges) often restrict the amount of trade that is feasible. It is easy to trade with a member of your family who lives in your house. You know you can trust them, they live near you, you speak the same language, and you share the same currency. Trading with your neighbors down the street isn't much harder. As transaction costs rise due to increased distance or cultural differences, the fewer wealth creating trades will be made. Still, ocean shipping is the cheapest form of transportation, so it is often cheaper to ship butter from New Zealand to Puerto Vallarta, Mexico than it is to transport butter there from inland neighboring Mexican states.

Trade's Wealth Creating Mathematical Certainty

To illustrate how trade is a positive sum game, envision two countries, the US and the UK, in a world where the only two products produced are ginger ale and beef. Table 3.1 reveals the output per worker per day in each country if they dedicate their entire day to the production of that good, either beef or ale. For example, a worker in the US is able to produce either 15 lbs. of beef or 60 liters of ale.

An **absolute advantage** exists if one can produce more output per unit of input. The US has an absolute advantage in the production of beef over the UK, because a US worker can produce more beef per day than can a UK laborer. Similarly, the UK is said to have an absolute advantage in the production of ginger ale, as one worker in the UK can produce more ginger ale than a similar worker in the US. In this case, it is apparent that one country is really good at producing one product while the other is good at producing another product.

TABLE 3.1	PRODUCTION OPTIONS FOR ONE WORKER IN EACH COUNTRY	
	US	**UK**
Beef (lbs.)	15	5
Ginger Ale (liters)	60	100

If the US and the UK in this example specialize and then engage in trade, two things will happen. The first is that wealth will be created, and the second is that both countries will be made better off. Assume that each country has exactly two workers. In a world of no trade, if one worker in each country produced each good, then world production would look as follows in Table 3.2

TABLE 3.2	WORLD PRODUCTION WITHOUT TRADE FOR TWO WORKERS IN EACH COUNTRY	
US production	**UK production**	**World production**
15 lbs. beef	5 lbs. beef	20 lbs. beef
60 liters ale	100 liters ale	160 liters of ale

Now assume that each country specializes in the product where they have an absolute advantage. Both US workers will produce beef while both UK workers will produce ginger ale.

TABLE 3.3	WORLD PRODUCTION WITH SPECIALIZATION	
US production	**UK production**	**World production**
30 lbs. beef	0 lbs. beef	30 lbs. beef
0 liters ale	200 liters ale	200 liters of ale

By engaging in specialization and the division of labor, world wealth increases. The same inputs are used in both scenarios, but in the free world trade scenario 10 more lbs. of beef and 40 more liters of ginger ale are produced. The world's **production possibilities frontier** expands under free trade. As long as both countries want both products, they can have more of them by using the same quantity of inputs, but allowing those inputs to specialize in what they do best.

Each country could be self-sufficient in the sense that they could make both beef and ginger ale, but both countries can have more of both products if they specialize and trade. Note that every time the US produces 15 lbs. of beef, they are forgoing 60 liters of ginger ale. Consequently, the opportunity cost of 1 lb. of beef is 4 liters of ginger ale (this is found by dividing 60 by 15). In this case, the US should be willing to trade a pound of beef to the UK as long as they get more than 4 liters of ginger ale in return (so that they get more than their own opportunity cost of producing it). Similarly, the UK could produce beef, but when it does so, it forgoes the production of 20 liters of ginger ale (100 divided by 5). The UK would not want to offer more than 20 liters of ginger ale for one pound of beef. Both countries will end up with more output if they trade one pound of US beef for somewhere between 4 and 20 liters of ginger ale. Thus, the terms of trade lie somewhere between 4 - 20 liters of ginger ale per pound of beef.

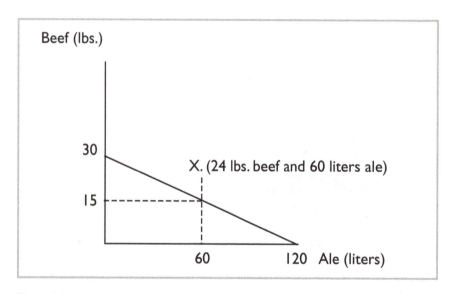

Figure 3.1   **US PPF WITH 2 WORKERS**

The **terms of trade** describes the rate at which one good (or service) is exchanged for another and typically lies between two countries relative opportunity costs of producing the good (or service).

Suppose the countries agree on a terms of trade of 10 liters of ginger ale for one pound of beef. If the US wants to consume 60 liters of ale, then it will have to trade 6 lbs. of beef. It will still have 24 lbs. left to consume. Note that in absence of trade, producing 60 liters of ale required the entire time of one worker, leaving only 15 lbs. of beef (the other worker's production) for consumption. This is illustrated in Figure 3.1, Point X containing 60 liters of ale and 24 lbs. of beef would be off of the production possibility frontier of the US in absence of trade, and yet is possible for consumption if the countries engage in trade. Similarly, Canada benefits by being able to now consume 6 lbs. of beef and 140 liters of ale, a combination they could not have consumed in absence of trade. In this way, free trade creates wealth!

What if a country has an absolute advantage in the production of everything? Would they ever benefit from trade? Assume a two country world represented by the levels of out put per worker per day represented in Table 3.4.

TABLE 3.4		
	US	**Canada**
Wheat (bushels)	10	8
Potatoes (bushels)	50	32

In this case, the US has an absolute advantage in both wheat and potatoes, as one worker in the US can produce more of either good than a worker in Canada. To determine whether or not the US will benefit from trade with Canada, one must first determine which country has a comparative advantage in the production of each good. A country has a **comparative advantage** if its opportunity cost of production is lower than the opportunity cost of production for the other country. If each country has a comparative advantage in a different product, both countries will benefit from trade.

The opportunity cost of producing one bushel of wheat in the US is 5 bushels of potatoes. In Canada, the opportunity cost of producing one bushel of wheat is only 4 bushels of potatoes. Canada gives up fewer potatoes to produce wheat than the US, and therefore Canada has a comparative advantage in wheat production. The opportunity cost of producing one bushel of potatoes in the US is one-fifth of a bushel of wheat. In Canada, the opportunity cost of producing one bushel of potatoes is one-fourth of a bushel of wheat. By having a lower opportunity cost of production, the US has a comparative advantage in potato production.

The opportunity cost of one bushel of potatoes is the reciprocal of the opportunity cost of one bushel of wheat. In this manner, every country is mathematically guaranteed to have a comparative advantage in the production of something. No matter how bad a country is at producing goods, it will be better at producing some goods than others and therein will be their comparative advantage.

In this case, as long as Canada receives between four and five bushels of potatoes for one bushel of wheat, both the US and Canada will gain from trade. Canada could grow potatoes, but would have to forgo 4 bushels of potatoes to produce a bushel of wheat. Canada must at least receive four bushels of potatoes to be made better off from trade. Likewise, the US could grow wheat, but would have to forgo the production of five bushels of potatoes to grow it. Instead, if the US grows the five bushels of potatoes and sell less than that to Canada for a bushel of wheat, they can consume more than they could without trade. Thus, even if one country has an absolute advantage in all goods, it still would benefit if they specialized according to their comparative advantage and traded.

Trade Agreements

In order to reduce global trade barriers following WWII, many countries got together to sign The **Global Agreement on Tariffs and Trade (GATT)**. The **World Trade Organization (WTO)** was formed to implement GATT and now has 153 members. The reduction in global trade barriers brought about through GATT has done more to increase world trade than have **regional trade agreements**.

With each round of trade negotiations, the WTO seeks to lower more trade barriers. Because the agreements apply equally to all 153 countries, they all must approve of the agreements before they can take effect. Therefore, the trade agreements with the largest potential to speed economic growth are also the politically most difficult to achieve. As a result, many countries have enacted **multilateral trade deals** between a smaller number of countries. Each round of WTO negotiations is named after the location where they begin.

TABLE 3.5[1]	TOP US TRADING PARTNERS, 2017 IN BILLIONS OF US $				
Rank	Country	Exports	Imports	Total Trade	Percent of Total Trade
1	China	$130	$506	$636	16.4%
2	Canada	$282	$300	$582	15.0%
3	Mexico	$243	$314	$557	14.3%
4	Japan	$68	$137	$204	5.3%
5	Germany	$54	$118	$171	4.4%
6	South Korea	$48	$71	$119	3.1%
7	UK	$56	$53	$109	2.8%
8	France	$34	$49	$83	2.1%
9	India	$26	$49	$74	1.9%
10	Italy	$18	$50	$68	1.8%

[1] Source US Census Bureau Foreign Trade Statistics

The European Union has a free trade deal among its members. The **North American Free Trade Agreement (NAFTA)**, enacted in 1994, lowered trade barriers between Canada, the US, and Mexico. This was an important deal for all three economies, as both Canada and Mexico rank among the top five biggest trading partners with the US.

NAFTA has helped all three North American economies grow. Unemployment in each of the countries fell in the late 1990's following NAFTA's ratification. In 2018, President Trump embarked on an effort to tweak NAFTA and rename it the United States-Mexico-Canada Agreement (USMCA). This rebranded agreement was awaiting Congressional approval at the time of this edition's publication. The **Free Trade Area of the Americas (FTAA)** was a proposal to form a free trade area for the Western Hemisphere, but formal negotiations for this treaty have been stalled since 2005. However, the US did pass the **Dominican Republic - Central American - US Free Trade Agreement (CAFTA)** in 2004.

The US also has **bilateral trade agreements** with Australia, Bahrain, Chile, Colombia, Israel, Jordan, Korea, Morocco, Oman, Panama, Peru, and Singapore. Exports to Peru doubled in the year after the Peruvian free trade agreement. While bilateral trade agreements don't reduce as many trade barriers as multilateral trade deals, they are easier to negotiate.

The Balance of Trade

In 1950, imports and exports made up less than 5% of the US economy. In 2017, US imports were 15% of US GDP while exports were 12% of US GDP. The US economy has become more globally integrated as a result of reduced trade barriers and lower transaction costs from technological advancements in transportation and communication.

In the 1960's and 1970's, the US ran a trade surplus with the rest of the world. Currently, the US runs a trade deficit. Table 3.6[2] illustrates the tremendous increase in both imports and exports that the US has experienced since 1960.

© Lightspring , 2012, under license Shutterstock, Inc.

---

[2] Source World Bank

TABLE 3.6	US BALANCE OF TRADE IN BILLIONS OF DOLLARS		
	Exports	Imports	Trade Surplus/Deficit
1960	25.9	22.4	3.5
1970	56.6	54.4	2.2
1980	272	291	-19
1990	535	616	-80
2000	1,070	1,449	-378
2010	1,289	2,330	-998
2017	2,351	2,351	-552

Some people mistakenly believe that a trade surplus is "good" while a trade deficit is "bad". The truth is that the most important trade statistic is the total dollar value of trade. The more specialized goods and services that are voluntarily traded, the more wealth gets created. If a country runs a trade deficit, they must also run a **capital account surplus**. When Americans buy goods from abroad, they must first exchange their dollars for foreign currency. When the US runs a trade deficit, someone outside of the US must be collecting US dollars. Countries running a trade surplus must be running a **capital account deficit**, where they are investing more in a foreign country than is being invested back.

These dollars can go to one of three places. If the dollars forever remain outside of the US and are used by people in other countries to exchange goods amongst themselves, then the US has successfully traded worthless pieces of paper for real goods and services. In other words, in this scenario the US never has to give anything of value in return for the goods it has received. If the dollars return to the US in the future, then the US will run a trade surplus at that point in time, as foreigners buy more US goods and services. Alternatively, the foreign owners of US dollars could store their currency in US financial institutions. This money is then made available for consumers, firms, and governments to borrow for consumption, investment, or spending. A trade deficit is only natural for a country that seeks to use foreign savings for their own investment in capital.

At any point in time, the **balance of trade** plus the **capital account** must equal zero. In early US history, the US faced relative capital scarcity, and as a result ran years of trade deficits while foreign savers poured money into US financial markets. As the US government now piles up trillions of dollars of debt, their need for a capital inflow to purchase this debt causes the economy to run a trade deficit. Budget deficits (spending more than is received in revenues) cause trade deficits, which is why the two are known as the **twin deficits**. Politicians who dislike the trade deficit often advocate increased trade barriers to reduce imports. Rather than lower wealth creating trade, politicians who earnestly want to reduce the trade deficit should focus their attention on lowering the budget deficit or increasing the domestic savings rate. A low amount of domestic savings relative to the domestic demand for borrowing will result in a trade deficit. If the borrowing fuels current consumption, future economic growth will be compromised. If the borrowing fuels investment in productive capital, then future economic growth will be enhanced.

Trade Barriers

There are four ways governments can restrict trade: a tariff, a quota, an embargo, or regulation. A **tariff** is a tax on imports. **Quotas** restrict the quantity of an import into a country, while **embargoes** outlaw all trade with a country. Countries can also use their regulatory powers to put foreign producers at a disadvantage in the market.

While both tariffs and quotas can be used to restrict trade, tariffs destroy less wealth than do quotas. If a tariff is placed on an imported good, then the sales price of that good will increase. Foreign producers will receive a lower price for their good, while consumers pay more for the good. The difference between what the producer receives and the consumer pays is the amount of the tariff paid to the government. While both foreign producers and domestic consumers are hurt by a tariff, the federal government does gain tax revenue and domestic producers of the good have increased revenue.

Under a quota, the federal government gains no tax revenue. By restricting the importation of goods, foreign producers are able to sell fewer products, but also face less competition for their products. As a result, they are able to charge higher prices to US consumers. Just as with tariffs, not only will US consumers pay more for imported goods under a quota regime, they will also pay more for domestically made goods as there will be less competition in the market to keep prices low.

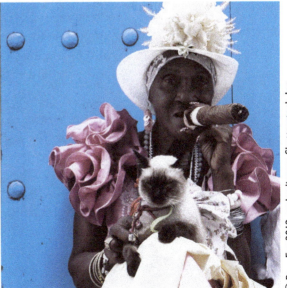

Because a tariff is applied equally to all foreign producers, the most efficient (low cost) producers will still have a competitive advantage over their less efficient competition. However, under a quota, government officials pick which companies get to sell their products in the market. This type of government selection encourages bribery and corruption and means that bureaucrats rather than consumers choose the products that are for sale. There is no guarantee under a quota system that the most efficient producers will be selected to export their goods.

Tariffs, quotas, and embargos all increase the price and quantity sold of domestically produced goods, as there is less competition from abroad. The US has had an embargo on trade with Cuba since 1960. The United Nations general assembly has passed annual resolutions ever since 1992 criticizing the embargo against Cuba. In fact, they state that such an embargo violates international law. Embargos do the most damage to a country's wealth because they outlaw all wealth creating trades between two countries. Embargos not only hurt the country at which they are directed, but also hurt consumers in the enforcing country by limiting access to goods and raising prices on domestically produced goods. Embargos are typically reserved for countries with which a country is at war, but are sometimes enacted for other political reasons.

Arguments for Trade Restriction

Given the wealth creating power of lower trade barriers, why do we live in a world awash in trade restrictions? The answer to this question is political rather than economic. There are many reasons used by politicians to support trade restrictions. Below are lists of the **protectionist** arguments along with their counterarguments. A protectionist is someone who advocates trade restrictions on imports.

1. **To protect US jobs**—There is a belief that restricting the importation of goods and services will cause Americans to buy more domestically produced goods. This increase in domestic demand is believed to increase the number of jobs available for Americans.

   Counterargument—Trade restrictions destroy more jobs than they create. As we illustrated in the earlier section on comparative advantage, forcing resources to abandon their comparative advantage will cause world production to fall. Resources in the US go from where they could create more production to areas where production is more difficult. Although some politically connected jobs are saved by protectionism, in net more job creation potential exists with trade.

   Example—The US restricts the importation of foreign grown sugar into the US in order to save sugar growing jobs in the US. Rather than let sugar come from the sugar cane fields of Jamaica or Brazil, politicians would rather have US citizens buy sugar from Florida sugar cane or plains state sugar beet growers. The result is that the price of sugar in the US is double what it is in the rest of the world. This does create jobs in the US sugar growing industry. However, it has destroyed even more jobs in the candy making industry, as large US candy makers have moved their production facilities overseas to take advantage of cheaper sugar inputs. Additionally, sugar has been replaced in American foods and sodas with high fructose corn syrup to avoid the high cost of sugar. Coke and Pepsi only use high fructose corn syrup in the US, and they do so because of government tariffs on sugar.

2. **To gain a price advantage**—If trade restrictions increase the price of foreign made goods, then more people will choose to buy American made goods.

Counterargument—If the US places a tariff on imports, other countries will retaliate with tariffs placed on goods and services exported from the US. Jobs will then be lost in export oriented industries.

Example—When the US placed a tariff on European made steel in 2002, the European Union threatened retaliation by placing tariffs on US made goods such as Harley Davidson motorcycles, Florida oranges, and cars made in Michigan. As a result, the US repealed the steel tariff rather than risk losing jobs in the motorcycle, car, and orange industries. Similar retaliatory tariffs were exchanged between China and the US in 2019.

3. **For political reasons**—The US may wish to punish countries they consider to be part of the "axis of evil"[3]

© Copestello, 2012, under license Shutterstock, Inc.

Counterargument—Political reasons are rarely consistent.

Example—When Fidel Castro came to power in Cuba during its communist revolution, private businesses and property were nationalized. The US has placed a trade embargo on Cuba until such time as they reimburse the former owners of the nationalized property for their losses, many of whom live in Florida. In fact, during the American Revolution the American government confiscated property from loyalists and forced them to move to Canada. These loyalists have never been reimbursed for their loss of property.

When Mao Zedong came to power in China during its communist revolution, private businesses and property were nationalized. Yet, the US trades with China even as they refuse to repay those who lost property during their revolution. The US does trade with some communist countries; it just does not trade with ones that have a huge expatriate presence in a presidential swing state. While the US economy is hurt by not trading with Cuba, it would be hurt even more by not trading with China.

---

[3] A term first used by President George W. Bush in his 2002 State of the Union Address

4. **For national security reasons**—It is not in the national security interests of the US to sell stealth bombers or nuclear weapons to countries that seek our destruction.

Counterargument—Everything is not a national security issue.

Example—In 2001, the US Army cancelled an order of black berets (hats) because of "national security interests". It was deemed not in American's national security interest to buy berets made in China[4]. Given that a beret can't actually stop a bullet anyway, it is difficult to surmise the national security interest. Nevertheless, the contract was awarded to an American company who couldn't meet the deadline and had to outsource the berets to Mexico.

5. **To prevent dumping**—If a country is allowed to sell its goods below cost, they will do so until they put domestic manufacturers out of business. Once that occurs, they can raise their prices and take advantage of consumers.

Counterargument—Selling below cost cannot be made up by selling in volume; a company just loses more. As a result, dumping rarely, if ever, happens. In reality, if a company sustains losses in order to force out competition, then as soon as they raise their prices, new entrants will arise to compete. Thus, dumping is typically not a successful strategy for foreign companies. Most likely, those businesses that claim dumping is occurring are actually just observing that their competitors are able to produce at a lower cost.

Example—The US made the claim that Europe was **dumping** steel in the US, which kept West Virginian steel companies at a disadvantage. However, when the WTO investigated, no dumping was found to have taken place.

If dumping were ever found to occur (say in plasma TV's) then US consumers would likely benefit. People in other countries would be paying for our consumption.

6. **To protect infant industries**—New industries may need time to develop without competitive pressures. Once they develop and become competitive, trade barriers can be reduced.

Counterargument—Once an industry benefits from restricted competition, it will be politically difficult to remove that protection, as existing workers would likely lose their jobs. Existing workers bear concentrated benefits to the protection, while consumers bear diffused costs. As such, existing workers will be easier to organize politically than general consumers.

---

[4] May 2, 2001 CNN.com "Army Berets won't be made in China"

Example—Alexander Hamilton advocated the **American System** of high tariffs on manufactured goods in the early 1800's. His argument was that once Americans learned how to manufacture textiles, they could then effectively compete with British firms which had already undergone the industrial revolution. As a result, by the time of the US Civil War, the US had a lower per capita income level than did Australia, whose colonies did not have high tariffs placed on British manufactured goods. So, the infant industry argument most likely slowed economic growth in the US during the 1800's.

7. **To avoid exploitation of the poor**—It is not fair to hire someone and pay them $2 an hour to work.

   Counterargument—Over a billion people currently live on less than $1.25 a day. To them a job that pays $2 an hour would greatly improve their ability to meet their and their families' needs and wants. By restricting trade with poor countries, protectionists increase world poverty rather than alleviating it.

   Example—When firms open factories that pay higher than average wages in a country, lines often form for job applications. While $10 a day might not sound like a good deal to a US worker, it is an eight fold increase in the per capita income of someone making $1.25 a day. So, their standard of living actually increases from such opportunities. Most would agree that forcing someone to work (slavery) or hiding from someone the full dangers of their work is immoral. However, barring this, individuals voluntarily choosing to work for wages that appear low to us are presumably doing so because it is better than any other options available to them. Consequently, if wealthy Americans boycott products made by workers being paid less than $10 a day, then they actually would be decreasing job opportunities for those individuals rather than increasing them.

8. **To protect the environment**—Companies will move their plants away from countries with tight environmental standards to countries with lower standards.

   Counterargument—Rising incomes are positively correlated with improved environmental conditions. When people are faced with the choice of pollute and eat or don't pollute and don't eat, they choose the former, just as the US did in its own history. As countries become wealthier, one of the

© Sergej Khakimullin, 2012, under license Shutterstock, Inc.

---

[5] *The Mystery of Capital: Why Capitalism Triumphs in the West and Fails Everywhere Else.* 2000.

things they demand is a cleaner living environment. As trade creates wealth, it also works to make the environment cleaner.

Example—The US used to let manufacturers dump hazardous byproducts into rivers and lakes. As the economy became wealthier, people were more willing to allocate money towards protecting the environment, and public opinion worked to create the clean air and clean water acts.

While trade creates wealth, not everyone is made better off in the short run as result of reducing trade barriers. If a person has invested in physical or human capital that is specialized in an industry that is not competitive and is only in existence due to government protection, then the removal of that protection will cost them their investment and/or their job. However, since trade crates wealth, more jobs will be created than are destroyed by reducing trade barriers. As that provides little solace to the person currently losing their job, trade agreements often contain language to provide financial support to workers who need new training in order to take advantage of the new jobs created by expanded trade.

Key Terms

Absolute advantage

American System

Balance of trade

Bilateral trade agreements

Capital account

Capital account deficit

Capital account surplus

Comparative advantage

Division of labor

Dominican Republic - Central American - US Free Trade Agreement (CAFTA)

Dumping

Economies of scale

Embargo

European Union

Free Trade Area of the Americas (FTAA)

Global Agreement on Tariffs and Trade (GATT)

Infant industries

Marginal benefit

Marginal cost

Multilateral trade deals

North American Free Trade Agreement (NAFTA)

Positive sum game

Production possibilities frontier

Protectionist

Quota

Regional trade agreements

Specialized

Tariff

Terms of trade

Transaction costs

Twin deficits

World Trade Organization (WTO)

Zero sum game

Questions for Review

1. Why is free trade a positive sum game?

2. a. What are four arguments in favor of erecting trade barriers? What are their counterarguments?

   b. What is the difference between a tariff, a quota, and an embargo?

   c. Who benefits from trade barriers? Who is hurt by trade barriers?

3. Who are the top US trading partners?

4. What is a trade deficit? A trade surplus? Which does the US have now? Why? How do each of these relate to capital account balances?

5. The numbers in the following tables illustrates how many units of a good can be produced in one day by one person in each country.

	US	China
jeans	32	12
computer chips	4	3

a. Which country has the absolute advantage in jean production?

b. Which country has the absolute advantage in chip production?

c. Which country has a comparative advantage in jean production?

d. Which country has a comparative advantage in chip production?

e. What is the opportunity cost of 1 chip in the US? In China?

f. What is the opportunity cost of 1 jean in the US? In China?

g. Would these two countries be willing to trade? If so, how many jeans would be traded for one computer chip?

Long Run Economic Growth

"Insanity: doing the same thing over and over again and expecting different results."

— *Albert Einstein*

© Kokhanchikov, 2012, under license Shutterstock, Inc.

Economies can grow extensively, intensively, or via specialization and trade. **Extensive economic growth** occurs when an economy produces an increased level of output due to an increase in the quantity of resources being used. If a country finds new natural resources, increases the size of its labor force, or builds more factories, it can produce more output. Extensive growth may or may not increase the average standard of living of a country's inhabitants. Economic growth in the first millennium and a half AD was largely extensive.

More people produced more aggregate wealth, but little gain was made in the development of human capital or technological advancement.

Intensive economic growth is growth caused by an increase in **productivity** (an increase in the quantity of output produced by a resource). If workers become more skilled, new technology is invented, or entrepreneurs find more efficient ways to produce and distribute products, then an increase in productivity results. Finally, growth can occur through the specialization of labor and gains from trade. This chapter discusses public policies that contribute to both extensive and intensive economic growth. Growth from specialization and trade was discussed in Chapter 3.

Extensive Growth

Why might a country desire extensive economic growth? Extensive economic growth may be desired for national security, to take advantage of economies of scale (where cost of production per unit falls as more is produced), or to increase solvency of government run pay-as-you-go pension schemes. In colonial American history, the British government favored a growing American population in order to be better able defend the North American British colonies against French or Spanish encroachment. As America's population grew, it was able to take advantage of economies of scale in transportation, urbanization, and the warehousing of goods. At the conclusion of the French and Indian War, Great Britain's incentive to increase the American population lessened, and it placed regulations on American colonists seeking to prevent their westward movement, so as to avoid conflicts over property with Native Americans. The next few sections examine policies that foster extensive growth in natural resources, labor, and capital.

Hong Kong

Extensive Growth Policies for Natural Resources

A **natural resource** is any material source of wealth that exists in a natural state. Natural resources can be broken down into renewable or non-renewable resources. **Non-renewable resources**, once depleted, are forever used up. **Renewable resources**, over time, can replenish themselves and, if properly cared for, can create wealth for generations to come. Every country has access to some natural resources. Russia has the most land of any country. Brazil has the most tropical rainforest. Saudi Arabia has the most proven oil reserves. Natural resources are not spread equally over the globe. Differences in access to highly valued natural resources can lead to differences in relative wealth between countries. Access to deep-water ports, moderate climates, scenic views, fertile land, timber, mineral deposits, and cheap energy sources (oil, natural gas, wind, solar, or tidal) differ greatly between countries. However, if differences in natural resources accounted for the lion's share of the difference in wealth between countries, Nigeria would be one of the wealthiest countries in the world and Hong Kong would be one of the poorest.

Natural resources are to wealth creation as potential energy is to motion. Just because a country has vast amounts of highly valued natural resources does not mean that it is wealthy. Nigeria is abundant in valuable natural resources but remains one of the poorest countries in the world. Africa, as a continent, has large quantities of oil, natural gas, diamonds, gold, and other valuable natural resources, and yet many African economies remain poor. Conversely, Hong Kong has access to few natural resources (other than its deep water port), and yet is one of the richest places in the world.

The legal structure surrounding resource rights can fundamentally alter if, and when, potential wealth gets turned into actual wealth.

The Importance of Property Right Protection

History is full of examples of individuals and nations who thought that the quickest way to acquire wealth was to invade other people and take their wealth. The Spartan economy was based upon conquest, Vikings invaded forcibly by the sea, and Spain sailed off with boatload after boatload of gold and silver from Latin America. Nonrenewable resources can especially be key sources of conflict (for example, conflict diamonds) when **property rights** to those resources are not clearly defined or enforced.

Countries that clearly define and enforce property rights grow faster than those with tenuous property rights. Countries that cannot defend themselves from foreign invasion, or police themselves to prevent theft, will likely be poor. In the absence of a rule of law, owning non-renewable resources is often more of a liability than an asset. When asked why he robbed banks, John Dillinger explained that that is where the money was.

Poorly defined property rights can lead to civil wars caused by struggles over non-renewable resources. This remains the chief impediment to growth in many African

© Nejron Photo/Shutterstock.com

countries. Consequently, high levels of potential wealth are no guarantee of actual wealth.

Further, natural resources only become actual wealth if they are used. Knowing that oil exists in ANWAR or the Gulf of Mexico does not make the US richer if legislation is passed that prohibits drilling there for oil. The US may have fertile soil, but if the government pays farmers not to grow crops, wealth isn't created. Botswana created wealth by mining the most diamonds of any country in 2008. Perhaps the biggest controversy regarding the use of nonrenewable resources is in determining which generation has the moral right to it, since once it is gone it can no longer be used by future generations. Norway creates wealth by taking oil and natural gas from the North Sea. It then takes the revenues from oil and natural gas sales and saves the money for future generations. In this way, they let future generations benefit from nonrenewable resources that are used today.

Property rights are also key to the continual usability of renewable resources. If waterways are overfished, the fish supply will not regenerate. If buffalo herds are killed off, they can't reproduce. If soil fertility is exhausted, it may take years to rejuvenate it. If forests are clear cut, they take years to grow again.

When renewable resources are owned by private individuals, those individuals have an incentive to maximize their wealth creation potential over time, thereby maximizing wealth creation. Ranchers don't typically slaughter their whole cattle herd in a year. Incentives change, however, when resources are commonly owned. US bison were commonly owned in the 1800's, and the only way to profit from a bison was to kill one and skin it. There was no incentive to preserve bison, so they almost went extinct. Nobel Prize winner, Elinor Ostrom, helped pioneer the field of **institutional economics**, which suggests that formal and informal institutions develop to aid in wealth creation. According to Ostrom, institutions form to allocate commonly owned assets like fish or fresh water.

The value of natural resources also changes over time. Middle Eastern oil wasn't highly valued two thousand years ago. The invention of the internal combustion engine changed that. Given that the future is uncertain, people don't know which resources, renewable or not, will be most valued in the future. Thus, the protection of renewable natural resources for future use is important.

Unfortunately, political pressure or bureaucratic self-interest often influences the management of government owned renewable resources. Bureaucrats often ignore current market prices and do things like subsidize logging in national forests, or prevent sustainable logging in the same.

© FUN FUN PHOTO/Shutterstock.com

Corn being farmed in front of an ethanol refinery

Both errors cause a misuse of scarce resources. One such example is when corn farmers have lobbied Congress to mandate its use in ethanol in order to drive up the price of corn. With increased profitability of corn planting, fewer other crops are grown, which drives up the cost of foods, both nationally and globally. US ethanol policy not only slows the US economy, but it also makes it harder for poor people in foreign countries to afford food.

In 2008, a bribery scandal came to light in the Denver office of the US Department of the Interior.[1] Government workers engaged in sex and drug abuse with oil company workers and took thousands of dollars of gifts while overseeing billions of dollars worth of energy contracts. These are just a few examples of resource mismanagement. A look into the former Soviet Union's environmental record suggests that government command and control policies over natural resources are not any more likely to yield optimal resource management.

Thus, natural resources, both renewable and nonrenewable, are potential sources of wealth creation as long as property rights are clearly defined and enforced, resources are efficiently managed, and government policies don't incentivize their disuse or misuse. Private ownership of natural resources allows wealth-creating incentives to guide the use and care of natural resources. Where private property rights are difficult to define and enforce, institutions, both formal and informal, can be created or allowed to evolve to address the use and care of commonly owned resources.

Extensive Growth Policies for Labor

Government policies can, and do, influence the quantity and quality of the work force.

Like natural resources, a country's population represents a potential source of wealth creation. Extensive growth in labor comes from either an increase in the numbers of laborers or an increase in the number of hours spent working.

Increases in the numbers of individuals in the labor force come from either increasing the population or an increase in the percentage of the existing population who take part in the labor force. An increase in the population can come from increased births (over time), increased **immigration** (more individuals moving into the country), decreased **emigration** (fewer individuals moving abroad), better health, and longer life expectancy. All of these factors can be influenced by changes in government policy.

Policies Influencing Family Size

What types of policies influence family size in the US? Most commonly, increased family size is related to policies that lower the cost of child rearing, such as the Family Medical Leave Act, child tax credits and deductions, and subsidized living expenses for children (food, clothing, shelter, education, and health care). Such policies all work to increase the rate of child bearing. Families in the poorest quintile in the United States have the highest average birth rate of any income quintile. Food stamps, public housing, public education, and Medicaid are all features of the US welfare state that lower the cost of child rearing to low income families. As incomes increase in the US, parents have access to less government support for child rearing and potentially greater access to reliable methods of birth control and tend to have smaller average family sizes.

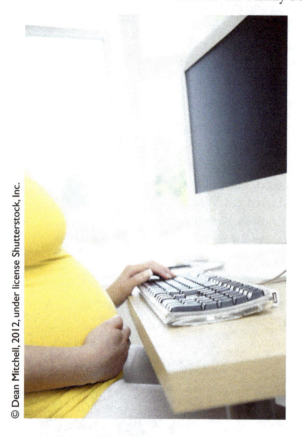

Changing average family sizes today translate into a different potential labor force of the future. But, these same policies may have a different short-term impact on the supply of labor. Researchers have noted that the presence of children in a family increase both the average wages and hours supplied to the labor force by men.[2] The opposite is true for women, though less so for women who are married, have more years of education, or have older children.[3] In sum, it is debatable whether or not policies meant to increase family sizes have a positive impact on the short-term supply of labor.

Changes in Immigration and Emigration

Another way to increase the labor supply is to allow workers to move into a county. Immigration and emigration are largely economic phenomenon, though war and persecution can also play key roles. An economy that has a net positive amount of immigration will see its population increase. Immigrants of working age bring some level of skills or education from their home country. In this way, the country to which they immigrate gains the advantage of their work without having had to pay for their rearing costs. Additionally, these new workers increase the domestic demand for goods and services, stimulating other areas of

---

[2] Shelly Lundberg and Elaina Rose, "The Effects of Sons and Daughters on Men's Labor Supply and Wages" Review of Economics and Statistics, May 2002, 84(2): 251–268

[3] Data: US Bureau of Labor Statistics

the economy beyond those in which the immigrants are employed.

Historically, immigrants into the United States have consistently worked more hours per year than native born workers. Government policies to restrict immigration, particularly among highly educated foreigners, have worked to slow down economic growth in the US. Policies that openly attract highly educated immigrants not only improve the quantity of the labor force, but work to increase its average skill level.

And yet, laws in the United States set the quota for immigrants below the true number wishing to immigrate. As a result, a black market is created for immigration. Foreigners sneak across the border or pay human smugglers to assist them in entering the US. Illegal immigration is not as economically valuable as legal immigration. Illegal immigrants lack the ability to use the justice system to enforce property rights. They waste valuable resources avoiding detection from immigration officials, and have an incentive to give birth to children in the US to decrease their odds of deportation. Because illegal immigration is considered criminal, the cost of engaging in further criminal activities is lowered for legal immigrants. Roughly 27% of federal prisoners are not citizens of the United States. An increase in legal immigration among skilled immigrants, along with the tightening of border security to prevent illegal immigration, would increase both extensive and intensive economic growth in the United States.

Access to Healthcare

Healthy workers miss fewer work days than do unhealthy workers. Better health coupled with extended life expectancy also allows workers to spend more years in the labor force if they so choose. By the end of their careers, elderly employees have amassed extensive job experience, which can increase labor productivity. Policies that discourage smoking (for example, a cigarette tax), and obesity (for example, building pedestrian infrastructure) can lead to healthier lifestyle choices and longer careers in the labor force. Public policies that improve health care or make it more affordable/accessible to workers can increase economic growth. And yet, in February 2014, the Congressional Budget Office released a report that the Affordable Health Care Act would reduce the number of full time jobs in the US by 2.5 million. While healthier workers work more hours per year, poor design of government health programs may actually cause the labor supply to shrink. And while programs such as Medicare and Medicaid increase access to healthcare, they do not directly increase the health of the current US workforce, as these programs are largely only available for individuals outside of the labor force.

Incarceration Rates

Not only do workers need to be generally healthy to work, they must be non-institutionalized in order to participate in the labor force. As of December 31, 2016, an estimated 6.6 million persons were under the supervision of US adult correctional systems, representing 2.6% of US adults. The US incarcerates more prisoners, and a higher percentage of its adult population, than does any other industrialized country.[4] Such a large incarceration rate hurts economic growth for two reasons. The first is that prisoners are kept from the labor market. Not only do they forgo current production, but also upon release, their ex-convict status reduces their employment prospects. Second, according to the Office of the General Counsel for the Federal Bureau of Prisons, the average cost of incarcerating a federal inmate in 2017 was $36,299.[5] As resources are used for prisons, they are diverted away from the private sector or from other government programs such as education.

One obvious change in government policy that would result in fewer incarcerations would be the decriminalization of illicit drugs. If rehabilitation and education replaced incarceration, economic resources could be reallocated to more productive uses.

Changes in Hours Worked and Labor Force Participation

Tax rates, labor laws, and social safety net programs all impact the amount of labor individuals supply to the labor force. Nobel Prize winning economist Edward Prescott illustrates the importance of marginal tax rates on labor.[6] In the 1970's, the average worker in Germany, France, and the United Kingdom all worked more hours per year the average worker in the United States. Successive changes in marginal income tax rates (upward in Europe and downward in the

[4] Source: April 2018, NCJ 251211 "Correctional Populations in the United States, 2016, US Department of Justice *Bureau of Justice Statistics*"

[5] Cite: 4/30/2018 Document Number: 2018-09062

[6] "Why Do Americans Work So Much More Than Europeans?" *Federal Reserve Bank of Minneapolis Quarterly Review* Vol. 28. No. 1. July 2004, 2–13.

US) during the 1980's resulted in workers in the United States working more hours than workers in each of these other countries by the early 1990's. When they are allowed to benefit from the fruits of their labor, workers work more hours per year. As marginal tax rates increases, workers find less marginal benefit in an extra hour of work and decide to work less.

Child labor laws, mandatory retirement ages, and minimum wage laws all work to decrease the amount of labor provided in an economy. Minimum wage laws outlaw the employment of individuals whose marginal revenue product (the amount of revenue they can bring in for their employer) is below that level. Not only do such laws reduce the employment of low skilled workers, they prohibit such workers from gaining experience.

Many governments have instituted some sort of social safety net to help care for the poor and indigent. The more generous the safety net is, the less attractive an extra hour of work becomes. In many cases, an extra hour of work causes such a reduction in safety net payments that work becomes unprofitable for individuals. In this way the safety net can act more like a web than a net. Welfare dependency is a symptom of poorly designed safety nets. The Welfare Reform Act of 1996 (PRWORA) increased the number of people in the labor force by limiting access to welfare and increasing work requirements for recipients. Since then, however, there has been a marked increase in disability claims.

Similarly, countries that have more generous unemployment insurance benefits have higher levels of unemployment and longer average bouts of unemployment than do societies with less generous benefits. Generous benefits result in people taking more time to find a job before heading back to work.

Thus, government policies can enable, or discourage, the quantity of work engaged in by a country's work force. As long as government policies discourage work, economic growth rates will be lower than they otherwise would be. Policies that promote an increase in the quantity and quality of work help to create wealth. Still, wealth does not necessarily accrue fastest to the hardest workers. Creating wealth by hand is often arduous. The wealth creation process is vastly accelerated with the addition of capital.

Extensive Growth Policies for Physical Capital

Greater Accumulation of Physical Goods

Producing wealth without the help of machines, tools, or factories is very difficult. For this reason, economic growth is highly correlated with capital investment. Societies with the highest levels of per capita output are those societies with the most capital. This is why the economic system of wealth creation is referred to as capitalism. The production of mass quantities of goods and services is only possible with the help of capital.

Unlike natural resources, capital cannot be found lying around under the ground, it has to be made. The creation of capital, then, represents an active decision to forgo current consumption in order to use today's resources to create capital for use tomorrow. Societies on the brink of starvation have little ability to forgo current consumption in pursuit of more prosperous future. The ability and willingness to engage in savings is a prerequisite for capital accumulation. Societies that save larger percentages of their income have faster capital accumulation rates than do societies with lower savings rates.

Governments can create an economic environment that is either friendly or hostile to the development of capital. Capital friendly policies include the solid definition and protection of private property rights, low marginal taxes on capital income, low regulation of the uses of capital and sale of its output, tax policies that encourage savings, monetary policies that provide a stable currency, and the provision of complementary public infrastructure. Because capital is mobile, countries that have capital friendly environments are able to benefit from both domestically and internationally funded capital formation in their country.

© Gina Sanders, 2012, under license Shutterstock, Inc.

Property Rights Protection

Government failure to define and protect property rights of capitalists often leads to high levels of theft, civil wars, the expropriation of capital by governments themselves, competition for private capital from government owned capital, and a regulatory environment that encourages taking rather than making. Individuals and firms do not make a habit of forgoing current consumption for investment in future capital unless they are relatively certain that they will be able to benefit from the capital they create.

Consequently, capital is not attracted to high crime areas, as profits lost to theft discourage capital formation. Civil wars likewise cause death and destruction of capital. People who do not think they will likely live very long are not apt to forgo current consumption. Firms who believe their capital is likely to get blown up are not likely to locate in war torn areas.

Some governments have historically attracted private investment in major industries from foreign firms only to nationalize the capital. Typically, government officials lack the technical knowledge to operate and repair said capital, so output falls as a result. At the same time, other firms then refuse to invest their capital in the country for fear of losing it to government control. Likewise, if private capitalists believe that a government can at any time compete with them using publicly owned capital, private capital dissipates. Government sponsored enterprises have access to the public tax revenues to cover operating losses, a benefit not typically shared by the owners of private capital.

Rent Seeking

Firms can gain wealth by producing goods people want to buy at prices they want to pay, or they can make money by lobbying governments to rig the economic playing field in their behalf. **Rent seeking** is the process of engaging in costly non-productive actions (such as lobbying) in search of profit. When government officials pick economic winners and losers, firms redirect their resources from wealth creation to lobbying the government. This often involves reducing physical capital and employing more labor (lobbyists). Theft and rent-seeking therefore destroy wealth.

Tax Incentives for Capital Accumulation

Because capital is mobile in the long run, countries that try to heavily tax income derived from capital find it more difficult to attract new capital than do countries with low marginal tax rates on capital income. Table 4.1 illustrates the variety of **corporate income tax** rates throughout the OECD. Ireland, with its corporate income tax rate that is approximately one-half that of the United States, has attracted capital that makes it one of the richest countries in the world.

The **capital gains tax** is a tax on the sale of capital that has appreciated in value. It is applied to the sale of assets ranging from factories, to houses, to shares of stock. High capital gains taxes serve as a disincentive to invest in assets that may appreciate in value. Entrepreneurs also face income taxes. High marginal tax rates on income derived from capital decrease the profitability of capital and therefore work to chase capital to lower taxed political jurisdictions.

TABLE 4.1	2018 OECD CORPORATE TAX RATES (COMBINED NATIONAL AND SUB-NATIONAL RATES)		
Country	**Tax Rate**	**Country**	**Tax Rate**
Hungary	9	Austria	25
Ireland	12.5	Chile	25
Lithuania	15	Netherlands	25
Czech Republic	19	Spain	25
Poland	19	United States	25.8
Slovenia	19	Luxembourg	26.01
United Kingdom	19	Canada	26.8
Estonia	20	Korea	27.5
Finland	20	Italy	27.8
Iceland	20	New Zealand	28
Latvia	20	Greece	29
Slovak Republic	21	Belgium	29.6
Switzerland	21.1	Japan	29.7
Denmark	22	Germany	29.8
Sweden	22	Australia	30
Turkey	22	Mexico	30
Israel	23	Portugal	31.5
Norway	23	France	34.43

Regulation and Infrastructure

Capital is most productive when its use is not heavily regulated and its output can be sold globally. Swiss banks for years have attracted deposits based on their low level of government regulations relating to the reporting of deposits to government authorities. Burdensome labor or environmental regulations also cause capital to seek less regulatory environments. Firms that find it difficult to liquidate their capital due to foreign investment controls or unstable currencies will be less likely to create capital in a country.

Most goods can be sold anywhere in the world. As a result, the decision to locate productive capital in any given geographical location will also be a function of ease of transport in getting their products to world markets. In this way, countries that support free trade policies attract capital. Production from their capital will be able to travel to other countries without facing punitive tariffs. Firms that locate in countries with high trade barriers find it difficult to export goods due to retaliatory trade barriers placed on products from their country.

Another aspect of getting goods and services to market is the existence of needed infrastructure. This infrastructure makes capital more productive by lowering the cost of getting products to market. Roads, ports, airports, railways, energy grids, and telecommunication systems all play a supportive role in lowering the transaction costs of doing business. Different governments choose to intervene to varying degrees in the infrastructure sectors. While some governments have nationalized railways, roads, and telecommunication companies, others have privately operated roads, railways, and telecommunication companies. Infrastructure ownership and operation tends to be more efficient when controlled by the private sector rather than the public sector. Private industry is much less likely to build a bridge to nowhere than are politicians.

Savings Incentives

By running up government debt, governments can crowd out private investment. As consumers and firms engage in savings, their savings can be used by other consumers for consumer loans, by businesses for investment, or by governments for government pending. As governments borrow increasingly large amounts of money, less saving is left over for private capital accumulation. Capital only can be formed once saving has occurred. The first step in increasing a national savings rate is to decrease the indebtedness of the public sector. As the US government paid down on its national debt following the US Civil War, private capital investment increased and an investment boom transpired.

The National Debt Clock in New York City February 13, 2019.

The other way to increase the national savings rate is to incentivize savings. Income, capital gains, and inheritance taxes act as disincentives for consumers to postpone current consumption. Governments that replace income taxes with sales (consumption) taxes and abolish estate taxes discourage consumption rather than savings. By allowing people to save tax-free for retirement or college, individual retirement accounts and college 529 savings plans increase the rate of return to savers and thereby incentivize savings.

It has been more than 200 years since the industrial revolution took hold in the UK and the Netherlands. Capital accumulation often itself works to stratify countries around the world into the **industrialized countries** (those with high levels of capital), the **industrializing countries** (those with increasing levels of capital), and the **non-industrialized countries** (those with little capital). Free market economies have often been referred to as capitalist economies because of the quick pace at which free market countries accumulated capital in the 19th and 20th centuries. As important as increased capital accumulation has been to economic growth in the previous two centuries, since the middle of the 20th century, it has been intensive economic growth and gains from trade that have contributed to the lion's share of economic growth in the industrialized world. The next sections examine policies that foster intensive growth.

Intensive Growth

Intensive economic growth occurs whenever productivity increases. Laborers can increase their productivity by obtaining human capital, skills, or knowledge that increases output per hour worked. Human capital can be gained through formal education or training (schooling), education or training that occurs within firm (such as with an apprenticeship or internship), or informally through learning by doing (experience).

Innovation and new technology can increase the productivity of natural resources, capital, and labor. For example, the invention and use of the internet revolutionized the way people and firms gather and use information, thereby increasing productivity in the economy. Productivity increases can also come via entrepreneurship. Intensive economic growth occurs when **entrepreneurs** discover new ways to combine resources to increase efficiency of production and distribution of goods and services. For these reasons, inventors and entrepreneurs play pivotal roles in increasing the standard of living from one generation to the next. The remainder of this chapter examines economic policies that influence intensive economic growth by encouraging or limiting the development of human capital, technology, and entrepreneurship.

Incentives for Human Capital Accumulation

Government policies affect not only the number of hours workers participate in the labor force, they also influence the productivity of those hours. Labor productivity, in part, is a function of human capital development. Policies that encourage, or increase, the education and skill level of the population (thereby increasing their **human capital**) can help to increase labor productivity. This benefits both the workers who are more productive (typically with higher wages) and the economy (with more output).

Government policies that encourage the accumulation of human capital speed economic growth. Highly skilled workers earn higher wages as a reflection of their enhanced productivity. Conversely, government policies that attempt to decrease income inequality (for example tax rates that are greater at higher income levels) reduce the marginal benefit to an individual of pursuing additional education or skills. If a high school dropout can make the same or almost the same as a medical doctor with ten years of post-high school education, then fewer people will take on the often arduous task of pursuing higher education.

The government in the US is directly involved in the operation of public schools from pre-school to post-secondary education. Policies that increase the education and skill level of students attending these schools will increase human capital levels. In 2015, an OECD study of 15 year olds in 72 countries found that the US ranked 41st in math, 24th in reading and 25th in science among the countries examined. Table 4.2 lists the top 10 countries in each discipline. Even as the United States spends more money per student on education than most other countries, the learning outcomes in the United States fail to land in the top ten. Reform of elementary and secondary education in the US, if it increases learning outcomes, would benefit economic growth.

The United States has arguably the premier university system in the world. One major difference between elementary education and university education in the US is that students are allowed to choose which university they attend (as long as they get admitted and can pay the tuition). In many elementary school districts, students are assigned a school to attend. Competition for students among colleges and universities helps to increase the value of a college education.

TABLE 4.2	**2015 PISA TEST SCORE RANKING**		
Rank	**Math**	**Reading**	**Science**
1	Singapore	Singapore	Singapore
2	Hong Kong	Hong Kong	Japan
3	Macao	Canada	Estonia
4	Taiwan	Finland	Chinese Taipei
5	Japan	Ireland	Finland
6	China*	Estonia	Macao
7	Korea	Korea	Canada
8	Switzerland	Japan	Viet Nam
9	Estonia	Norway	Hong Kong
10	Canada	New Zealand	China*

College and university faculty are more likely to work for private colleges and universities than are elementary school teachers. They are also less likely to be unionized than their elementary school counterparts. While the federal government aides low income students with Pell Grants to attend the university of their choice (including private religious schools), many elementary school districts do not allow this type of voucher program. The school choice movement argues that the government should give parents a choice of elementary and secondary schools that their children can attend without having to pay private tuition. Doing so would increase competition among schools. However, the idea of school choice is typically unpopular among teachers unions and has not been widely implemented in the US.

Only 48 percent of Native-born Americans held postsecondary degrees as of 2017.[7] Low college graduation rates in the United States are partly a reflection of how poorly many children are educated at the elementary and secondary education levels. Over one-third of college students in the US now must take remedial classes because their skill set was not college ready.

In an effort to make a college degree more affordable, US government policies give tax breaks for educational expenses, tax breaks for saving for college (529 savings plans), interest deductibility of student loans, and grants for low income students (Pell Grants), and in some cases offer student debt forgiveness. These incentives, however, do nothing to ensure that the education pursued with this government help actually improves a student's preparedness for the workforce.

[7] OCED Education at a Glance, 2018.

TABLE 4.3	RANK OF COUNTRY'S BY PERCENTAGE OF 25–34 YEAR OLDS WITH COLLEGE DEGREE			
Rank	**Country**		**Rank**	**Country**
1	Korea		6	Ireland
2	Canada		7	Australia
3	Japan		8	United Kingdom
4	Russia		9	Luxembourg
5	Lithuania		10	Switzerland

While taking out student loans to gain a medical education often makes sense, acquiring massive student debt for an unfinished degree, or a degree in underwater basket weaving, does little to boost the worker productivity of students and becomes wasted taxpayer money. Roughly 44 percent of all students who enter a four year college in the US fail to receive a college degree.[8] This results in billions of dollars in wasted resources. Government policies that throw untargeted money at education serve to slow down economic growth by misallocating resources. Targeted educational policies, such as the use of technical training schools, can go a long way to ensure that education spending results in an increase in human capital.

Human capital levels can also increase by increasing the number of highly educated/skilled immigrants a country allows to enter. Policies that openly attract highly educated immigrants not only improve the quantity of the labor force, but work to increase its average skill level. Allowing foreign students who graduate from US universities to stay in the United States would go a long way to increasing human capital levels in the United States.

All of these factors encourage human capital formation and in this way foster intensive economic growth. Like increases in human capital, innovations in technology can increase productivity and lead to intensive growth. We now turn to examine the government policies that aid in the development of new technology.

Policies That Encourage the Creation of New Technology

The most notable source of government involvement in innovation is the protection of intellectual property rights. Societies that allow inventors to reap the

---

[8] http://www.thefiscaltimes.com/Articles/2010/10/28/High-College-Dropout-Rate-Threatens-US-Growth.aspx

economic rewards of their invention incentivize invention and innovation. The Founding Fathers of the United States thought that the protection of intellectual property rights was so necessary for economic growth that they included patent protection in the US Constitution. As the economy becomes more internationalized, international protection of intellectual property rights becomes increasingly important. This topic has been a major point of negotiation in global trade talks.

Table 4.4 ranks the top ten innovating countries in 2018.[9] Governments can incentivize private innovation through tax credits to firms for research and development costs, or they can directly award prizes to private firms who solve a specified public problem. The British Longitude Act of 1714, under Queen Anne, offered a prize up to 20,000 British Pounds to anyone who could invent a technology to correctly determine longitude while at sea within 30 nautical miles.

In this case, the British government identified a pressing national security need and incentivized the private sector to devote resources to solving the problem. An English clockmaker by the name of John Harrison invented the marine chronometer, thereby solving the problem.

In the US, The National Science Foundation works to fund research and development through grants to researchers. Alternatively, the government could identify technological innovations they wish to see and directly employ government researchers. For instance, researchers at the National Institute of Health work on federally approved and sponsored health research. Having governments pick and fund specific research projects turns research and development into a political animal where politicians determine where innovation should occur rather than letting the market determine it. Note that government sponsored research runs the risk of appealing to special interest groups rather than the general public.

---

[9] Global Innovation Index 2018 released jointly by WIP, Cornell University, INSEAD and the 2018 GII Knowledge Partners, the Confederation of Indian Industry, PwC's Strategy & and the National Confederation of Industry (CNI) Brazil and Brazilian Micro and Small Business Support Service (Sebrae)

TABLE 4.4	GLOBAL INNOVATION INDEX		
Rank	**Country**	**Rank**	**Country**
1	Switzerland	6	United States of America
2	Netherlands	7	Finland
3	Sweden	8	Denmark
4	United Kingdom	9	Germany
5	Singapore	10	Ireland

Such special interest groups can include those whose jobs are in peril as a result of the new technology. The development of ATM's, for instance, has reduced the need for bank tellers. The development of handheld computers has decreased the demand for hard cover books or printed newspapers. Governments are often approached by industries whose future prosperity is threatened by new technology to set rules against the adaption or use of the new technology. Governments that restrain from granting such regulatory or tax preferences to dying industries are able to provide a technologically friendly economic growth environment. Few would seek to prevent the creation of a cancer vaccine, even though such a vaccine could make oncologist jobs obsolete. Yet, often politicians bend to lobbyists making similar arguments concerning the preservation of jobs made obsolete by new technology. Although some individuals may lose their jobs as a result of technological innovation, such innovations increase economic growth and therefore increase the standard of living for generations to come.

©Vasily Smirnov, 2012, under license Shutterstock, Inc.

Even beyond explicit government policies toward invention and innovation, lies a society's acceptance of change. If a traditional society (such as the Amish) is resistant to technological or scientific advancement, then members of that society will be less likely to use their talents inventing new technologies or making new discoveries. A social ethic that embraces technological advance and educates its citizens accordingly works to create an innovation friendly economic environment. Likewise, entrepreneurship is important for such innovations to be put into use. The next section examines policies that foster entrepreneurship.

Policies That Encourage Entrepreneurship

The economy is ever changing. Firms come and go. Jobs are gained and lost. According to the US Census Bureau, virtually all new job creation between 1977 and 2005 came from firms that were less than five years old.[10] Older firms, on average, were net job destroyers in this time period (meaning more jobs were lost in these firms than were created). Joseph Schumpeter referred to this violent churning of the economy as a process of **creative destruction**. Innovation and changing wants cause the production mix of an economy to change over time.

The Changing Mix of Output in the US

Table 4.5 illustrates how the US economy has changed its mix of outputs since WWII. As a percentage of GDP, the agriculture and manufacturing sectors in the US have seen dramatic declines in their relative importance to output. On the other hand, the industries which experienced the most growth were in the sectors of finance, professional services, education, and healthcare.

TABLE 4.5 % OF US GDP CONTRIBUTED BY SECTOR[11]			
Sector	1947	1987	2017
Agriculture, forestry, fishing, and hunting	8.2	1.7	.9%
Mining	2.4	1.5	1.7%
Utilities	1.4	2.7	1.5%
Construction	3.6	4.4	4.3%
Manufacturing	25.6	17.4	11.6%
Wholesale trade	6.4	6	5.9%
Retail trade	9.5	7.3	5.9%
Transportation and warehousing	5.8	3.2	3%
Information	2.8	4.2	4.8%
Finance, insurance, real estate, rental, and leasing	10.5	18	20.9%
Professional and business services	3.3	8.1	12.1%
Educational services, health care, and social assistance	1.9	5.9	8.4%
Arts, entertainment, recreation, accommodation, and food services	3.3	3.2	4%
Government	12.5	13.9	12.7%

---

[10] http://www.kauffman.org/newsroom/u-s-job-growth-driven-entirely-by-startups.aspx

[11] Source: Bureau of Labor Statistics

TABLE 4.6	TOP 10 DYING INDUSTRIES (2007–2017)[12]		
Rank	**Country**	**Rank**	**Country**
1	Videotape and disc rental	6	Land subdivision
2	Other apparel knitting mills	7	Directory and mailing list publishers
3	Magnetic median manufacturing and reproducing	8	Hosiery and sock mills
4	Photofinishing	9	Telephone apparatus manufacturing
5	Port and harbor operations	10	Newspaper publishers

Table 4.6 lists the top ten industries that contracted the most from 2007 until 2016. The wireless revolution has aided the decline of more than one of these industries, as videos on demand, downloadable songs, online newspapers, and other technologies have decreased the demand for many products such as CD's, video rentals, and printed newspapers. Why buy CD's in a store when you can download songs online? Why rent a movie from a store when you can stream movies online? Why buy physical newspapers when you can read them online?

Similarly, the creation and mass marketing of the automobile contributed to the destruction of many industries such as horse and buggy producers, blacksmiths, whip and saddle makers, stable boys, and dirt carters (manure removers). This caused many people to lose their jobs. The newly unemployed had to gain new education or skills to find a job in industries which were growing. William C. Durant, a leading buggy manufacturer left the buggy industry for the automobile industry where he later founded General Motors.

The high turnover rate among the largest firms is well illustrated through an examination of the Dow Jones Industrial Index. The **Dow Jones Industrial Index (DJIA)** is an index of the some of the largest firms publicly traded on the NASDAQ and the New York Stock Exchange. Table 4.7 illustrates how the makeup of the DJIA has changed over time. No company has been continuously listed in the DJIA from 1896 until 2019. General Electric was the last original Dow component to be replaced. It was replaced with Walgreens Boots Alliance in June, 2018. Apple replaced AT&T in March, 2015. Wal-Mart, the nation's top retailer only joined the Dow in 1997 when it replaced Woolworth.

Markets don't make themselves; individuals make them. Retail goods don't sell themselves; the Sam Waltons of the world sell them. Cars don't make themselves; the Henry Fords of the world build them. Software doesn't write itself; the Bill Gates of the world write it.

---

[12] Cite: Samuel Stebbins and Evan Comen, 24/7 Wall Street Published 9:23 a.m. ET Dec. 28, 2017 | Updated 3:13 p.m. ET Jan. 4, 2018

© Sai Yeung Chan, 2012, under license Shutterstock, Inc.

© VIPDesignUSA , 2012, under license Shutterstock, Inc.

Free markets and the protection of property rights are necessary but not sufficient conditions to generate meaningful long term economic growth. Games, no matter how just the rules, need players to play and entertain. Economic growth, no matter how free the markets and just the rules, needs **entrepreneurs** to build and create.

It would take a whole textbook to list every major development in the American economy and the corresponding entrepreneur. Entrepreneurship leads to economic growth as individuals have ideas that they act upon. Some are big ideas, some are small ideas. Some are good ideas, and some are downright foolish.

Eighty percent of new businesses fail within the first five years. Starting a new business is a risk. Yet, a successful economy needs creative risk takers. It is no coincidence that the rapid industrialization of the US in the late nineteenth century occurred during the heyday of American capitalism. Entrepreneurs were free to improve the world and make a buck in the process. The tycoons of yesteryear were able to amass great personal fortunes, but they also improved the lot of the poor by providing electricity, better transportation, improved communication, and better products at lower prices. America would be poorer if the tycoons had not been allowed to create wealth. Unfortunately, many tycoons that brought industrialization to the US are demonized as being "Robber Barons." This pejorative term is very misleading. Robbery and wealth creation through voluntary exchanges are altogether opposites. Entrepreneurs don't amass money for themselves by forcibly taking it from other people. They offer better products or lower prices than their competitors and people freely buy their products because they believe said products will improve their lives.

Entrepreneurs wear many hats. They invent new products, innovate new product lines, improve the quality of products, increase the efficiency of existing production and distribution, engage in **arbitrage**, take risks, and connect sellers with buyers and financiers with producers. They can also see where existing products sold by existing companies in existing markets can be altered to produce more wealth.

TABLE 4.7 DOW JONES INDUSTRIAL AVERAGE COMPOSITE COMPANIES

2019	1976	1928	1896
3M	Allied Chemical	Allied Chemical	American Cotton Oil
American Express	Aluminum Company of America	American Can	American Sugar
Apple	American Can	American Sugar	American Tobacco
Boeing	American Telephone & Telegraph	American Tobacco	Chicago Gas
Caterpillar	American Tobacco	American Smelting	Distilling & Cattle Feeding
Chevron	Bethlehem Steel	Atlantic Refining	General Electric
Cisco Systems	Chrysler	Bethlehem Steel	Laclede Gas
Coca-Cola	DuPont	Chrysler	National Lead
DowDuPont	Eastman Kodak Company	General Electric Company	North American Utility
ExxonMobil	Esmark (Swift and Co)	General Motors Corporation	Tennessee Coal & Iron
Goldman Sachs	Exxon Corporation (Standard Oil NJ)	General Railway Signal	US Leather
The Home Depot	General Electric Company	Goodrich	US Rubber
Intel	General Foods	International Harvester	
IBM	General Motors Corporation	International Nickel	
Johnson & Johnson	Goodyear	Mack Truck	
JPMorgan Chase	Inco (International Nickel)	Nash Motors	
McDonald's	International Harvester	North American	
Merck and Company	International Paper Company	Paramount Publix	
Microsoft	Johns-Manville	Postum Incorporated	
Nike	Minnesota Mining & Manufacturing	Radio Corporation	
Pfizer	Owens-Illinois Glass	Sears Roebuck & Company	
Procter & Gamble	Proctor & Gamble Company	Standard Oil (NJ)	
Travelers	Sears Roebuck & Company	Texas Company	
UnitedHealth Group	Standard Oil of California	Texas Gulf Sulphur	
United Technologies	Texaco Incorporated	Union Carbide	

TABLE 4.7	DOW JONES INDUSTRIAL AVERAGE COMPOSITE COMPANIES (CONTINUED)		
Verizon	Union Carbide	US Steel	
Visa	United Technologies Corporation	Victor Talking Machine	
Wal-Mart	US Steel	Westinghouse Electric	
Walgreens Boots Alliance	Westinghouse Electric	Woolworth	
Walt Disney	Woolworth	Wright Aeronautical	

Government Created Obstacles: Bailouts, Tax Codes, and Regulations

Government sponsored bailouts represent a complete rejection of the importance of entrepreneurs and the process of creative destruction in wealth creation. Existing firms sometimes use the political process to protect themselves from competition. They may lobby for trade restrictions against foreign competition, for regulation of competing industries, for tax breaks for their firms or for direct and indirect government subsidization of their business or industry. They also often lobby for regulations placed on new entrants into their industry. Existing businesses with existing employees have more political clout than hypothetical businesses that do not yet exist or that are yet to grow large.

© Sai Yeung Chan 2012, under license Shutterstock, Inc.

In contrast, if a firm is allowed to fail, its assets do not disappear. They are sold off to the highest bidders, who, in turn, will put them to use in more efficient ways than they were previously employed, lest the purchasers too go out of business. Workers don't die when the firm for which they work stops production. They become potential laborers for other firms in the same or even in different industries. The sign of a healthy growing economy is not one where existing firms never shed jobs, but one in which existing firms are allowed to shed jobs and free up labor to engage in more efficient production.

The US doesn't need a vibrant horse drawn buggy industry in order to thrive. Preventing the growth of one firm or industry (via taxes, regulation, or other means) to protect another firm or industry cripples not only entrepreneurship, but also cripples economic growth by inefficiently redistributing scarce resources. Clinging tightly to existing jobs will only cause fewer new jobs to be created.

Markets are constantly evolving. By taking advantage of individual information known to Hayek's "men on the street," individual entrepreneurs are able to create, innovate, and meet the needs and desires of the people around them.

Entrepreneurship is as natural to humans as breathing. It involves people trying to make the world a better place for themselves and the world around them. When Thomas Edison made and mass marketed electric lights, he not only improved his own wealth, but materially improved the lives of everyone else who could now have light after sunset without candles—except for employees of the candle industry who now needed to look elsewhere for jobs.

Governments can both foster and hinder entrepreneurship through government regulations and the tax code. Tax codes that provide low marginal tax rates applied equally to all firms benefit entrepreneurs more than tax codes with high marginal rates and special tax breaks to politically connected firms. Since start-ups tend to be small and politically unconnected, being hit with higher taxes than their larger competitors only serves to disadvantage to them.

Regulations regarding the formation of a business or regulations regarding hiring and firing of employees are particularly important to small startup firms. Table 4.8 shows the average number of days it takes in different parts of the world to register a new business venture. Table 4.9 shows the top ten best and worst countries in which to do business. The factors that went into the calculation included ease of starting a business, dealing with construction permits, registering property, getting credit, protecting investors, paying taxes, trading across borders, enforcing contracts, and ease of closing businesses.

Because entrepreneurs create wealth, it should not be surprising that the countries that are most receptive to doing business rank among the wealthiest economies in the world. Those that erect the most barriers to private industry rank amongst the poorest countries in the world. Perhaps the most important set of economic growth policies revolve around letting people improve their own lives and the lives of those around them.

© Toria, 2012, under license Shutterstock, Inc.

TABLE 4.8 — DAYS TO REGISTER A NEW BUSINESS[13]

Region	# of Days	Country	# of Days	Country	# of Days
North America	3.55	New Zealand	.5	Somalia	70
OECD	8.37	Canada	1.5	Brazil	79.9
Europe & Central Asia	11.64	Hong Kong	1.5	Eritrea	84
Middle East & North Africa	18.5	Georgia	2	Suriname	84.5
East Asia & Pacific	20.3	Australia	2.5	Haiti	97
Sub-Saharan Africa	24.05	Singapore	2.5	Cambodia	99
Latin America & Caribbean	30.95	Jamaica	3	Venezuela	230

TABLE 4.9 — FORBE'S 2017 LIST OF BEST AND WORST COUNTRIES[14]

Rank	Country	Rank	Country
1	United Kingdom	152	Libya
2	Sweden	153	Yemen
3	Hong Kong	154	Syria
4	Netherlands	155	Gambia
5	New Zealand	156	Haiti
6	Canada	157	Chad
7	Denmark	158	Equatorial Guinea
8	Singapore	159	Guinea-Bissau
9	Australia	160	Republic of the Congo
10	Switzerland	161	Central African Republic

[13] Source: Doing Business Project of the World Bank, 2017.

[14] Source: https://www.forbes.com/best-countries-for-business/list/#tab:overall

Thus, there are many acts that the government or society can take to encourage capital accumulation and technological innovation. Such actions lead to economic growth, but are not always politically popular, despite the overwhelming evidence of their overall benefits to society. Likewise, lower trade barriers lead to wealth creation and yet are often politically unpopular.

Convergence

Increased trade between countries has caused individual countries to become more globally integrated. As a result, natural resources, labor, capital, technology, and entrepreneurship, have moved between national boundaries at increased speed. Because of this free flow of inputs, ideas, and outputs, **convergence theory** suggests that countries with a lower per capita GDP should grow faster than countries with a higher per capita GDP, until their economies catch up. As poor countries catch up, their economic growth rates slow down, causing their per capita GDP to converge with richer countries.

Countries in the world can be placed into one of three categories. **Industrialized countries** (the first world) have the highest levels of per capita GDP along with the highest levels of capital accumulation. Examples include the US, Canada, Japan, Hong Kong, Australia, New Zealand, South Korea, and most of Western Europe. **Industrializing countries** (the second world or emerging markets) have lower per capita GDP than industrialized countries but higher levels than the non-industrialized countries. Examples include: China, India, most of Eastern Europe, most of South America, much of Southeast Asia, Mexico, and Russia. **Non-industrialized countries** (the third world) are the poorest countries in the world. These countries are disproportionately located in Africa and Central America.

All things being equal, entrepreneurs will move capital and technology to where they can pair them with cheaper labor. Accordingly, the non-industrialized economies of the world should have the highest economic growth rates as they attract **foreign direct investment** in capital and gain access to foreign technology. Industrializing countries should have the next highest growth rate followed by the industrialized world. As countries get closer and closer to the per capita income levels of the industrialized world, their economic growth rates should slow down. Playing economic catch up is typically easier for an economy than leading the economic pack. From bicycle racing to car racing, the headwind is born by the first cyclist/car and other racers are able to draft. Likewise, poorer economies can economically draft off of richer ones.

TABLE 4.10	2003–2017 AVERAGE YEARLY GROWTH RATES		
Region	**% Growth**	**Country**	**% Growth**
China	9.41%	US	1.90%
India	7.64%	EU	1.38%
Least Developed	6.07%	Japan	0.93%
Middle Income	5.80%	Yemen	-3.0%
High Income	1.78%	South Sudan	-6.8%

Does convergence theory hold? It is largely holding for the industrialized world. Table 4.10 shows average GDP growth rates from 2002–2012 in selected counties as reported by the World Bank. Emerging markets are attracting entrepreneurs, capital, and technology at faster rates than the industrialized world.

Who benefits? Should industrialized countries be concerned? Actually, this process of wealth creation benefits inhabitants both in and out of these countries. A rising level of capital and technology works to increase wages, per capita GDP, and consumption levels of citizens of the industrializing world. It not only benefits those in developing nations but it also benefits producers in industrialized countries who gain access to cheaper production and wider markets for their goods and services. It likewise benefits consumers in the industrialized world who now have access to cheaper goods and services.

Convergence, as evidenced by many non-industrialized countries, is not an economic given. Capital and technology have to be moved to third world countries by entrepreneurs, both domestic and foreign. Capital doesn't move itself. If the economic rules of the game discourage entrepreneurship in a country, then convergence won't happen, or its pace will be diminished. Many poor countries continue to stay poor because their cultural/political rules of the economic game are not conducive to entrepreneurial actions. High levels of debt, brutal dictatorship, hyperinflation and civil war make economic growth difficult. As we shall see in the next chapter, the protection of property rights is key to ensuring economic growth and development.

Poorly defined or enforced property rights are a leading cause of the lack of convergence amongst many of the world's poorest countries, according to work done by Hernando De Soto.[15] If entrepreneurs are not allowed to benefit from their market innovations, they will not engage in them. For countries that are failing to converge, better property right enforcement is key to enabling their economies to grow.

---

[15] *The Mystery of Capital: Why Capitalism Triumphs in the West and Fails Everywhere Else.* 2000.

Key Terms

Arbitrage

Capital gains tax

Convergence theory

Corporate income tax

Creative destruction

Dow Jones Industrial Index

Emigration

Entrepreneur

Extensive economic growth

Foreign direct investment

Government sponsored bailout

Human Capital

Immigration

Industrialized countries

Industrializing countries

Institutional economics

Intensive economic growth

Natural resource

Non-industrialized countries

Non-renewable resources

Productivity

Property right

Renewable resources

Rent seeking

Questions for Review

1. What is extensive economic growth? How does it differ from intensive economic growth?

2. Is the existence of large natural resource deposits in a country helpful or harmful to economic growth? Why?

3. List and explain three US government policy changes that would result in more extensive growth from the use of natural resources.

4. What are property rights? Why are they important to the use of resources?

5. Give three examples of government policies that may unintentionally discourage work. Why would politicians or citizens support such policies?

6. List and explain three US government policy changes that would result in a larger US work force.

7. Which country has the highest corporate income tax rate in the OECD? The lowest rate? How does the corporate income tax rate influence capital formation?

8. Why is capital important to wealth creation?

9. What role does saving play in capital creation? How does public debt affect private capital accumulation?

10. What is human capital? How is it developed?

11. What government policies discourage human capital development? What policies encourage it?

12. Name three of the countries that finished in the top ten in all three academic disciplines measured by the OECD educational attainment study. Where did the US place?

13. List and explain three US government policy changes that would result in a more skilled US work force.

14. Why is technological innovation important to wealth creation?

15. What public policies promote more rapid technological advances?

16. What is entrepreneurship? How do government bailouts limit entrepreneurship?

17. Why is entrepreneurship important to wealth creation?

18. What government policies promote or deter entrepreneurial activity?

19. a. What is convergence theory?

    b. Is convergence theory holding in reality? Who benefits from convergence?

    c. What impediments to economic convergence exist?

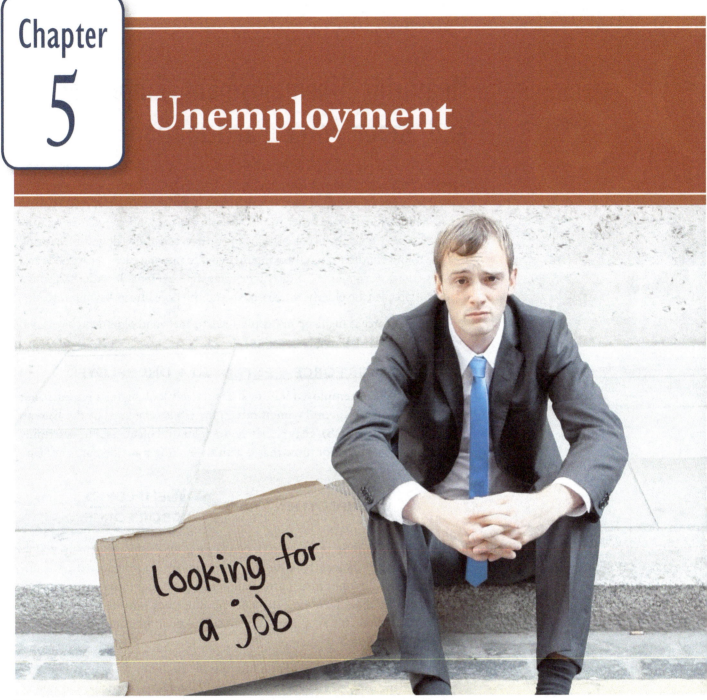

© Lasse Kristensen, 2012, under license Shutterstock, Inc.

H ave you ever been stuck in traffic in the middle of the day and wondered to yourself "Don't these people blocking my lane have jobs?" It turns out that in 2018, only 60.6% of Americans aged 16 and older had a job.[1] Including kids under age sixteen, fewer than half of Americans have a job. While this does not mean that the US unemployment rate is over 50%, it does mean that the US is not producing anywhere close to their production possibilities frontier. In this chapter, we examine what it means to be unemployed and consider policies which affect unemployment rates.

---

[1] Source: US Bureau of Labor Statistics

Measuring Unemployment, Employment, and Labor Force Participation

Why do so few people have a job? Not everyone wants a job, and some who want one have not yet found one they are willing to take. If work was completely enjoyable, it would be called play. Work serves as a means of producing income, but some individuals have other means. People who are independently wealthy do not have to work in order to consume. They can draw down on existing wealth. Young children can rely on their parents to provide them with goods and services. The government even distributes transfer payments in order to protect groups of people (the elderly, the disabled, and the poor) from having to work.

The labor force is made up of people aged 16 years and older who have a job or who are actively looking for one.

$$\textbf{LABOR FORCE} = \textbf{EMPLOYED} + \textbf{UNEMPLOYED}$$

One is considered **unemployed** if he or she is actively looking for a job but is not working. The official **unemployment rate** in the US is calculated by the **Bureau of Labor Statistics (BLS)**. They survey households and businesses to determine the percentage of the **labor force** that is actively looking for a job but is not currently working.

$$\textbf{UNEMPLOYMENT RATE} = \frac{\textbf{UNEMPLOYED}}{\textbf{LABOR FORCE}}$$

From children, to retirees, to stay at home parents, to slackers, many people choose not to actively look for a job and therefore are not considered to be unemployed. Thus, the labor force participation rate is a better indicator of production possibilities than the unemployment rate. The labor force participation rate is the percentage of the working age civilian, noninstitutionalized population that is either employed or unemployed.

The US has experienced a large increase in the **labor force participation rate** of women.[2] Between 1972 and 2018, the labor force participation rate of women grew from 43.9% to 57.5%. The overall US labor force participation rate grew from 60.4% in 63.1% in the same period, even as the rate for men actually fell from 78.9% to 69.0%. While these demographic changes have done little to the unemployment rate, they greatly impacted both the employment rate and the level of production in the economy.

$$\frac{\textbf{LABOR FORCE}}{\textbf{PARTICIPATION RATE}} = \frac{\textbf{LABOR FORCE}}{\textbf{WORKING AGE CIVILIAN NON-INSTITUTIONALIZED POPULATION}}$$

[2] Ibid.

Unemployment is considered to be undesirable because it creates both **human costs** and **economic costs**. When people want a job in order to meet the needs of themselves and their loved ones but cannot find one, people experience a number of human costs. Human costs are costs related to the physical, psychological, and social costs incurred by the absence of wealth creation. A loss of income can translate into an inability to meet one's physical needs for food, shelter, clothing, or health care. A loss of a job may also affect one's sense of self-worth. Unemployment is positively correlated with social ills such as crime, suicide, and abuse.

From an economic perspective, unemployment represents lost production. As multiple people who want jobs go without them, an economy loses out on their production and creates less wealth. The larger the unemployment rate, the greater the forgone production and loss of wealth production. Figure 5.1 illustrates historical unemployment rate fluctuations.[3]

Source: US Department of Labor: Bureau of Labor Statistics

Figure 5.1 **CIVILIAN UNEMPLOYMENT RATE 1948–2018**

---

[3] Federal Reserve Bank of St. Louis

Who Is Most Likely to Experience Unemployment?

Some groups of people are more likely to experience bouts of unemployment than others. Unskilled, blue collar workers are more likely than skilled, white collar workers to become unemployed. Less educated workers often have a much higher unemployment rate during a recession than do college graduates. Teenagers, because they have less job experience, and typically less education, have much higher unemployment rates than do older workers. During the Great Recession and the decades leading up to it, less educated workers experienced particularly large rates of unemployment as the number of manufacturing jobs declined. Less educated workers were particularly hard hit because of the decline in manufacturing jobs. This left fewer jobs for low skilled labor. Unemployment rates also tend to vary by race, gender, and location. Table 5.1[4] represents a snapshot of unemployment in January 2018.

TABLE 5.1	JANUARY 2018 UNEMPLOYMENT RATES						
US	3.9%						
Race or Ethnicity			**Age**			**Education (age 25+)**	
White	3.5%		16–19	12.5%		No high school	5.6%
Black or African American	6.5%					High school	4.1%
Hispanic or Latino	4.7%					Some College	3.7%
Asian	3.0%					Bachelor's Degree	2.2%
Gender			**Nativity**			Bachelor's Degree +	2.0%
Male	3.9%		US Born	3.8%			
Female	3.8%		Foreign Born	3.4%			
Sate			**State**				
Iowa	2.4%		Alaska	6.3%			
Hawaii	2.5%		West Virginia	5.1%			
New Hampshire	2.5%		Louisiana	4.9%			

In order to properly understand unemployment and its costs, we need to understand first its causes. There are four different categories of unemployment: seasonal, frictional, structural, and cyclical unemployment.

---

[4] Ibid.

Types of Unemployment

Seasonal Unemployment

Seasonal unemployment is caused by a change in seasons. Construction and agriculture are two industries that are weather dependent. There are fewer jobs in these industries during the winter months. When calculating the unemployment rate, the BLS reports seasonally adjusted data so that the unemployment rate that is reported already controls for a change in seasons. Seasonal unemployment is a natural part of the economy, and it is not as troubling as some other forms because it is temporary and will adjust with the seasons.

Unemployed lifeguards in the winter represent seasonal unemployment

Frictional Unemployment

Frictional unemployment is caused by a natural movement of people from one job to the next. Few people stay at the same job their whole life. Frictional unemployment includes those who are changing jobs to search for better jobs as well as those just entering or reentering the labor force. New college graduates searching for jobs are frictionally unemployed. Like seasonal unemployment, frictional unemployment is a natural part of the economy. This type of unemployment is also not particularly troubling because it is also temporary and actually is beneficial for the economy as people sort into better jobs. To prevent this type of sorting would be inefficient.

Unemployed recent college graduates represent frictional unemployment

Structural Unemployment

Structural unemployment is caused when people lack the skills necessary to perform jobs currently in demand by the market. A high school dropout may really want a job, but may lack the needed skills to be able to take advantage of job openings in fields that require specific knowledge. It could be that a person has amassed quite a bit of knowledge in the study of philosophy, but philosophers may not currently be in great demand in the economy. The existence of multiple job openings for trained nurses does little to help the philosopher find a job, unless he or she goes to school and gains the training necessary to become a nurse.

Not all sectors of an economy expand or contract at the same rate. People remain unemployed when they lack the skills needed to fill job openings or refuse to gain skills currently in demand by the market. When an economy experiences

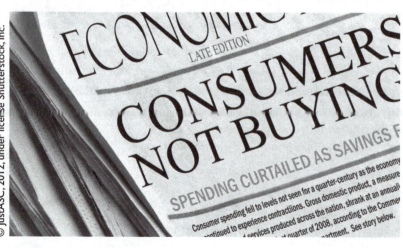

Those unemployed due to mismatched skills represent structural unemployment

an increase in technology or capital investment, certain skills often become unneeded or replaceable. The automobile put a huge dent in the employment prospects of wagon makers and wheel wrights.

Luddites were a group of Englishmen who rebelled against the industrial revolution (and machines), mistakenly thinking that machines cause unemployment. While new technology or capital will make some jobs obsolete, they create the need for new jobs, albeit perhaps ones that require a different skill set. To say that no person should ever suffer from structural unemployment is to deprive the world of new technology and capital. To end structural unemployment, the world would have to return to one where all production was made by hand, where life was indeed solitary, nasty, brutish, and short.

Knowing that structural unemployment is part of a dynamic growing economy doesn't provide much solace to the person who just lost a job that they had the skill and training to do. A society who wants a growing economy, however, must come to grips with the fact that changes in employment are necessary components of a thriving economy. Societies that provide easy access to worker retraining will have an advantage in minimizing the human and economic costs associated with structural unemployment.

Cyclical Unemployment

Cyclical unemployment is caused by a reduction in output following downturns in the economy. As unsold inventories of goods begin increasing, producers lower production of future output until they see the demand for their goods and services increase. It takes fewer people to produce fewer goods and services, and therefore employees get laid off. This reduction in output will be permanent in some industries (and individuals unemployed in those industries will suffer from structural unemployment), while the reduction in output will be temporary in other industries, as demand for their good or services rebounds with a growing economy.

Recessions lead to cyclical unemployment

Full Employment

The optimal amount of unemployment is not zero. A growing economy that allows the freedom to choose and switch between places of employment for workers will always have some frictional, seasonal, and structural unemployment. Government policies to outlaw these types of unemployment would result in slavery and long term slowing of economic growth rates. Economists consider **full employment** to be when cyclical unemployment is zero.

While no one knows what the unemployment rate would be if there were no cyclical unemployment, economists theorize that it would be between 5 and 5.5%. This theoretical level of zero cyclical unemployment is commonly referred to as full employment or **NAIRU** (the non-accelerating inflation rate of unemployment). When the unemployment rate falls below this level, inflation tends to increase. The shortage of skilled laborers in the marketplace forces prospective employers to offer higher wages in order to attract workers to their firms. The increased labor cost that results from a shortage of workers increases the cost of production of goods and services. These cost increases are passed on to consumers in the form of higher prices. So, inflation results when unemployment falls below NAIRU.

Government Policies and Unemployment

Government policies can, and do, alter both employment and unemployment rates. The provision of a social safety net (income support for the indigent) reduces the human costs associated with unemployment. If a person who loses their job can collect **unemployment insurance** payments from the government, they can continue to pay for food, clothing, and shelter as they look for a new job. Unemployment insurance payments in the United States are typically paid out up to 26 weeks following job loss. However, in times of recession, the US government often increases the duration for which one is eligible for benefits. The tradeoff is that the more generous the unemployment insurance is, the longer the average bout of unemployment lasts. A sure-fire way to increase the unemployment rate is to make unemployment less undesirable.

Many European countries allow unemployed workers to collect up to 80% of their former salary for up to two years. As a result, most European countries have higher levels and longer average bouts of unemployment than the US.[5] Robert Barro demonstrated that by extending unemployment insurance benefits during the 2008–2009 recession, the US government actually increased the unemployment rate.[6]

---

[5] "Explaining European Unemployment" *NBER Reporter: Research Summary* Summer 2004

[6] "The Folly of Subsidizing Unemployment" *Wall Street Journal* August 30, 2010

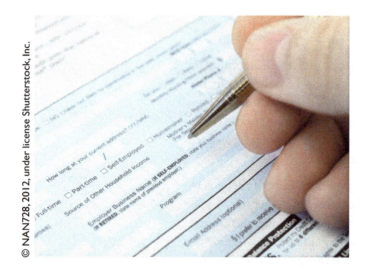

© NAN728, 2012, under license Shutterstock, Inc.

Likewise, **minimum wage** laws increase unemployment amongst the lowest skilled workers in the economy. Such laws outlaw all work whose net product is less that the prescribed wage. Young high school workers who can only generate $6 of new revenue from their employer will not be hired if the minimum wage rate is set at $7.25 an hour. Countries with higher minimum wage laws see higher levels of unemployment, particularly among young people. Requirements placed on employers regarding health coverage for their employees have a similar effect as minimum wage laws in discouraging employment.

Labor force rules regarding the ability to hire and fire workers also affect a country's unemployment rate. Firms that find it difficult to fire inept employees are less likely to hire new full time employees until they are certain that said employees merit hiring. The irony is that the more tightly a society clings to existing jobs, the less likely it is to create new jobs and, as a result, it will experience greater levels of unemployment.

Employment has grown fastest in US states that have adopted **right to work laws**. These laws make **labor union** membership voluntary. Between 1993 and 2003 in right to work states, non-farm private sector jobs increased by 24% compared to a 14% growth rate for forced union states.[7] Real income grew by 37% in right to work states compared to 26% in forced dues states during the same time period.

According to the BLS, a majority of union members in the US are now government workers rather than private sector employees. Private sector union membership has been falling since WWII, while federal employees only gained the right to unionize and **collectively bargain** in the 1960's, with legislation signed by President Kennedy. While unions are often portrayed as being beneficial for workers, economic evidence indicates that unions slow economic growth and increase overall unemployment in the economy.[8]

While unemployment can be a problem for the person or family suffering from it, policies designed to reduce the human or economic costs of unemployment need to be carefully designed so that they don't end up causing more, rather than less unemployment. In theory, the government could hire more

---

[7] Source: US Department of Labor

[8] Richard Vedder "Right-To-Work Laws: Liberty, Prosperity, and Quality of Life" Cato Journal, Vol. 30, No. 1 (Winter 2010)

workers during a recession, but government rules make it hard to fire them later. Evidence from the Great Depression indicates that government jobs prolong unemployment.[9] While many obtained artificially created government jobs following the Great Depression, they put off looking for lasting jobs and thus delayed the transition back into private sector employment.

As of the writing of this book, there were only two periods of post WWII American history when the US unemployment rate hit double digits: between September 1982 and June 1983 where it topped out at 10.8%, and in October 2009 when it hit 10.1%. Table 5.2[10] illustrates the US unemployment rate since 1920 in presidential election years. The US electorate has had a tendency to hold the US President accountable for the unemployment rate. Unemployed workers make for discontented voters who tend to turn on incumbents.

So, politicians often are motivated to take actions to reduce short run unemployment, despite the fact that in the long run such actions may actually do more harm than good. Likewise, similar tradeoffs exist when battling inflationary pressures. The next chapter examines inflation.

TABLE 5.2	HISTORIC US UNEMPLOYMENT RATES		
1920	5.2%	1972	5.6%
1928	4.2%	1976	7.7%
1932	23.6%	1980	7.1%
1936	16.9%	1984	7.5%
1940	14.6%	1988	5.5%
1944	3.2%	1992	7.5%
1948	3.8%	1996	5.4%
1952	3.0%	2000	4.0%
1956	4.1%	2004	5.5%
1960	5.5%	2008	5.8%
1964	5.2%	2012	7.9%
1968	3.6%	2016	4.7%

[9] Jim Powell. *FDR's Folly, How Roosevelt and His New Deal Prolonged the Great Depression* 2003.

[10] Ibid.

Key Terms

Bureau of Labor Statistics

Collective bargaining

Cyclical unemployment

Economic costs

Frictional unemployment

Full employment

Human costs

Labor force

Labor force participation rate

Labor union

Luddites

Minimum wage

NAIRU

Right to work laws

Seasonal unemployment

Structural unemployment

Unemployed

Unemployment insurance

Unemployment rate

Questions for Review

1. How is unemployment defined in the US? Would a stay at home parent be classified as unemployed? What about a student who is not seeking work and is not currently working?

2. Is the unemployment rate or the labor force participation rate a better indicator of production? Why?

3. How has the labor force participation rate of women changed in the last fifty years? For men? Why do you think these changes have occurred?

4. Why do many European countries perpetually have higher unemployment rates than the US?

5. What is meant by full employment? Where is the economy relative to their PPF curve if the economy is operating below full employment?

6. List and describe four types of unemployment. Which of these types is most disconcerting to the economy and why?

7. What government policies lead to increased unemployment rates?

8. Why is unemployment considered to be harmful?

9. Suppose the Island of Yore has 40,000 non-institutionalized civilians over the age of 16. Of these individuals, 25,000 are working. 5,000 are not working but are actively seeking work. The remaining 10,000 are either stay at home parents or are retired. What is the unemployment rate and labor force participation rate for Yore?

Chapter 6

Inflation

"Inflation is as violent as a mugger, as frightening as an armed robber and as deadly as a hit man."

— *Ronald Reagan*

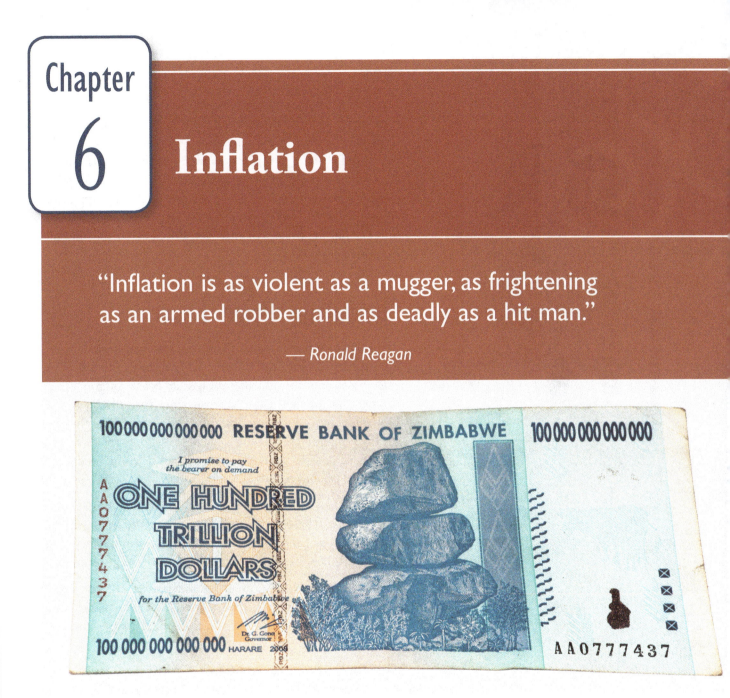

© Anton_Ivanov/Shutterstock.com

Have you ever heard your grandparents talk about the good old days when a candy bar cost less than a quarter and a coca cola could be purchased for a dime? Before there existed stores where everything cost $1 (or below $5), there were five and dime stores. In fact, the prices of individual goods and services change constantly. A gallon of milk is not the same price every time you go to the grocery store; nor do all grocery stores charge the same price for milk. Changes in the relative prices of goods and services reflect changes in people's ability and desire to buy a product relative to the changing costs (including opportunity costs) of producing them. Rising milk prices may reflect an increased love of dairy products by the masses, or it could reflect higher feeding costs for

© Andrey Armyagov, 2012, under license Shutterstock, Inc.

the dairy cows. The prices of all products don't change at the same rate or even in the same direction. The price of an HD TV may fall, even as corn prices increase. **Inflation** is said to have occurred when there is an increase in the average price level. Likewise, **deflation** is a decrease in the average price level. This section will explain how average prices are measured and explore the impact of changing prices on society and on economic growth.

Measuring Price Levels

The most common measure of average prices in the US is the **consumer price index (CPI)**. The CPI measures the collective price movements of a theoretical market basket of goods and services that the average urban consumer typically buys. The basket includes specific products that fall under one of the following categories: food and beverages, housing, apparel, transportation, medical care, recreation, education, communication, and other personal goods and services.[1]

The price of the market basket is measured every month and is compared to the price of the same basket in a base year in order to convert it to an index. The CPI is not a perfect **cost of living index**, but it is the one used for most **cost of living adjustments (COLAs)**, including those used by the federal government.

In order to calculate the CPI, the Bureau of Labor Statistics takes the current price of the market basket, divides it by the price of the market basket in a base year (currently the base period is 1982–1984), and multiplies the result by one hundred:

$$\text{CPI} = \frac{\text{CURRENT PRICE OF MARKET BASKET}}{\text{PRICE OF MARKET BASKET IN BASE YEAR}} \times 100$$

The rate of inflation from one year to the next can be calculated using each year's CPI in the following manner:

$$\text{INFLATION RATE} = \frac{\text{CPI MOST RECENT YEAR} - \text{CPI EARLIER YEAR}}{\text{CPI EARLIER YEAR}} \times 100.$$

Through the 1700's, 1800's and early 1900's, the US economy routinely experienced both inflation and deflation. Inflation rates have tended to spike during major wars, as governments have sought to help pay for war expenses by expanding the money supply. The only years in which the US inflation rate exceeded 20% were 1777, 1778 (American Revolution), 1813 (War of 1812), 1864, 1865 (US Civil War), and 1917 (WWI). The US went from 1955 until 2009 without

---

[1] For more information on current CPI calculations visit http://www.bls.gov/cpi.

Inflation Rate

Inflation Rate

Figure 6.1   **INFLATION RATE**

a single year of annual deflation. This was the longest period in US history where deflation was absent.

If a change in a single product's price improves the efficiency of markets by sending signals to consumers and suppliers, then such a price change will improve the allocation of scarce resources and enable wealth creation. This does not mean that all individuals will be happy to see the price change. A baker who sees the price of cake and cookies fall due to a low carb diet fad will not be happy with the price change. However, it will act as a signal to move resources out of baking and into another industry that will better meet the needs and wants of consumers. Rising gasoline prices will not make drivers happy, but will act as signals to move resources to oil production and gasoline refinement (or to producing cars that have a smaller reliance on petroleum for fuel).

In recent years, Zimbabwe and Venezuela have experienced bouts of hyperinflation. In 2008, the monthly Zimbabwean inflation rate reached over seventy-nine billion percent. In 2018, Venezuelan inflation topped one million percent. In both cases the hyper-inflation was caused by massive printing of currency by monetary authorities. Each country experienced a major economic contraction as a result of the hyperinflation, with over a million Zimbabweans and two million Venezuelans fleeing their home country in search of better economic conditions elsewhere.

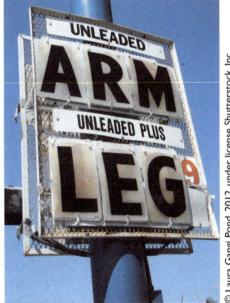

The Impact of Changing Prices

Changes in individual prices affect different people differently. So too do changes in the average price level. There are people who are helped by inflation, and there are people who are hurt by it. Likewise, deflation impacts groups and individuals differently.

Inflation can be a problem for individuals and businesses because it can increase consumer and business uncertainty, increase advertising costs, hurt people on fixed incomes and those who like to hold onto cash, hurt lenders who don't correctly anticipate inflation, and hurt taxpayers with bracket creep or capital gains taxes that are not indexed for inflation. Each of these problems is discussed below.

Increased Consumer and Business Uncertainty

As inflation rates rise, they also tend to be more variable. This makes long term business planning more difficult. Uncertainty with regard to the prices businesses will charge in the future or wages they will have to pay makes it difficult to agree to make long term investments or engage in long term labor contracts. Inflation, if correctly predicted, doesn't cause these problems. If a business owner knows that the inflation rate for next year will be 2% and she knows that she wants to give her employees a 1% real wage increase, then she will have to increase their nominal wages by 3%. A **nominal wage** is what physically appears on the labor contract, whereas **real wages** discount nominal wages by the amount of inflation.

NOMINAL WAGE INCREASE − INFLATION RATE = REAL WAGE INCREASE

If an employer gives her employees a 3% raise but inflation turns out to be 5%, then her employees will be taking a real pay cut, not on paper, but in terms of their ability to buy other goods and services with their pay check. They will have more physical money, but that money will be able to buy fewer goods.

Because all prices don't change at the same rate, the producers whose prices rise the fastest may benefit from inflation, while the producers whose prices rise the slowest will be hurt. The opposite is true for consumers. Higher prices for the things they buy make consumers worse off, but lower prices for the things they buy make them better off.

Increased Search Costs

Because prices are changing more quickly during periods of high inflation or deflation, it becomes more difficult for consumers to know if they are getting a good deal on what they are buying. This increases the **search costs** for consumers who want to make sure they are not overpaying for products they spend a lot of their income on.

Increased Advertising Costs

As prices rapidly change, it becomes more costly for a business to advertise their prices. Restaurants usually advertise the price of the food on their menus. Often these menus are laminated. The faster prices change, the more often a restaurant will have to create and laminate new menus. During periods of **hyperinflation** (over 200%), business begin advertising on chalk boards or dry erase boards rather than in print, media, or billboards because the costs of producing, printing, or painting a new ad become too high relative to how long that new advertisement will be useful. The costs of advertising a business's prices are called **menu costs.**

Following years of double digit inflation, upon visiting Buenos Aires, Argentina in 2019, the authors of this text encountered restaurants with laminated menus whose prices were written with erasable markers. The more often prices have to be changed, the more businesses have to pay in labor costs to change them. These higher costs of production create a feedback loop which creates even more inflation

People on Fixed Incomes and Those Holding onto Cash

As prices rise, the **purchasing power** of any one dollar decreases. Each dollar buys fewer goods or services. People who are on fixed incomes (the elderly on a fixed pension, or a child on a fixed allowance) are hurt by inflation because their income doesn't increase to keep pace with higher prices. Conversely, they would benefit from deflation. Social Security checks receive a COLA based upon the CPI, so social security recipients whose buying patterns mimic the average urban consumer aren't hurt by inflation. And, if inflation is overstated then recipients are actually better off.

People who save cash in coffee cans, under their mattresses, or in their wallets, or in non-interest bearing checking accounts are hurt by inflation. As prices rise, the purchasing power of this money falls. As such, in an inflationary environment, a dollar today is worth more than a dollar a year from now. When one of the textbook author's grandmothers died, a stash of money was found in coffee cans in her basement. This money had less purchasing power when it was discovered than it did when it was stashed, because prices have risen considerably since then. The **present value** of a dollar is equal to its future value controlling for inflation and the opportunity cost of earning interest on the dollar.

$$\textbf{PRESENT VALUE OF \$} = \frac{\textbf{FUTURE VALUE OF \$}}{\textbf{(1 + NOMINAL INTEREST RATE)}^{\textbf{\# OF YEARS IN THE FUTURE}}}$$

Lenders

In order to protect themselves from inflation, savers need to place their savings in financial institutions that pay them a rate of return that is equal to, or larger than, the rate of inflation. If future inflation rates were known, then savers could perfectly protect their money from inflation. However, future inflation is not known. Savers and lenders who underestimate future inflation can be hurt. If they place their savings in a certificate of deposit that pays a 2% rate of return, while the inflation rate turns out to be 5%, they will lose 3% of the purchasing power of their savings. Lenders who charge a 4% rate of interest on their loan will lose money if the rate of inflation turns out to be 5% (losing 1% of their purchasing power instead of making money on the loan). Conversely, borrowers who lock in a nominal interest rate expecting low inflation would benefit from a high and rising rate of inflation as they will pay back their loans with less valuable dollars. The **nominal interest rate** is the actual rate the bank charges the borrower or pays the depositor. The **real interest rate** is the nominal interest rate adjusted for inflation.

NOMINAL INTEREST RATE − INFLATION RATE = REAL INTEREST RATE

Bracket Creep and Capital Gains Taxes

When a business or person buys an asset, that asset appreciates in value, and if they decide to sell it, they will owe a capital gains tax. This tax is not indexed for inflation. If Bob buys one share of stock for $10 and sells it at $20 during a period of time with 100% inflation, then Bob will have to pay a capital gains tax on the $10, he *made* in nominal terms even though his real wealth didn't increase at all. The higher the inflation rate, the more people end up paying taxes on inflation rather than on real gains to their wealth. Likewise, if tax brackets are not indexed for inflation, then higher nominal incomes caused by inflation could push people into higher tax brackets, even if their real income has not increased.

Deflation

Like inflation, deflation can cause business and consumer uncertainty while increasing menu costs. These costs are minimized with stable prices. People on fixed incomes and people who like to hold onto cash benefit from deflation. As long as one's income doesn't fall, deflation allows one to consume more with his or her income. Drug dealers, because they deal in cash to avoid detection, may prefer deflation to inflation, as long as the price of their drugs falls slower than other prices.

In the late 1800's, many farmers took out loans during a period of deflation. This meant that the price of their corn and wheat fell each year as they tried to pay back their farm loans. This caused a number of farmers to lose their farms. Unexpected deflation can harm borrowers while it helps lenders. Still, the price of corn fell less quickly than the cost of shipping the corn over railroads, so farmers benefited relative to railroad companies from the deflation.

The biggest fear of deflation is that producers won't invest in new capital to build new products if the price of their output is falling. However, during the deflation of the late 1800's the price of capital goods fell more quickly than did prices of consumer goods. Investment increased, causing one of the fastest economic growth spurts in US history.

Deflation could also cause consumers to engage in less consumption as they believe that future prices will fall further. This could lead to excess inventories on the part of firms. Furthermore, if deflation is accompanied by unemployment, falling prices may make labor market adjustment more difficult. Workers are more likely to tolerate falling real wages if their nominal wages increase rather than decrease.

To summarize, groups of people that tend to be hurt by inflation tend to be savers (the wealthy), lenders (banks), small business owners, consumers, people on fixed incomes (generally the elderly), and taxpayers. Groups that tend to be hurt by deflation are debtors, and businesses whose prices would fall faster than others. The United States government may be hurt by deflation more than inflation, because they are less likely to collect as much income tax, sales tax, or capital gains tax revenue and they need to make interest payments on their large debt. Even though deflation is preferred to inflation by most consumers (voters), the Federal Reserve (the US central bank) has purposely tried to prevent deflation since WWII in order to protect business investment and government debt. We will discuss more in later chapters how actions of the Federal Reserve and the federal government can lead to inflation.

Problems with Inflation Measurements

Despite our best efforts, inflation is difficult to accurately measure and is believed by many economists to be overstated. Inflation estimated by the Bureau of Labor Statistics is believed to be overstated by a full percentage point for a number of reasons. For one, the CPI does not take into account changes in quality. Even a low tech television bought today has many more features and a much greater clarity than a high tech television purchased in 1950, and yet this is not reflected by the CPI. Likewise, new products are often introduced in the market at a cheaper price than existing products, and yet new products are not included in the CPI until the average household is purchasing the newer version. For example, Blu Ray players, Phones, microwaves, and many other types of technology have fallen greatly in price since their introduction to the market and yet are only slowly incorporated into the CPI. So, the CPI does not reflect the reduction in the cost of technology in a timely fashion. In fact, by the time these new products are included, many consumers are buying a newer type of technology.

The CPI also overstates inflation as it assumes that individuals buy the same products regardless of changes in price. If a consumer goes to the store and sees that bacon prices are $7 a pound, they likely will choose to purchase a different breakfast meat or none at all. The CPI assumes that market baskets stay constant, and in this way further overstates inflation. In a similar manner, during economic slowdowns, consumers are more likely to purchase products at discount stores, and the CPI does not account for this change in consumer behavior that lowers the prices they are paying.

Even if the CPI were a perfect measurement, it still would not equally reflect changes in the purchasing power for all sectors of the population. Consumers are affected differently by rising prices in different sectors, and yet the CPI is calculated based on weights representative of the average household. The typical college student can tell you that tuition prices have risen much faster than the rate of inflation, and so inflation is a poor measure for their changes in buying power. Likewise, older members of the population are generally more affected by the rising cost of medical care than is exhibited by the CPI alone.

Causes of Inflation or Deflation

There are three main things that cause a change in the average price level: an overall increase in the cost of production (called cost push inflation), an overall increase in demand for goods and services (called demand pull inflation), and an increase in the money supply. The first two causes account for most short term fluctuations in the average price level. The latter is the only explanation of why prices today are higher than they were a generation ago.

Almost all production involves hiring laborers and using energy. As wages or energy prices increase, these costs are passed along to consumers. The double digit inflation of the late 1970's and early 1980's can in part be explained by an increase in the price of oil caused by collusion within **OPEC (Organization of Petroleum Exporting Countries)**. As their collusive agreement fell apart, the price of oil fell, and so did the inflation rate. During times of war, demand for goods and services typically increases in order to support the war effort. This causes inflation during the first part of military buildup, until people start cutting back on the purchase of consumer goods.

Nobel Prize winning economist Milton Friedman once said that, "Inflation is always and everywhere a monetary phenomenon." The oldest macroeconomic theory that is still in use is the **quantity theory of money**. It is an accounting identity that shows that long term changes in price levels are connected to long term changes in the supply of money. Inflation is all about the relative scarcity of money vs. goods and services.

THE QUANTITY THEORY OF MONEY: MV = PY

The left hand side of the equation is how much money is spent in the course of a year. To find this, one must take the amount of money in circulation (M) and multiply it by the number of times each dollar is spent over the course of the year (V), the **velocity of money**. The right hand side of the equation is Nominal GDP. It is the average price level (P) multiplied by Real GDP (Y). As output occurs, money is used to pay for the factors of production. The dollar value of output must be equal to the amount of money being spent during the same time period.

To isolate the average price level, one can divide each side of the above equation by real GDP (Y).

$$P = \frac{MV}{Y}$$

If there is no real economic growth and the velocity of money remains unchanged, then the only way that the average price level could increase is to increase the **money supply**. Though the velocity of money is not constant from one year to the next, it remains relatively constant from one generation to the next (though it is increasing due to computers and ATMs).

Put another way, If V is constant, inflation occurs when the money supply increases faster than real RGDP, and deflation occurs when the money supply goes up more slowly than real GDP. When gold was used as the source of money, inflation was caused when the supply of gold increased faster than economic growth. This is what happened in Spain circa 1600's when they brought boatloads of gold back from the Western Hemisphere.

The US has a **fiat currency** (a currency with no intrinsic value) and consequently, they can increase or decrease the supply of money any time they wish. Long run inflation or deflation occurs as a result of active government or central bank policies. Deflation did not just vanish on its own during the last half of the twentieth century; it was prevented due to central bank policies.

There is some controversy between two Noble Prize winning economists Milton Friedman and Friedrich Von Hayek as to the cause and effect of changes in the money supply and real GDP. Between 1929 and 1933, real GDP fell by 29%, prices fell by 25%, the money supply fell by 33% and the velocity of money fell as well. Did the reduction in the left hand side of the quantity theory of money cause a decline in the right side, or the other way around? Friedman supposes the former while Hayek supposes the latter.

Milton Friedman and Anna Schwartz argue in "The Great Contraction, 1929–1933" that the decline in the supply of money caused credit markets to freeze up and caused otherwise sound banks to close do to a lack of available liquidity. These bank failures and credit shortages caused business investment to nearly vanish.

Friedrich Von Hayek argues that the reduction in the velocity and the money supply was caused by a slowdown in investment. He argues that business investment declined not because of a credit crunch but because they were already operating well under full capacity and had no need to expand. This lower demand for loans caused the supply and velocity of money to decrease.

In the 2008–2009 contraction, the central bank acted as if Friedman was correct. They provided liquidity to banks and financial institutions to keep them from failing. By increasing the money supply, the Federal Reserve attempted to boost business investment and GDP. Still, banks sat on new reserves and business borrowing did not recover. Businesses that were operating below capacity had little desire to invest in new capital. In the end, both economists provide insight into the correlation between the money supply and real GDP.

Providing short term liquidity to prevent solvent banks from closing can help to prevent an economic slowdown brought on by a collapse of the financial sector. The financial sector is needed to align lenders and borrowers. In their absence, business investment becomes very difficult. On the other hand, as the phrase goes, "you can lead a horse to water, but you can't make it drink." An increase in the money supply does not guarantee that businesses will want to invest when they are uncertain or pessimistic about the future, or if they are paying down debt from previous investments. Further, if inefficient banks are kept open with bailouts despite poor lending decisions, then banks may have an incentive to continue to make risky decisions that inhibit economic growth.

Thus, inflation and unemployment are both serious macroeconomic issues that can have large impacts on society, and yet, as we will see in later chapters, fiscal and monetary policies designed to relieve one of these issues typically increases the other. This tradeoff is one policymakers must evaluate when deciding if and how to react to changes in the macroeconomy.

Key Terms

Consumer price index

Cost of living adjustment

Cost of living index

Deflation

Fiat currency

Hyperinflation

Inflation

Menu costs

Money supply

Nominal interest rate

Nominal wage

OPEC

Present value

Purchasing power

Quantity Theory of Money

Real interest rate

Real wage

Search costs

Velocity of money

Questions for Review

1. a. Who is hurt by inflation? Why

   b. Who is helped by inflation? Why?

   c. Who is hurt by deflation? Why?

   d. Who is hurt by deflation? Why?

2. a. What is the CPI? How is it calculated?

   b. Why does the CPI overstate the true burden of inflation?

3. What is the present value of $400 received five years from now if the nominal interest rate is 3%?

4. If the nominal interest rate is 8% and the inflation rate is 2%, what is the real interest rate?

5. If the inflation rate is 4% and you want to give your employees a 5% increase in their real wage, by how much would you need to increase their nominal wage?

6. What causes inflation and deflation?

7. Why has deflation largely disappeared in the US?

8. In the land of Sanders only two goods are consumed, fried chicken and coleslaw. The price of a bucket of fried chicken was $10.00 in 1990 and $14.00 in 2000. The price of a serving of coleslaw was $1 in 1990 and $2 in 2000. The typical Sanderian consumed 25 buckets of chicken and 20 servings of coleslaw a year in 1990.

   a. What is the price of the market basket in 2000?

   b. What is the CPI for 2000 using 1990 as the base year?

   c. If the CPI for 1995 is 130, with 1990 as the base year, then what was the rate of inflation between 1990 and 1995?

   d. If the CPI for 1995 is 130 and the CPI for 1996 is 133, what is the rate of inflation between 1995 and 1996?

   e. If the CPI for 1991 using 1990 as the base year is 85, state briefly what must have happened to the prices between 1990 and 1991.

9. Suppose that in the country of Topper, they consume only two goods: basketballs and towels. In the base year of 2010, residents on average bought 10 towels and 100 basketballs. The price in 2010 for basketballs was $12 while towels cost $7. In 2020, basketballs cost $10 while towels cost cost $12.

   a. What is the CPI of 2020 using 2010 as the base year?

   b. If the CPI of 2015 was 110, then what was the rate of inflation between 2015 and 2020?

Chapter 7

Business Cycles and Financial Institutions

"All the world's a stage.
And all the men and women merely players.
They have their exits and their entrances;
And one man in his time plays many parts."

—*William Shakespeare - As You Like It*

Much like a Shakespearean play, the economy is inhabited by many different actors, each of whom plays multiple roles. Any effort to model the economy must begin with an outline of who the actors are and how those actors relate to each other. In reality, individuals make economic decisions for themselves and for their dependents. Modeling individual decision making is the realm of microeconomic study.

The study of macroeconomics generally considers the actors in the economy to be groups of people, like consumers. This is not to say that all consumers are homogeneous. Rather, it enables the researcher to examine trends in choices made by large numbers of people. Broad economic statements such as, "consumer spending will increase as a result" does not mean that all consumers will, or should, buy more. The assumption is that each individual actor will act according to their own enlightened, rational self-interest.

The purpose of this chapter is to introduce chief actors of the economy, explain their relationship to each other, and to examine the factors that lead to business cycles.

Macroeconomic Actors

Consumers

Every individual in an economy is a **consumer**, since everyone must consume in order to survive. Consumers purchase goods and services in an attempt to meet their material needs and wants. Consumers are limited in their consumption by the scarcity of resources. Goods and services are not free, so consumption has to be paid for. The sources of payment include income, gifts, transfer payments, or debt. Income comes from labor **(wages)**, capital **(interest)**, land **(rent)**, and entrepreneurship **(profit)** under the control of the individual consumer.

Not all consumers earn income. Young children, from an economic perspective, could be termed "unproductive eaters". Children, and other dependents, consume as a result of resources given to them. Some consumers rely on transfer payments. A **transfer payment** occurs when the government gives money or resources to a consumer without a good or service provided in return.

Should a consumer wish to purchase a good or service without first earning or receiving the needed money to do so, they have the option of borrowing money. By taking on debt, the consumer is pledging a portion of their future income to the lender in exchange for current consumption.

Consumption can consist of goods or services made domestically or abroad. Consumers can do more than just consume their entire income. They could also pay taxes, save, or give their income to charity. After tax income is called **disposable** (discretionary) **income**. Savings can occur in or apart from financial institutions. Some people hold savings in a coffee can or under a mattress. Others place their savings in financial institutions that offer a positive rate of return on the savings.

Financial Institutions

Financial Institutions are firms that coordinate savers with borrowers. A saver, be it an individual, a government, or a firm, voluntarily agrees to postpone current consumption, government spending, or investment in order to gain a return on their savings that would increase their consumption, government spending, or investment ability in the future. Banks, credit unions, credit card companies, stock markets, commodity markets, bond markets, insurance companies, and pension plans are all examples of financial institutions.

First Bank of the United States

Banks, Credit Unions, and Credit Card Companies

Consumers can defer consumption by placing a fraction of their current income in a financial institution. If they go to their local bank or credit union, they could place their money in a **checking account**, a **money market account**, a **savings account**, or in a **certificate of deposit**. Money placed in a checking account won't typically generate interest income for the saver, but checking accounts offer easy access to the money. Access to money is called **liquidity**. Money markets are less liquid than checking accounts, but more liquid than savings accounts or certificates of deposit. A certificate of deposit specifies a period of time during which the money may not, without a fine, be withdrawn from the bank. Typically, banks entice savers to agree to less liquidity by paying higher interest rates on the savings.

Banks, credit unions, and credit card companies facilitate consumer and small business borrowing. Every time a consumer uses a credit card, they take out a loan from the credit card company. Often these loans are interest free if the entire loan is paid off by the billing due date. Otherwise, the interest rate charged by credit card companies tends to be much higher than that charged by local banks, but not as high as rates charged by **cash advance stores**. This higher interest rate reflects the higher risk associated with making loans for nondurable consumer goods. It's virtually impossible for a credit card company to repossess the double bacon cheeseburger that was bought with a credit card.

Whether or not a bank or credit card company gives a loan to an individual or small business is dependent upon the likelihood of repayment. **Credit scores** are proxies for the credit worthiness of consumers. A low credit score means a person does not have a history of making on time payments of their debts. Low credit scores limit the availability of credit to an individual while increasing the interest rate they will have to pay to secure the loan.

There are **usury** laws in many states against charging excessive interest rates for loans. Some people believe that lenders who charge high interest rates to people with bad credit scores are taking advantage of those individuals. The truth is that if lenders can't charge enough interest to cover the likelihood of default, loans to high risk borrowers would not be made. Usury laws work to create a black market for loans where an illegally high rate of interest is charged by **loan sharks**. Loan sharks make illegal loans to people with very poor access to legal credit at high interest rates. Because the loans are not enforceable by law, loan sharks often must resort to the threat or action of physical violence in order to collect on their loans.

If a small business is looking to expand, they may need to take out a small business loan from a bank. In order to determine whether or not said expansion is a profitable idea, the owner needs to compare the expected marginal benefit of the business expansion with the marginal cost. The opportunity cost of investment is the interest rate. The higher the interest rate is for a small business loan, the less profitable new investment projects will be. Even if the business owner uses her own money, the interest rate is the opportunity cost of investment. If a business owner can earn a 3% rate of return by expanding their business but can save money in a certificate of deposit at 5%, then the rational business owner would choose not to expand their business, even if they did not have to take out a loan to do so.

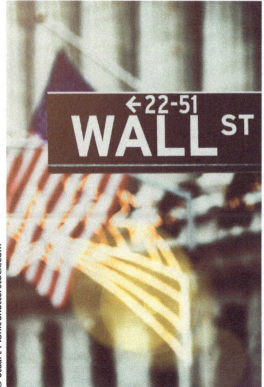

© Stuart Monk/Shutterstock.com

Stock and Commodity Markets

Rather than take a loan out from a financial institution, owners of a firm could sell a portion of their equity stake in the firm in order to raise money for a capital investment. A **share of stock** is part ownership in a firm. Stock markets are institutions where partial ownership of corporations are bought and sold. A saver may forgo current consumption in order to buy part ownership in a company they expect will make money in the future. As a part owner of the company, they are entitled to a share of the company's future profits. The **New York Stock Exchange (NYSE)** is the largest stock market in the United States, while **NASDAQ** is the second largest stock market in the United States. Both are located in New York City.

The current price of a share of stock depends upon potential buyers and sellers of that share agreeing to a price for the transaction. People have varying expectations as to the future profitability of a corporation. As people's expectations begin to diverge from each other, they begin buying and selling shares based on their beliefs. All buyers and sellers of stock are speculators in that they are all acting on imperfect information regarding the future profitability of the firm.

The **Dow Jones Industrial Average** (DJIA or Dow) is a composite index of 30 of the country's largest corporations' stocks. It is the most often quoted index of how the stock market is doing. If the Dow goes up from one day to the next, it is often said that the stock market is up. This does not mean that the price of all stocks went higher, nor does it mean that all thirty stocks on the Dow went higher. Individual stock prices can increase or decrease independent of the Dow or **NASDAQ Composite** (an index of how companies listed on the NASDAQ perform). The **S&P 500** is a broader index of 500 companies on the NYSE, while the **Russell 2000** is an index of 2000 companies listed on the NYSE.

People who are optimistic that the stock market indices will increase in the near future are called **bulls**. People who are pessimistic that the stock market indices will increase in the near future are called **bears**. A **bull market** is a stock market whose indices are increasing while a **bear market** is a stock market whose indices are decreasing.

Bull markets occur as people begin expecting an increase in companies' future profits. As such, stock market movements attempt to predict future performance of the economy. The stock market crash of 1929 was a reflection of changes in expectations about the future profitability of US businesses. The important thing to understand is that changes in the stock market do not cause changes in economic output. Changes in economic output cause changes in the stock market. The stock market crash of 1929 was caused by the Great Depression rather than being the cause of it.

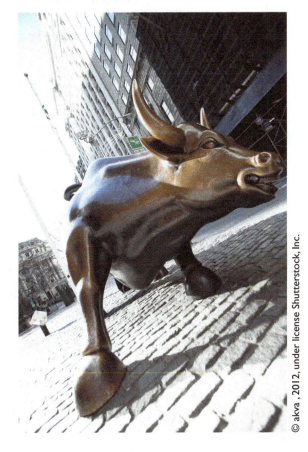

When a corporation earns a profit, it can **retain earnings** to be used for future investment or it can pay **dividends** to shareholders. Dividends are taxed as shareholder income. In this way, income produced by corporations is taxed twice. Corporate profits are taxed at the corporate income tax rate and dividends are then taxed at the personal income tax rate. The use of retained earnings avoids this problem of double taxation by reinvesting earnings into the firm instead of paying stockholders a dividend.

Savers could hold their savings in assets called **commodities** with the hope that their value will increase over time. Popular commodities include precious metals such as gold and silver, industrial metals such as copper and aluminum, West Texas Intermediate (crude oil), crops such as corn and soybeans, and livestock such as lean hogs or live cattle. Not everyone who thinks that the price of lean hogs will increase will want said hogs running around their living room.

Fortunately, commodity markets have evolved to allow, for periods of time, people to own commodities without actually taking delivery of them. **Futures contracts** even allow individuals to buy and sell commodities that exist only in the future.

Bond Markets, Mutual Funds, and Pensions

Alternatively, savers may wish to place their funds in a bond market. A bond market is an institution that allows people to buy and sell the right to collect debt. A corporation or a government may wish to issue bonds in order to finance a capital improvement. A bond is an IOU that promises to pay the owner a certain amount of money over a fixed amount of time. These IOU's (bonds) are then bought and sold in bond markets. By purchasing a bond, a saver takes the risk that the debtor may default on their obligation to pay their debts. The greater the perceived likelihood of default, the greater the interest rate savers will need to be offered in order to get them to voluntarily lend their money. Bond rating agencies, such as **Moody's** or **Standard & Poor's**, make estimates about the credit worthiness of corporations and governments. In order to encourage individuals to accept a lower interest rate on government debt, the US government makes income earned from interest on government bonds tax exempt.

Rather than put all of one's life savings in a single stock, bond, or commodity, it is less risky to diversity one's **portfolio**. **Mutual funds** are collections of assets (stocks, bonds, commodities) that diversify one's assets through the purchase of a single fund. Mutual funds exist for virtually all tastes and preferences from environmentally conscious mutual funds to mutual funds that specialize in vice (gambling, tobacco, and alcohol).

Pensions are another popular way to save. They are so popular that many employers offer a pension plan for their employees as part of their compensation packages. Typically pensions are either defined benefit plans or defined contribution plans. A **defined benefit pension plan** specifies how much money a retiree will receive each year upon retirement. If a firm offers a defined benefit pension, they are legally obligated to place an actuarially determined amount of savings aside to meet all future pension promises. A **fully funded pension** system meets these actuarial requirements. Often, government pension systems are not fully funded. A **pay-as-you-go pension** system pays current retirement benefits out of current revenue.

Most private employers who offer a pension now offer a **defined contribution pension**. They contribute to an employee's **individual retirement account** a fixed amount each pay period. The amount of money an employee has upon retirement depends upon the rate of return generated by the assets in the retirement portfolio. Most retirement plans allow for the diversification of savings into stock, commodity, and bond markets.

Firms

Firms also play a key role in the economy as institutions that produce goods and services for consumers to consume. Firms include **sole proprietorships** (one owner), **partnerships** (owned by two or more partners), and **limited liability corporations** (owned by shareholders). Firms employ resources (natural resources, labor, human capital, physical capital, technology, and entrepreneurship) in order to engage in production. They also pay taxes, donate to charity, and borrow money to invest in new capital.

The money to build a new machine, tool, or factory must come from savers. Savings predate investment. Firms use financial institutions such as banks, the stock market, and bond markets to borrow money from savers, both foreign and domestic. Firms can also use retained earnings to finance future investment. The choice of where to place the investment, domestically or abroad, is also made by firms. Their choice of where to engage in investment and production is a function of both the cost of production and the ability to get their products to their prospective consumers, both domestic and foreign.

When firms engage in production, they generate revenue which allows them to pay wages to their laborers, interest on their borrowed capital, rent on their borrowed land, and profits to their owners. This generates income for consumers. Firms also pay taxes which include capital gains taxes, corporate income taxes, license fees, and personal income taxes paid by owners of the firm. These taxes generate revenue for the government.

In a dynamic, growing economy, new firms begin production while inefficient firms go out of business. Firms that produce goods and services and sell them at prices consumers want to pay grow, while firms that produce goods and services that people don't want or charge prices people don't want to pay shut down. When firms fail, their resources are freed up for use by more productive firms. Government bailouts of firms prevents this reshuffling of resources to their most efficient usage.

The Government

Federal, state, and local governments are collectively referred to as "The **Government**". Governments can collect taxes, engage in government spending, enact transfer payments, receive **intergovernmental transfers**, borrow, save, and regulate the economy.

Taxes can be placed on consumers or businesses. Spending can be on goods and services made domestically or abroad. Transfer payments can be made domestically or abroad to consumers, businesses, or other governments. Regulations can be placed on consumers, businesses, or lower levels of governments. While some state and local governments are required to balance their budget every year, others, including the US national government, have no such requirement. When governments spend and give away more money than they receive in taxes and intergovernmental transfers in a given year, they run a **budget deficit**. When they receive more in taxes and intergovernmental transfers than they spend and give away, they run a **budget surplus**.

In the United States, the Constitution enumerates powers held by Congress and the national government. Other powers are reserved for states, as noted in the 10th Amendment. This system of divided government power is called **federalism**. By reserving some power to states, federalism allows for competition between the fifty states in attracting firms and consumers to produce and set up shop in their state. Such competition allows states to experiment with spending, taxing, borrowing, and regulatory rules to determine the mix that best meets the needs and wants of people living within each state. It also holds state and local governments accountable for poor decisions by offering US citizens a choice to live under different tax levels, spending levels, or regulatory rules.

The Foreign Sector

Finally, the **foreign sector** is the most broadly defined economic actor. It represents consumers, financial institutions, firms, and governments that exist outside the borders of a country. Recall that **exports** are goods and services produced within a country and purchased by foreigners. **Imports** are goods and services produced outside of the country but purchased within the country. A **trade deficit** occurs if the dollar value of imports exceeds the dollar value of exports. A **trade surplus** occurs if the dollar value of exports exceeds the dollar value of imports.

Foreign firms can build capital in a country not their own. This is called **foreign direct investment (FDI)**. Foreigners can also borrow and save in a country's financial institutions. Japanese consumers could place money in the NYSE, and an American bank could make a loan to the Greek government. National laws and international treaties regulate domestic economic actors who engage in transactions with the foreign sector. In a globalized economy, it is not uncommon for a firm in Country A to take a loan from a bank in Country B in order to invest in new capital in Country C in order to export their product to Country D. The more integrated the world economy becomes, the more important a proper understanding of the foreign sector becomes.

Figure 7.1 illustrates how the actors in the macroeconomy interact. As production occurs, owners of resources are rewarded with income. This income is then used to purchase more output, which in turn, produces more income. The circular logic of the economy begets the name of the model, the **Circular Flow Model**. During periods of economic expansion, products are produced, people get paid, and they buy more output, causing more stuff to be made and more people to be paid. During periods of economic contraction, fewer products are made, so fewer people get paid, which results in them being able to buy even less output, causing output to fall more. The remainder of this chapter will analyze changes in the business cycle that result when the actors listed here change their actions from one day to the next and therefore affect the growth rate of the economy.

Business Cycles

While each economic actor can engage in multiple actions for various reasons, there are certain actions that cause firms to engage in more production. As consumers, firms, governments, and foreigners purchase more goods and services, existing inventories of unsold goods falls. This acts as a signal to producers to increase their output. Short run changes in output are the result of either changes in demand for the output of firms or a change in the firm's cost of production, which leads to changes in the supply of output. These changes create **business cycles**, or a cycle of increases and decreases in real GDP.

As displayed in Figure 7.2, business cycles contain expansions and contractions. A single business cycle contains one of each. An **expansion** occurs whenever Real GDP is increasing. It means that the economy is growing and so the PPF is shifting outward. Another commonly used term for an expansion is a recovery. When an expansion reaches it highest level of RGDP it is said to be at its **peak**. The opposite of an expansion is called a contraction. A **contraction** occurs whenever Real GDP is falling from one quarter to the next. The contraction's lowest level of real GDP is called the **trough**. A **recession** typically describes a contraction lasting for at least two consecutive quarters. However, the National Bureau of Economic Research dates recessions and defines a recession as "a significant decline in economic activity spread across the economy, lasting more than a few months, normally visible in real GDP, real income, employment, industrial production, and wholesale-retail sales."[1]

---

[1] For more information see Source:
Public Information Office
National Bureau of Economic Research, Inc.
1050 Massachusetts Avenue
Cambridge MA 02138
USA

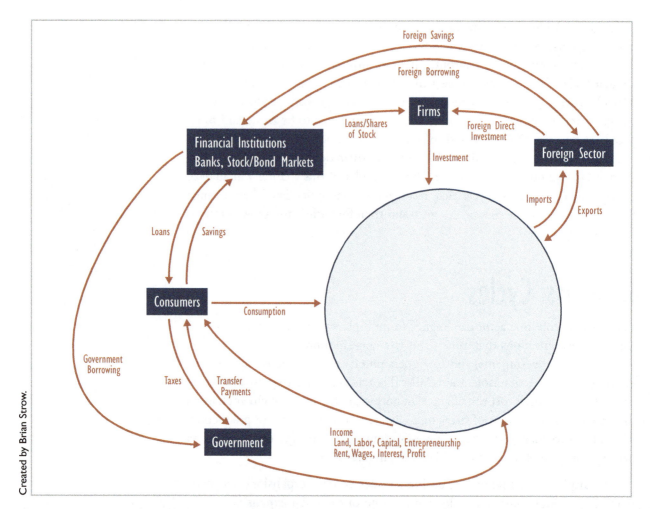

Created by Brian Strow.

Figure 7.1   **CIRCULAR FLOW DIAGRAM**

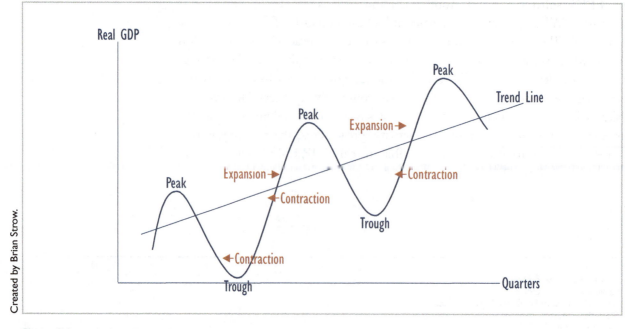

Created by Brian Strow.

Figure 7.2   **THE BUSINESS CYCLE**

TABLE 7.1	HISTORIC RECESSION DURATIONS
Starting Month	**Duration**
June 1857	18
October 1860	8
April 1865	32
June 1869	18
October 1873	65
March 1882	38
March 1887	13
July 1890	10
January 1893	17
December 1895	18
June 1899	18
September 1902	23
May 1907	13
January 1910	24
January 1913	23
August 1918	7
January 1920	18
May 1923	14
October 1926	13
August 1929	43
May 1937	13
February 1945	8
November 1948	11
July 1953	10
August 1957	8
April 1960	10
December 1969	11
November 1973	16
January 1980	6
July 1981	16
July 1990	8
March 2001	8
December 2007	18

Source: Public Information Office National Bureau of Economic Research, Inc. 1050 Massachusetts Avenue Cambridge MA 02138 USA

The NBER has identified 33 recessions since 1854. The average length of recessions from 1854–1945 was substantially longer than the average length since. However, the Great Recession of 2007–2009 stands out as an anomaly to this trend, lasting 18 months, and with effects of the recession lasting even longer. At the date of publication of this book, the NBER's Business Cycle Dating Committee had not made an announcement since its June 2009 announcement that the economy had started expanding. In other words, the economy has been in an expansion for the last decade according to the NBER. Since 1945, the average expansionary period has lasted 58.4 months, or just under 5 years.

Case Study: The Great Recession (2007–2009)

According to the National Bureau of Economic Research, the US economy entered into a recession in December 2007 and ended the recession in June 2009. In the popular press, the event was known as "The Great Recession". The unemployment rate rose from 4.4% in May of 2007 to a high of 10% in October 2009. The unemployment rate did not return again to 4.4% until March 2017, almost a full decade after its initial rise. During the recession, the US economy logged five quarters of negative economic growth. For the first time since 1954, the economy experienced deflation in 2009 as the consumer price index fell by .35%.

TABLE 7.2	REAL GDP GROWTH BY QUARTER DURING THE GREAT RECESSION				
	2008				**2009**
Q1: -2.3%		Q3: -2.1%		Q1: -4.4%	
Q2: 2.1%		Q4: -8.4%		Q2: -0.6%	

What caused this dramatic contraction? In a nutshell, the recession served as a market correction for excessive debt fueled growth between 1997 and 2007. Households, firms, and governments enabled higher levels of spending by taking on ever greater levels of debt. Table 7.3 shows that each of these sectors dramatically increased their debt levels during the decade before the recession. In total, between 1997 and 2007, US debt increased by $30.5 trillion, while US GDP only increased by $5.5 trillion. Ultimately, debt has to be repaid and debt fueled spending has to be curtailed, which leads to an economic slowdown.

TABLE 7.3 US DEBT IN THE TRILLIONS OF $		
	1997	2007
Business Debt	4.8	10.6
Household Debt	5.5	13.8
Financial Sector Debt	5.3	16.2
Federal Government Debt	5.5	9.2

Investment and the Burst of the Housing Bubble

Home prices rose 84% between 2000 and 2006. This sharp increase in home prices drove home builders to pick up the pace of new home construction. However, this run up in home prices was unsustainable. In turn, this made the increase in home construction unsustainable. Home prices fell 26% from their peak before they began to recover in 2012. New home construction crashed, taking the economy down with it.

Between the second quarter of 2006 and the third quarter of 2009, only one quarter saw an increase in investment spending in the US. Every other quarter recorded a decrease in investment spending, including a -38.8% decline during the first quarter of 2009. Private residential fixed investment (housing) started its decline in 2005 and fell a cumulative 57% between 2005 and 2009. Private nonresidential fixed investment, by contrast, did not begin its decline until 2008 but had declined 17% by 2009. Clearly, the decline in new home and apartment construction triggered the downturn, but why did the housing bubble get started?

Problems of this size rarely have singular causes. In the case of the housing bubble, the increase in home prices were aided by lower than normal interest rates, easing home mortgage standards, market speculation, and a public policy push to increase rates of home ownership. The effective federal funds rate (prime interest rate) was kept below 2% for three years, beginning in December 2001, to help the economy recover from the 2001 recession. Not since 1961, had the federal funds rate been so low. This lowered the cost of borrowing, which indeed prompted more people to borrow larger amounts of money for their home.

Since housing prices were going up, some began to believe that they could always make money by flipping homes. It did not matter if they could afford the house they bought, because they could always sell it for more if they had to—until they could not. Many lenders eager to make money from loan organization fees and gain favor with pro-housing government politicians began relaxing lending standards to people with poor credit. As long as home prices kept rising, even people with bad credit were unlikely to default on their home loan. They would merely sell their house, pay off their debt, and bank the profit. When home prices began to fall, people walked away from their mortgages in large numbers because they owned more on their home loan than they could sell their home for. This left banks with huge financial losses which translated into fewer loanable funds available for firms to borrow and invest.

Consumption and the Fall of the Dow

The Dow Jones Industrial Average fell from 14,164 on October 9th, 2007 to 6,470 on March 6th, 2009. This reduction in people's retirement savings likely triggered a reduction in consumption due to the wealth effect. Rising unemployment rates could have also made it more difficult for consumers to engage in spending. Nevertheless, during the recession, real consumption spending only fell 2.3% from its pre-recession pace, and it began recovering in early 2009. Clearly consumption was much more resilient than investment was in the economic downturn.

Net Exports and the Trade Deficit

The US had an annualized trade deficit of only $97 billion in the third quarter of 1997. By the third quarter of 2006, the US trade deficit had increased to $806 billion. This increase was in the trade deficit a sign that US consumers, firms, and governments were ramping up their spending by borrowing increasingly large amounts of money from abroad. As the US economy entered recession, firms and consumers were forced to cut down on foreign borrowing in order to begin to repay previous debts. By the second quarter of 2009, the trade deficit had fallen to $339 billion.

The moral of the story is that short term economic growth can be fueled by borrowing money from abroad. However, borrowing to increase current consumption or to increase the size of homes does nothing to improve economic productivity or long run economic growth. When the time comes for these debts to be repaid, spending will fall and economic growth will become more difficult to obtain. Nobel winning economist F.A. Hayek long ago noted that business cycles are often caused by the bursting of credit bubbles. The Great Recession was just another case in point.

Conclusion

Just as macroeconomic actors all contribute to and draw from the economy, a number of factors lead to shifts in production that drive business cycles. Government policies also play a role in either incentivizing or slowing down spending and production.

Government policies often have multiple and conflicting motives. Policies such as increasing the minimum wage, forced usage of union labor, and environmental protections are imposed to protect workers and the environment. The tradeoff is that these regulations increase the cost of production and therefore slow down economic growth. Each government regulation would need to be examined on a case by case basis to determine if the marginal benefit to workers or the environment exceeded the marginal cost imposed upon society through slower growth.

Government policies on war and immigration can affect the productive capacity of an economy at any given time. More resources lead to more output. Changes in business taxes along with changes in education policy can also affect the cost of production.

The economy is ever changing. Changes made by any number of actors have the potential to cause business cycles in the US economy. Consumers, firms, governments, and foreign economic actors all play a part in a growing economy. While the economy grows, it does not always do so at an even rate. The following chapters will examine how John Maynard Keynes modeled short run business cycles in the economy along with his policy prescriptions for governments and central banks. This analysis will also include critiques of his prescriptions.

Key Terms

Bear

Bear market

Budget deficit

Budget surplus

Bull

Bull market

Business cycles

Cash advance store

Certificate of deposit

Checking account

Circular Flow Model

Commodity

Consumers

Contraction

Credit scores

Defined benefit pension plan

Defined contribution pension

Disposable income

Dividend

Dow Jones Industrial Average

Expansion

Exports

Federalism

Financial institutions

Firms

Foreign Direct Investment

Foreign sector

Fully funded pension

Futures contract

Government

Imports

Individual retirement account

Interest

Intergovernmental transfers

Limited liability corporations

Liquidity

Loan sharks

Money market account

Moody's

Mutual funds

NASDAQ

NASDAQ Composite

New York Stock Exchange

Partnership

Pay-as-you-go pension

Peak

Portfolio

Profit

Recession

Rent

Retained earnings

Russell 2000

Savings account

Share of stock

Sole proprietorship

Standard & Poor's

S&P 500

Trade deficit

Trade surplus

Transfer payments

Trough

Usury

Wages

Questions for Review

1. What roles are played by each of the economic actors in the economy?

2. What is a stock market? What is the biggest stock market in the US?

3. What is a bond market? How do government bonds differ from corporate bonds?

4. a. Compare and contrast the following savings instruments: a checking account, a savings account, a money market account, and a certificate of deposit.

   b. Compare and contrast defined benefit and defined contribution pensions.

   c. Compare and contrast fully funded and pay-as-you go pensions. What are the advantages and disadvantages of each?

5. What is a recession? How does it differ from a contraction?

6. Suppose that RGDP rises from quarter 1 to quarter 2. What phase of the business cycle are we in?

7. Suppose that RGDP falls from quarter 1 through quarter 2? What phase of the business cycle are we in? What determines if this phase is called a recession or not?

8. What is a bull market? What is a bear market?

9. What phase of the business cycle is the economy currently in?

10. True or false: if RGDP was growing at a rate of 3% in the first quarter, and growth slows to a rate of 2% in the second quarter, then we are in a contraction.

Aggregate Demand and Aggregate Supply

A myriad of economic actors make decisions relative to making their lives better, their company's profits higher, or their re-election more likely. John Maynard Keynes developed the aggregate demand and aggregate supply model to attempt to explain unemployment, inflation, and output by examining the demand for domestically made goods and services relative to their supply. This chapter outlines the aggregate demand and supply model and discusses how shifts in aggregate demand or supply affect the macroeconomic equilibrium. The chapter then examines the natural adjustment process back to full employment and explores supply side economics.

Aggregate Demand

Aggregate demand (AD) is the sum total of all domestic goods and services that consumers, businesses, the government, and foreign actors want to buy at any given price level. It is theoretically derived by adding the demand for apples to the demand for cars to the demand for bread to the demand for every other good or service. Mathematically, aggregate demand equals the demand for consumption plus investment plus government spending plus net exports at each price level. Recall that these are the same variables used to calculate GDP via the expenditure approach.

$$AD = C + I + G + NX$$

For individual goods and services, the **law of demand** states that as prices fall, the quantity demanded of a good or service increases. The aggregate demand curve is downward sloping because consumers, businesses, governments, and foreigners can all afford to buy more goods and services as prices fall. This is due to three factors: the wealth effect, the interest rate effect, and the foreign trade effect.

The **wealth effect** occurs when lower prices enable economic actors to engage in greater purchases of goods and services with the same amount of income. In this way, consumers feel wealthier, as their money goes further due to the lower prices. At the same time, lower price levels typically lower the cost of borrowing money. This leads to an **interest rate effect**. As the cost of borrowing money falls, firms will be better able to afford investment in new capital, consumers will be more likely to purchase homes and durable consumer goods, and governments will find it cheaper to borrow and spend. Even if firms, consumers, or governments are using their own funds for these purchases, the opportunity cost of doing so decreases as prices fall. Finally, lower domestic prices will encourage residents and foreigners to purchase more domestically produced goods and services, thereby lowering imports and increasing exports. This is known as the **foreign trade effect**. All three of these effects cause the aggregate demand curve to slope downward such that as price levels fall there is an increase in the aggregate quantity demanded.

Note that when the prices of individual goods are aggregated, they yield an **average price level**. In reality, the average price level is measured and reported by examining a market basket of goods defined by the Bureau of Labor Statistics. As such, prices of individual products can change at different rates or even in different directions from the government reported average price level. Rather than stand for an actual price, the y-axis is meant to measure changes in the average price level (i.e. inflation or deflation). Recall that an increase in the average price level is inflation, while a decrease is deflation.

The x-axis of the aggregate demand curve represents the RGDP, or the total value of all goods and services produced in the economy, controlling for price levels. In this way, the x-axis is a measure of actual economic output. An increase in RGDP reflects economic growth, while a decrease in RGDP is an economic contraction. Figure 8.1 illustrates how aggregate demand is the sum of each individual demand curve in an economy.

Figure 8.1
CREATION OF AGGREGATE DEMAND VIA THE SUMMING OF INDIVIDUAL DEMAND CURVES

Aggregate demand constantly shifts as actors in the economy act and react to each other. Aggregate demand shifts to the right (increases) when consumption, investment, government spending, or net exports increase. Aggregate demand shifts to the left (decreases) when consumption, investment, government spending, or net exports decrease. Many factors can cause consumption, investment, government spending, investment, and net exports to change; changes in any of these will likewise shift Aggregate demand. In Figure 8.2, AD represents the initial level of aggregate demand while AD' represents the new level of aggregate demand following a change in consumption, investment, government spending, or net exports.

Figure 8.2
SHIFTS IN AD

Changes in the demand for output can be broken down into changes in one of four categories: consumption (C), investment (I), government spending (G), and exports (X). To understand short term fluctuations in output, one must understand what causes the demand for consumption, investment, government spending, and exports to change. Output changes as economic actors make different choices. If everyone made the same choice every day, there would not be business cycles. The next section will explain factors that change the demand for each category of output.

Factors Which Shift Demand for Output

Changes in Consumption

The level of current consumption depends upon the prices of goods and services relative to consumers' income levels, the level of consumers' wealth, the amount of tax burden on consumers, the availability of credit, and consumers' expectations about the future.

As people's incomes increase, so does their consumption of goods and services. Milton Friedman's permanent income hypothesis states that consumers will spend a relatively constant percentage of all new permanent income. They will not increase consumption based on temporary income changes. Temporary income tends to increase savings rather than consumption. If more is better, then as people's capacity to purchase goods and services increases, so too will their actual consumption.

As people's wealth increases, so does their ability to engage in consumption. If Bob's income remains unchanged, but he notices that the value of the house he owns doubled in the last year, he is wealthier. Bob can now afford to consume more (assuming he wants the same amount of money available in retirement) as before the increase in house prices. In this way, US consumer spending increased faster than incomes during the housing boom of the early 2000's.

Consumers can not purchase goods and services with money that is taken from them by the government. All things being equal, an increase in taxes results in a decrease in consumption. Conversely, a decrease in taxes will result in an increase in consumption, as long as people view the tax change as permanently altering their disposable income.

The purchase of higher priced consumer goods, such as automobiles, often occurs on credit. The more that credit is made available to consumers or the lower the rate of interest, the more likely they are to shift future consumption forward. A decrease in credit availability or the price of credit, all things being equal, will reduce current consumption.

Consumers make consumption decisions not just based on current information, but also based upon expectations about the future. If consumers are confident that they will not get fired from their job, then they are more likely to engage in consumption than if they are uncertain about the future. Expectations of higher future prices, increases in income or wealth, increased availability of credit, and lower expected tax rates all will cause consumers, on average, to engage in more current consumption.

Policies That Target Consumption

Current consumption generally increases when taxes are lowered and when consumers are confident that future government policies will lead to lower taxes and more economic growth. Governments have often attempted to increase consumption by redistributing money from high income individuals to low income individuals on the belief that lower income individuals will spend a larger percentage of their income than did the people who once held the money. While this policy attempts to increase consumption, it also works to decrease investment, because the expectation of future income transfers decreases the future profitability of current investment. Policies designed to boost short run consumption typically come at the cost of decreased future consumption due to slower economic growth.

Changes in Investment

Business investment is even more volatile than consumption. Since WWII, investment has grown at one-third the rate of growth for consumption, but has had two and a half times the variance. During the same time period, investment levels had ten times the variance of either net exports or government spending.

Firms exist to make profit. In their pursuit of profit, they often employ new machines, tools, factories, or software. The purchase of new capital is investment. Investment decisions are based on the expected benefits over time from the fixed capital vs. the marginal costs of employing the capital.

The opportunity cost of investment is the interest rate. The higher the interest rate, the more costly it is for firms to borrow money to buy new capital. As interest rates fall, more and more capital projects become profitable. Thus, one source of variance in investment is a change in interest rates.

Similarly, changes in access to business credit can alter the pace of investment. When business credit becomes more scarce, current investment falls. As business credit standards loosen, more entrepreneurs gain access to start-up capital and investment increases. As more loans are made by banks in a fractional reserve banking system, the money supply increases. This in turn causes a decrease in interest rates. In this way, increased business investment leads to even more business investment. On the contrary, when firms begin investing less, fewer loans are made, the money supply shrinks, causing interest

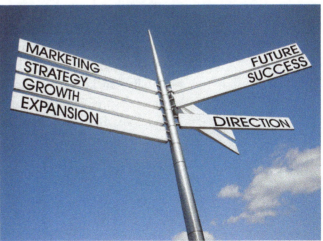

© joingate, 2012, under license Shutterstock, Inc.

rates to rise and other investment projects to become more costly. As a result, the economy tends to experience booms and busts in investment, which cause and/or exacerbate business cycles.

Other factors that affect investment are the price of capital, business confidence, and business taxes/regulations. As the price of capital falls, firms are able to upgrade their capital for a lower cost. Conversely, if the price of capital increases, such as due to an increase in the price of steel raising the price of machinery, then fewer firms can afford to make new investments. The falling price of steel in the 1870's caused railroad firms to replace iron rails with steel rails. Even though steel rails for years had been more durable than iron rails, their cost had remained prohibitively high.

An increase in business taxes and regulations on capital works to decrease the amount of new private sector investment. Taxes on capital, such as the capital gains tax, alter the capital to labor ratio that firms find to be profit maximizing. As taxes or regulations on capital increase, it becomes more profitable to substitute labor for capital and increases the likelihood that any new capital is built overseas. Business investment represents the true mobility of capital. While an existing factory is hard to move, when it comes to replacing the factory (i.e. new investment), capital is very mobile. New investment today translates into a larger stock of capital for tomorrow, so decisions by the government in terms of regulations or taxes on capital now not only affect today's level of investment, but tomorrow's level of potential output.

The last major source of investment variability is business confidence/uncertainty. When businesses think that their business will grow in the future, they are more likely to invest and expand their productive capacity. As firms become pessimistic about their future, new investment is curtailed. As firms face greater uncertainty due to changing regulations or taxes, this added uncertainty causes a decrease in current investment. Investment has a multi-year lifespan, so that the more uncertain business owners are about the relative profitability of capital over time, the less new investment will materialize.

John Maynard Keynes suggested that business investment is determined by "animal spirits" and is therefore unpredictable. However, because most investment in capital is expensive (relative to current cash flow) capitalists have an economic incentive to make informed investment decisions. To suggest that capitalists act irrationally based upon "animal spirits" neglects reality. Good capitalists make money and have more money to invest in the accumulation or more capital in order to seek more profits. Ill-informed capitalists lose their capital and have no further profits to invest. Time is on the side of informed investment decisions.

Policies That Target Investment

Government policies to increase investment come in two varieties: increasing investment over time (including now), and increasing investment in the short run (at the expense of future investment). In order to increase investment over time, governments can create a tax and regulatory environment that is conducive to investment. Legal changes that make taxes and regulations more capital friendly will boost investment levels both now and later.

The second strategy does not increase capital accumulation over time, but merely alters when in time investment occurs. For instance, if the Federal Reserve increases the money supply in order to lower interest rates, they lower the cost of borrowing with the intent of spurring current investment. Inflation neutral monetary policy dictates that today's loosening of monetary policy necessitates a future tightening. In this way, the Federal Reserve signals that today's investment will cost less, and tomorrow's investment will cost more. Therefore, tomorrow's investment should be moved forward to today. Likewise, investment tax credits which apply to now, but not later, provide an incentive to move investment forward.

To the extent that this strategy is effective, an economy gets more investment today accompanied by less investment tomorrow. The 2009 "Cash for Clunkers" program saw a temporary increase in car sales followed by a large reduction in car sales as consumers planning to buy cars in the near future just moved up their consumption by a couple of months. Excessive use of monetary easing or investment tax credits causes artificial investment bubbles that can, and do, burst.

In order to bring the US out of the 2001 recession, the Federal Reserve eased monetary policy and increased the money supply, which caused businesses to bring investment forward. Because monetary policy was so loose for so long, a large amount of investment was brought forward. In fact, so much was brought forward that excess capacity was created in everything from industrial plants, to condos, to office space. This excess capacity caused investment to come to a virtual halt in the US, helping to trigger the 2008–2009 economic recession.

Changes in Government Spending

Changes in government spending are less predictable than changes in private sector spending. People's actions concerning their own money tend to be more predictable than government officials decisions concerning other people's money. The political reward system is such that it is often in the short term benefit of politicians to increase spending and cut taxes. Because politicians face elections in the short term, they tend to emphasize these politically popular policies rather than policies that focus primarily on long run economic growth. Still, there have been periods of US history where politicians have decreased government spending, most notably at the conclusion of major military conflicts.

Historically, governments around the world have tended to spend more money in times of war than in times of peace. Constituents are usually not asked to forgo their normal government spending programs in order to finance military action.

So, rather than cut other government spending or raise taxes, most countries over time have financed wars through increased government debt. The most notable swings in government spending in the United States indeed have revolved around military conflicts such as The American Revolution, The War of 1812, The Spanish American War, The US Civil War, WWI, WWII, The Cold War, and conflicts in Korea, Vietnam, Iraq, and Afghanistan. The decrease in military spending following wars is known as the **peace dividend**, because money that had been diverted to the war effort is now returned to meeting the needs and wants of consumers and businesses.

A second cause of fluctuating government spending is the phase of the business cycle. In response to slow economic growth or recessions since the 1930's, US politicians have often advocated the expansion of government spending in order to help stimulate the economy. President Herbert Hoover increased government spending on public works projects at the beginning of The Great Depression. President Barack Obama increased government spending for almost all government programs as a response to the 2008 recession.

Robert Higgs has shown that major increases in government spending due to shocks such as wars and recessions never fully dissipate. Instead, government spending levels rarely return to pre-crisis levels. They almost always remain higher. For politicians, spending and the power derived from it can be addictive.[1]

Policies That Target Government Spending

Government policies that cause government spending to change over time include balanced budget rules, pay as you go rules, or binding spending constraints. Governments with binding spending constraints, either in terms of dollars, a percentage of output, or as a function of tax receipts, have less discretion over changing government spending than do governments with no such rules.

As governments become more in debt, future government spending becomes imperiled. Therefore, a strategy of government borrowing to increase current government spending can lead to less government spending over time. Historically, the government's decisions to go to war also have had profound impacts on current spending levels for domestic causes.

[1] Robert Higgs. "Crisis, Bigger Government and Ideological Change: Two-Hypotheses on the Ratchet Phenomenon." *Explorations in Economic History* 22 (1985): 4.

Changes in Exports

People in other countries change the amount of goods and services they buy from the US for a variety of reasons. Because all people in other countries are consumers, the same factors the affect United States consumption affects foreign consumption. These factors include the prices of goods and services, foreign incomes and wealth levels, foreign tax burdens, the availability of credit, and their expectations about the future. As foreign consumers buy more generally, they also tend to buy more US exports. Therefore, increases in things like foreign income or foreign wealth increase the US's ability to sell goods abroad. In this way, one doesn't have to be altruistic to hope that other countries become wealthier over time. One can root for a growing world economy because it will benefit United States exporters and therefore the US economy.

© kentoh, 2012, under license Shutterstock, Inc.

Of particular note to foreign consumers or businesses is the relative price difference of products between countries. When one country's prices increase relative to those of another, fewer consumers, both domestic and abroad, will want to buy that country's goods and services. Conversely, when the relative prices of a country's goods fall, more people around the world will want to buy them.

Policies That Target Net Exports

Government policies that cause net exports to increase in the short term include increased trade barriers, export subsidies and depreciation of their currency's value. However, in the long run other countries retaliate by putting trade barriers on US exports, devaluing their currency, and subsidizing their country's exports. Over time, these actions serve to lower exports and slow down economic growth.

Over time, a country can increase its net exports by lowering its national debt and, after time taxing consumption rather than production. By lowering its national debt, governments take away the option of foreigners storing domestic currency in government bonds. Instead, they would be forced to buy goods, services, or assets in the domestic economy, thereby spurring exports. Tax codes that tax production handicaps producers selling to the international market. Tax codes that tax consumption shift some of the domestic tax burden to international producers.

Thus, any factor that causes a change in consumption, investment, government spending, or exports also causes a change in GDP. At the same time, the economy is influenced not just by what is demanded but also by what is supplied to the economy. We turn our attention now to aggregate supply.

Injections and Leakages

These spending categories (consumption, investment, government spending, and exports) are known as **injections**. To sum up demand side explanations for business cycles, when consumption, investment, government spending, or exports increase, GDP increases. When they fall, GDP falls. After all, GDP calculations are made by summing up consumption, investment, government spending, and net exports.

In the short run, consumers could choose to save more and consume less. Because an increase in saving causes a decrease in consumption, savings are known as a **leakage** in the short term. Leakages are items that if increased, tend to slow down GDP in the short run. Savings can make their way back into the economy through investment, but it may take time for this to occur. Likewise, taxes and imports are two other common leakages. When taxes increase on consumers, they cannot afford to engage in as much consumption. When taxes are increased on businesses, they cannot afford to engage in as much investment. While these taxes may find their way back into the economy via higher government spending, there is no requirement that they do so.

When consumers choose to buy foreign made products, they replace domestic consumption (and therefore production) with products that increase foreign production. While the purchase of foreign goods increases foreign incomes and could therefore cause future exports to increase, there is no guarantee that people in other countries, once wealthier, will want to buy more American made products. Yet, free trade overall increases wealth.

Aggregate Supply

Aggregate supply is the sum total of all goods and services firms and governments are willing and able to produce at any given price level. It is theoretically derived by adding the supply of apples to the supply of cars to the supply of bread to the supply of every other good or service. Figure 8.3 illustrates this relationship.

The aggregate supply curve's shape varies from flat to upward sloping and then to vertical. At any given point in time, an economy can only produce on or within its production possibilities frontier. When output in the economy is extremely low, as is the case in a severe recession, a large number of productive resources are unused, and the country is operating inside its production possibilities frontier. Multiple existing factories are idle, skilled workers are laid off, and land is left fallow. In this state of affairs, producers are said to have **excess capacity**. Firms can increase production without substantial increases in cost by employing workers that are already trained and utilizing capital that was sitting unused. In this way, aggregate supply is relatively flat at low levels of economic output because production can increase without increases in the price level.

At the other extreme, when production is near full capacity, the aggregate supply curve is vertical. The vertical portion of aggregate supply represents the constraint resulting from the production possibilities frontier. Even if consumers want to buy more products, producers cannot operate above full capacity. So despite higher price levels, production cannot increase beyond this point without economic growth, and so aggregate supply is vertical here.

For most levels of production, aggregate supply is upward sloping. As production increases toward full capacity, more and more resources are employed in the production process. The most fertile land is plowed first. The most productive capital and workers are also employed first. As production increases, producers needing more resources are then forced to employ less productive resources in the production process. This increases the cost of production and yields higher prices for output. As a result, in this range of aggregate supply, increased output corresponds to a higher price level.

Just as aggregate demand shifts from changes in a variety of factors affecting GDP, aggregate supply shifts when anything changes the cost of producing. As the cost of production increases, aggregate supply shifts to the left (decreases); at any given price level, producers will now be able to bring fewer products to market. As the cost of production decreases, aggregate supply shifts to the right (increases); at any given price level, producers will now be able to bring more products to market. The cost of production can be affected by changes in government regulations, business taxation, the quantity of resources available for production, resource productivity, wars, and natural disasters.

While different industries will face different changes in their cost structure and different technological innovations affecting productivity, aggregate supply is meant to measure overall changes in the cost of production. Changing

Figure 8.3
CREATION OF AGGREGATE SUPPLY FROM INDIVIDUAL SUPPLY CURVES IN THE ECONOMY

Figure 8.4
SHIFTS IN AS

energy and labor costs, for instance, tend to have widespread impact on numerous firms. In Figure 8.4, AS represents the initial level of aggregate supply while AS' represents the new level of aggregate supply following a change in the cost of production.

Factors That Shift Aggregate Supply

Business cycles can also be caused by quick and unexpected changes in the cost of production faced by a majority of firms in a country. These include changes in the cost of inputs, changes in productivity or technology, changes in the quantity of inputs (such as with immigration, natural disasters, war), changes in government regulations, and changes in business taxes.

When OPEC increased the price of oil in the 1970's the US economy suffered. Energy is a major input into the production process and the increase in the price of energy increased both production and distribution cost of goods throughout the US economy. This worked to slow the economy down.

In the 1990's, the internet revolution dramatically lowered information and communication costs. This increased worker productivity and lowered the cost of production for many goods and services throughout the economy. As a result, the economy grew quickly.

Wars and natural disasters decrease the productive capacity of an economy by destroying existing capital. This destruction lowers current output while creating the need to rebuild capital which can increase the pace of economic growth following the end of military hostilities. Germany and Japan's economies were devastated by the Allied troops' bombings. However, following WWII, both economies grew quickly, as they worked to replace destroyed capital.

Once again, government policies can affect the cost of production. In particular, increases in government regulations and business taxes increase the cost of production which in turn, slows down production and therefore decreases economic growth by decreasing aggregate supply.

Macroeconomic Equilibrium

Theoretically, the intersection of the aggregate demand and aggregate supply curves represents the **macroeconomic equilibrium**. This is where the quantity of domestic goods and services demanded in the economy equals the quantity of domestic goods and services supplied. This equilibrium dictates the current price level, the current level of RGDP, and the current unemployment rate. An increase in aggregate demand or a decrease in aggregate supply causes inflation (the equilibrium average price level increases). A decrease in the aggregate demand or an increase in aggregate supply causes deflation (the equilibrium average price level decreases).

Likewise, RGDP changes as a result of a change in aggregate demand or aggregate supply. An increase in RGDP occurs when aggregate demand or aggregate supply increases. RGDP decreases as aggregate demand or aggregate supply decreases. While the x-axis explicitly represents output or RGDP, it implicitly represents unemployment. Reductions in output are typically accompanied by a reduction in the workforce, as fewer workers are needed to produce fewer goods and services. Economic growth is usually accompanied by an increase in the workforce, as more workers are needed to produce a larger number of goods and services. As such, a decrease in aggregate demand or aggregate supply causes an increase in unemployment, while an increase in aggregate demand or aggregate supply causes a decrease in unemployment. The one caveat to note is that changes to aggregate supply caused by changes in worker productivity can cause output to change without changing levels of unemployment. Figures 8.6 and 8.7 illustrate the changing price levels and changing output levels that result.

Recall that full employment is where cyclical unemployment equals zero, but the overall unemployment rate is between 5 and 5.5%. When aggregate demand and aggregate supply intersect at the full employment level of output (FE), the economy is said to be at equilibrium at its "happy place." This is illustrated in Figure 8.5. The next section discusses what happens when the economy moves away from this "happy place" due to shifts in aggregate demand or aggregate supply.

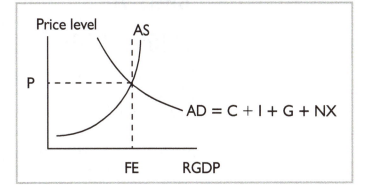

Figure 8.5
THE ECONOMY AT ITS "HAPPY PLACE"

Figure 8.6

Figure 8.7

Shifts Away from Full Employment Equilibrium

Once upon a time (the 1930's), in a land far, far, away (the United Kingdom), John Maynard Keynes proposed the aggregate demand and aggregate supply model to explain current levels of unemployment and inflation and to provide theoretical analysis with policy alternatives to reach full employment. Full employment (the economy's happy place where no cyclical unemployment occurred) was seen as the ideal place to which the economy should be directed.

Unfortunately, the economy routinely suffered "shocks" that knocked it out of the full employment equilibrium. These shocks were modeled as being exogenous to the economy. That is, they came out of nowhere, and were not expected events. In reality, no one knows the future, so every day contains shocks to someone. Furthermore, these shocks are not exogenous to the economy but rather they are endogenous, as they result from actions made by actual economic actors taking part in the economy. Nevertheless, the analysis of the Keynesian model will treat "shocks" as being exogenous. This section examines the scenarios created when such shocks occur.

Recessionary Gap

A **recessionary gap** is caused by aggregate demand being "too low." It intersects aggregate supply to the left of full employment. Anything that would cause a reduction in consumption, investment, government spending, or net exports, then would lead to a recessionary gap. The result is high unemployment, a decrease in output, and deflation.

Assume the economy is operating at full employment. Next, assume that businesses become pessimistic about their future profitability and this pessimism leads to a decrease in new investment. This unexpected decrease in business investment is considered to be an exogenous shock to the economy. Recall that aggregate demand is composed of consumption, investment, government spending, and net exports. As investment falls, aggregate demand falls as well. Consequently, aggregate demand will intersect aggregate supply to the left of full employment, and the economy is said to be experiencing a recessionary gap.

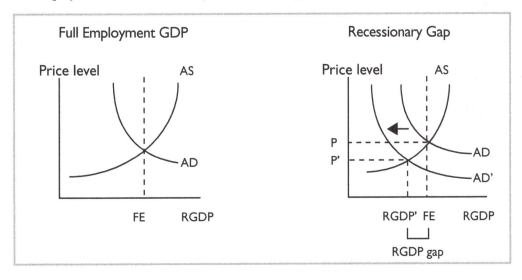

Figure 8.8   **A RECESSIONARY GAP RESULTS FROM A DECREASE IN AGGREGATE DEMAND TO A LEVEL BELOW FULL EMPLOYMENT**

© Slavoljub Pantelic, 2012, under license Shutterstock, Inc.

As aggregate demand falls, real GDP decreases (to RGDP' in Figure 8.8). Since fewer businesses want to buy new capital, workers are laid off, and less capital is produced. As a result, unemployment increases. All things being equal, there will also be downward pressure on prices. While lower output and higher unemployment are generally viewed as negative economic phenomena, deflation helps creditors and consumers buy more with their income, but could hurt producers or debtors.

The recessionary gap is so named because a prolonged decrease in output is referred to as a recession. The RGDP gap refers to the gap between current RGDP and full employment RGDP. In other words, it is the amount of production the economy is forgoing due to cyclical unemployment. Note that no one actually knows the size of a recessionary gap while it is occurring. It is anyone's guess as to what level of RGDP corresponds to full employment. Economic data regarding the present output levels of the economy are neither immediate nor wholly accurate. Recall from Chapter 2, GDP data are calculated for each quarter of the year. The government's final estimate of a quarter's production only comes three months after the completion of the quarter. This estimate still is not perfect for reasons also cited in Chapter 2.

© mostafa fawzy, 2012, under license Shutterstock, Inc.

The Great Depression in the US is said, according to this model, to have been a really large recessionary gap. Consumption[2] and investment[3] dramatically slowed down in the US economy. The Smoot-Hawley Tariff also caused US exports to decline. This fall in consumption, investment, and exports caused a large downward shift in US aggregate demand. As a result, the unemployment rate reached 25%, real GDP fell by 33% between 1929 and 1932, and deflation led to a 33% fall in prices.

Inflationary Gap

What happens when aggregate demand shifts in the opposite direction? First assume once again that the economy starts out operating at full employment. Now suppose the government declares war on another country and dramatically ratchets up military spending. This increase in government spending will cause a shift rightward in the aggregate demand curve. When the aggregate demand

---

[2] Peter Temin argued that an unexplained fall in consumption led to the Great Depression.

[3] John Maynard Keynes argued that an unexplained fall in investment led to the Great Depression.

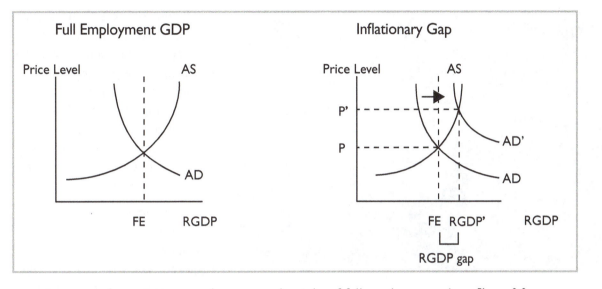

curve intersects the aggregate supply curve to the right of full employment, the economy is said to be experiencing an **inflationary gap**.

As the government demands to buy more tanks, more workers are hired to produce them. Unemployment falls, while real GDP increases. These two economic phenomena are usually considered to be good things. More people have jobs and more output is being made. Still, output that is available to consumers typically falls in times of war. The production of tanks, fighter jets, and ammunition requires the use of scarce resources. As the production of military equipment increases, the production of consumer and investment goods decreases. In WWI, the US converted Ford automobile plants into tank factories. More tanks led to fewer autos.

The inflationary gap derives its name from the fact that this increase in aggregate demand has resulted in an increase in the average price level, i.e. inflation. There is also now a gap between full employment RGDP and current RGDP, as is illustrated in Figure 8.9 as RGDP shifts to RGDP'. As more products than normal are demanded, buyers bid against each other for access to scarce output. As output increases, it does so by utilizing less productive inputs (less fertile land, lower skilled labor, etc.). The use of less productive inputs drives up the production costs to firms, who in turn pass some of these cost increases on to buyers. Those groups that are most hurt by inflation, such as creditors, small businesses, and people on fixed incomes, will not see the inflationary gap as a good thing.

Thus, an inflationary gap is caused by aggregate demand being "too high." It intersects aggregate supply to the right of full employment. Anything that would cause an increase in consumption, investment, government spending, or net exports past full employment would lead to an inflationary gap. The result is low unemployment, an increase in output, and inflation. In a sense, the economy has overheated.

Figure 8.9
AN INFLATIONARY GAP IS CAUSED BY AN INCREASE IN AD BEYOND FULL EMPLOYMENT

© K.L. Kohn, 2012, under license Shutterstock, Inc.

In the 1960's, military spending increased due to the Vietnam conflict. At the same time, the government began implementing President Lyndon Johnson's Great Society programs. This increase in government spending pushed the US economy into an inflationary gap. While unemployment rates fell, inflation rates soared.

As the aggregate demand curve shifts, there is a tradeoff between unemployment and inflation. As aggregate demand increases, unemployment falls, but inflation increases. As aggregate demand decreases, unemployment increases but inflation decreases. Because unemployment and inflation are often observed moving in opposite directions, some people began to believe that they must always do so.[4] The **Phillips Curve** was introduced to economics by William Phillips and it represented an inverse relationship between unemployment and inflation. However, the Phillips Curve proved to be incorrect once the economy was observed suffering from stagflation, or a decrease in aggregate supply.

Stagflation

What happens when aggregate supply decreases? Again assume that the economy is operating at full employment. Suppose that the government declares industry carbon emissions bad for the environment and introduces a tax on all carbon emitted in the production process. This increase in government regulation and taxation will cause a decrease in the aggregate supply curve. When the aggregate supply curve decreases (so that now it intersects the aggregate demand curve to the left of full employment), the economy is said to be experiencing **stagflation**.

As the cost of production increases, firms are willing to sell less output at every price. This reduction in output puts the economy in a contraction and causes workers to be laid off, thereby creating higher unemployment. The increased cost of production gets passed on to consumers via higher prices (inflation).

Stagflation derives its name from the fact that output is stagnant (not growing) while the economy is experiencing inflation. The presence of stagflation during the late 1970's served to disprove the Phillips curve. Unemployment and inflation can indeed rise at the same time if production costs in the economy are increased.

---

[4] Phillips, A. W. (1958). "The Relationship between Unemployment and the Rate of Change of Money wages in the United Kingdom 1861 to 1957". *Economica* 25 (100): 283–299.

The stagflation that occurred in the 1970's developed as OPEC dramatically increased the price of oil. Oil is (and was even more so then) an important energy source for the production and transportation of goods in the economy. As the price of oil increased, the US economy experienced a simultaneous increase in unemployment and inflation. As a presidential candidate, Jimmy Carter's campaign coined a new economic term called the misery index. The **misery index** is the unemployment rate plus the inflation rate. Carter used the misery index to point out how the economy had gotten worse under President Ford. Unfortunately for President Carter, rising oil prices continued during his term to increase the misery index from 12.72 to 19.72. This contributed to his loss to Ronald Reagan in the 1980 presidential election.

Thus, stagflation is caused by aggregate supply shifting to the left such that it intersects aggregate demand to the left of full employment as shown in Figure 8.10. Anything that would cause an increase in the cost of production would result in stagflation. The result is high unemployment, a decrease in output, and inflation. Rising prices accompanied by higher unemployment and lower output is by most accounts the worst possible economic problem for an economy to face.

Figure 8.10
STAGFLATION RESULTS FROM A DECREASE IN AS BELOW FULL EMPLOYMENT

Long Run Economic Growth

So far, the problems caused by aggregate demand shifting away from full employment or aggregate supply shifting leftward have been discussed. What happens when aggregate supply shifts rightward? Actually, increases in aggregate supply are good for the economy. This scenario is illustrated in Figure 8.11.

When the cost of production falls or resources increase, aggregate supply shifts to the right. Firms are able to produce more output at every possible price level. This increase in output is called long run economic growth, and as such, the production possibilities frontier for the economy shifts outward. More

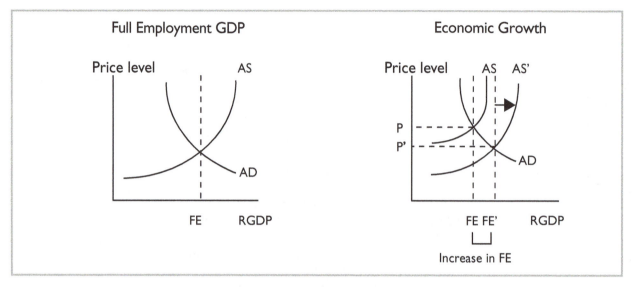

Figure 8.11
ECONOMIC GROWTH IS CAUSED BY AN INCREASE IN AGGREGATE SUPPLY BEYOND FULL EMPLOYMENT

production options become available for the economy, corresponding to a higher average standard of living.

If the decrease in the cost of production arises from increased worker productivity, then as the aggregate supply curve shifts rightward, so too does the full employment level of output. Each worker, if more productive, can make more output per unit of input; therefore, the full employment level of output will be greater and a new "happy place" for the economy will be created. If the increase in the aggregate supply curve is due to an increased number of resources, then the full employment output will again be increased. In this way, the full employment level of output for today's economy is larger than where it was fifty years ago.

The internet revolution of the 1990's dramatically lowered information costs for producers and consumers in the economy. This caused a reduction in the cost of production for many firms. As a result, the US economy experienced a period of low unemployment accompanied by low inflation and fast economic growth. (In absence of Federal Reserve policy, there would have been deflation).

Indeed, few people complain about the absence of inflation, fast economic growth, and low unemployment. This is why the "Holy Grail" of economics revolves around shifting the aggregate supply curve to the right and why the authors of this text devote so many chapters to analyzing how that can happen.

John Maynard Keynes is considered by many to be the father of modern macroeconomics. His analysis of short term fluctuations in the economy served as the discipline's standard for half of a century. It is important, however, to note that his analysis was entirely limited to the short run economy. The **short run economy** is considered to be an economy during a single business cycle. Prior to the 1930's, the study of political economy was primarily interested in analyzing the **long run economy**. The long run economy is considered to be an economy over multiple business cycles. Adam Smith's *Wealth of Nations* was an analysis of the long run economy. He examined why some countries were wealthier than others over time. The next section highlights how the economy works to self-correct from shocks and explores the idea behind supply side economics, while providing examples of both from US economic history.

Say's Law

The predominant strain of economic thought in the eighteenth and nineteenth centuries was known as the **Classical School**. Adam Smith, David Ricardo, Jean-Baptiste Say, Thomas Malthus, and James Mill were some of the major economists associated with this school of thought. Their view of the short and long run economies are best summed up by **Say's Law**. Say's Law states that "products are paid for with products."[5] A restatement of this principle is that production creates the wealth needed for consumption, or supply creates its own demand.

According to Say's Law, there could be some firms whose products are unwanted by consumers, therefore causing a glut of those specific products. This glut, however, was balanced by a shortage of goods that consumers actually desired. As producers whose products are unwanted go out of business, resources are freed up to be used by firms whose products consumers demand.

In this way, swings in unemployment rates are primarily due to increases in structural unemployment as workers are forced to leave industries whose products are not in demand. It takes time for them to be retrained and gain employment in industries whose products are in demand. The classical school believed that this change in production and employment would happen naturally as individuals responded to incentives that they faced. Short term fluctuations in unemployment were temporary, and in the long run, the economy would always return to full employment on its own. In the long run, then, the economy faces a vertical aggregate supply curve at full employment.

Says Law contradicts **under-consumption theory**, popularized by Keynes. Under-consumption theory states that the economy, if left alone, will experience general gluts of output where consumers are unable or unwilling to consume that which has been produced. Cyclical unemployment, he surmised, then became the chief cause of fluctuations in the unemployment rate. People were unemployed because of a lack of aggregate demand. Under-consumption theory is a rejection of Say's Law. It assumes that consumption drives production rather than production being the catalyst of consumption. When it comes to advocating policies to intervene in the short run economy, economists who adhere to under-consumption theory focus on changing aggregate demand. Those who believe in Say's Law focus either on letting the economy self-correct, or on policies designed to increase aggregate supply. Adherents to Say's Law tend to focus on the long run health of an economy. On the other hand, those who advocate

---

[5] Treatise and Coordination of Economic Activity. 1803. 153

Keynesian views of intervention in the economy tend to hold Keynes' view that "In the long run we are all dead."[6] Put another way, long term ramifications of market intervention are not important to **neo-Keynesians**. Their focus is on solving today's problems today regardless of future implications.

The Self-Correcting Economy

Self-Correction in a Recessionary Gap

As previously noted, adherents to Say's Law believe that specific gluts in specific industries will work themselves out over time. As consumers do not buy a firm's output, that output piles up. Firms cannot indefinitely afford to pay their workers or pay for the use of other resources without generating revenue from the sale of their products. As firms go bankrupt, the resources they were using are freed up to be used by firms who are producing products that people want to buy at prices they want to pay.

In this way, bankruptcies and business failures are a way to reallocate resources to the location in which they are most valuable. This process thus increases economic efficiency.

Market self-correction consists of a different dynamic under Keynesian analysis. Since general gluts or general shortages exist in the Keynesian view, markets cannot self-correct simply by moving resources from one industry to the next. From this perspective, a solution must require a change in all industries. How, then, will an economy self-correct from a recessionary gap, an inflationary gap, and stagflation under the Keynesian framework?

Recall that a recessionary gap is caused by aggregate demand being too low. Unemployment is higher than normal; prices and output are lower than they were at full employment. Unemployment can be viewed as a surplus of workers. More people want a job than are currently being hired in the market. Markets clear surpluses by placing products on sale. Any clothing store that has a surplus of jackets will have to put the jackets on sale in order to move their inventory.

The economy works the same way with a surplus of workers; it figuratively places them "on sale." Because there are a number of people unemployed during a recessionary gap, there is greater competition among workers for any given job opening. This competition for jobs by workers enables producers to offer lower wages than normal and still hire skilled workers. In the recessionary gap, **real wages** (which represent the purchasing power of workers' hourly labor) are bid down.

A change in the real wage is the self-correcting mechanism of the economy. As producers are able to pay less for labor, the cost of production falls. This

---

[6] *A Tract on Monetary Reform* (1923).

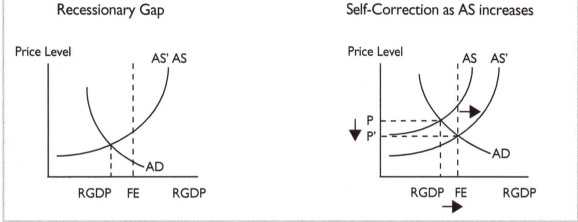

decrease in the cost of production causes aggregate supply to increase. As long as cyclical unemployment exists, there will be downward pressure on real wages, shifting aggregate supply rightward until it again intersects aggregate demand back at full employment. This is illustrated in Figure 8.12

Keynes acknowledged that a decrease in real wages would indeed bring the economy back to full employment. However, he stated that wages are "sticky downwards." People don't like taking pay cuts, and unions which represent workers will fight wage decreases. Therefore, Keynes chief critique of the self-correcting economy during the recessionary gap is that it took too long to work.

Note that for the self-correcting economy to work, people don't necessarily have to take nominal pay cuts, though that does sometimes happen. People just have to have a reduction in their real wages. If an inflation rate of 3% exists, while workers receive a nominal wage increase of 1%, then real wages fall by 2%. A change in nominal wages minus the inflation rate equals the change in real wages. Typically during a recession, people's wages don't tend to keep up with inflation, and they take real wage cuts. Another way to take a real wage cut is to require more worker output for the same salary. This too would lower the cost of production to firms allowing room for aggregate supply to increase and for the economy to self-correct.

Figure 8.12

THE SELF-CORRECTION PROCESS IN A RECESSIONARY GAP

Self-Correction in an Inflationary Gap

The inflationary gap is exactly the opposite of the recessionary gap. Output and prices are higher than normal, but unemployment is lower than normal. In fact, the economy, by cutting into frictional and structural unemployment, is facing a shortage of workers. As an economy approaches its production possibilities frontier, producers can only produce more of their output if other producers produce less. The scarcity of qualified workers becomes more acute than normal.

As producers compete with each other to hire or retain qualified employees, real wages are bid up. As it becomes more expensive to compensate workers, aggregate supply decreases. The upward pressure on real wages will continue shifting the aggregate supply curve leftward until it intersects the aggregate demand curve back at full employment.

Workers don't tend to protest wage increases. Producers cannot profit if they lack the needed workers to produce more output. As a result, unlike the recessionary gap, the economy can self-correct quickly out of the inflationary gap. On the downside, inflation, which is already a problem, gets worse as the economy returns to full employment. Figure 8.13 illustrates the resulting increase in inflation.

Figure 8.13
THE SELF-CORRECTION PROCESS IN AN INFLATIONARY GAP

Self-Correction in Stagflation

The market self-corrects from stagflation in the same way as it does from a recessionary gap. High levels of unemployment continue to put downward pressure on real wages, shifting the aggregate supply curve rightward until it again intersects the aggregate demand curve back at full employment. The problem, just as in the recessionary gap, is that wages may be sticky downwards. Figure 8.14 shows the self-correction process in stagflation.

The Self-Correcting Economy in American History

Throughout the eighteenth, nineteenth, and early twentieth centuries, the American economy self-corrected with relative ease. Large increases in unemployment were accompanied by large reductions in real wages. Unregulated labor markets adjusted quickly to changing market conditions. This occurred even as large numbers of Americans moved from the agricultural industry to the manufacturing and service industries.

Throughout the twentieth century, the labor market took longer to adjust to market conditions. Increased union membership in the first half of the twentieth century created a climate where existing workers obtained more leverage over their wages at the expense of the currently unemployed. Government mandating of minimum wages also prevented market correction in wages for low skilled jobs. If the labor market for unskilled labor will only clear at a wage below the legally allowed minimum, then mandated minimum wages prevent this adjustment and result in higher unemployment levels.

The development of unemployment insurance benefits and government work programs also reduced the pace of labor force adjustment. In the past, the loss of a job necessitated a quick search for a new job, lest a worker be unable to meet the needs of themselves or their dependents. These safety nets reduce the immediate urgency of finding a new job and therefore reduce the downward pressure placed on real wages, slowing their decline and prolonging the return to full employment.

As the percentage of laborers employed by the government has increased, so too has the percentage of employees who have been awarded tenure. University professors, school teachers, and many government workers have labor contracts that do not permit firings without explicit employee malfeasance. While the real wages of tenured employees can, and do, fall during recessions, the market is prevented from reallocating labor between industries.

Homeownership can also impede self-correction in labor markets. A laborer who loses his job may only be able to find a new job in a different city or state than where he currently lives. Increased home ownership rates cause labor to be less mobile. One reason that unemployment stayed so high for so long after the 2007–2008 recession is that homeowners had a difficult time selling their homes and relocating due to the large number of unsold homes on the market.

Figure 8.14
THE SELF-CORRECTION PROCESS IN STAGFLATION

Thus, while the economy will eventually return to full employment on its own, this process is not instantaneous due to sticky wages and institutional constraints. For this reason, many politicians (who will seek reelection in the short term rather than the long term) advocate for government intervention in order to stabilize macroeconomic situations. While such interventions have substantial costs of their own, they may appear to help the situation in the short run. It is the topic of taxing and spending interventions by the government that we turn to in our next chapter on fiscal policy.

Key Terms

Aggregate demand

Aggregate supply

Average price level

Classical School of
Economic Thought

Excess capacity

Foreign trade effect

Inflationary gap

Injections

Interest rate effect

Law of demand

Leakage

Long run economy

Macroeconomic equilibrium

Misery index

Neo-Keynesians

Peace dividend

Phillips Curve

Real wages

Recessionary gap

Say's Law

Short run economy

Stagflation

Under-consumption theory

Wealth effect

Questions for Review

1. What causes consumption levels to change?

2. What causes investment levels to change?

3. What causes government spending levels to change?

4. What causes exports to change?

5. a. What government policies can spur current consumption?

   b. What government policies can spur current investment?

   c. What government policies can spur current government spending?

   d. What government policies can spur current exports?

   e. What causes the cost of production to change?

6. Identify which component(s) of GDP change(s) as a result of each of
   these scenarios:

   a. capital gains taxes are increased

   b. the DOW rises

   c. mortgage rates fall

   d. new tariffs are implemented

7. What causes a recessionary gap? An inflationary gap? Stagflation? What
   causes long run economic growth?

8. What problems arise from a recessionary gap? Inflationary gap?
   Stagflation?

9. Below is a list of economic shocks. List whether they cause a recessionary gap, an inflationary gap, stagflation, or long run economic growth. Also graph the impact of these shocks on aggregate demand or supply and note what happens to prices, unemployment, and real GDP as a result of each shock:

   a. Consumers decide to go on a spending binge because they want to live for today.

   b. Foreigners decide to boycott US made goods due to America's invasion of foreign countries.

   c. A drought decimates US agricultural output for the year.

   d. New solar power technology dramatically lowers energy costs.

10. What factors cause aggregate demand to increase? Decrease? What factors shift aggregate supply?

11. Examine each of the following events. What impact will they have on aggregate demand, aggregate supply, the average price level, RGDP, and unemployment? Graph the shift in AD or AS and label the changes that occur as a result.

   a. The United States experiences an increase in worker productivity.

   b. Interest rates increase making it more expensive to borrow money.

   c. The European Union bans the importation of US made products.

   d. The federal government raises the minimum wage to $100 an hour.

   e. The federal government lowers the corporate income tax rate.

   f. The federal government spends $100 billion on building new bridges in the United States.

   g. The federal government imposes a carbon tax on all carbon emissions from US plants.

   h. Consumers become optimistic that the economy will begin to grow quickly in the near future.

12. What is Say's Law? What does it imply? Why is the rejection of Say's Law the starting point for Keynes's advocacy of fiscal policy?

13. How does the economy self-correct out of a recessionary gap? Out of an inflationary gap? Out of stagflation? Graph each of these scenarios.

14. What was Keynes's chief gripe with the self-correcting mechanism coming out of the Great Depression?

Chapter 9

Keynesian Fiscal Policy and Supply Side Economics

fiscal

fiscal *adj* **1** of government f
taxes. ◆ *n* **2** short for PROCURATOR

fish ◆ *n*. *pl* fish, fishes **1** cold

Keynesian Fiscal Policy

Keynesian fiscal policy was born out of the Great Depression. Keynes theorized that government intervention in the economy could bring the economy back to full employment faster than the economy could self-correct. By changing the rates of taxing and government spending, the government could manipulate aggregate demand until it intersected aggregate supply back at full employment.

The practice of Keynesian fiscal policy is meant to smooth business cycles. **Expansionary fiscal policy (fiscal stimulus)** is an increase in government spending or a reduction in taxes that is meant to increase aggregate demand.

Expansionary policy is typically used in response to a recessionary gap or in the case of stagflation in order to lower unemployment. When the economy overheats, as it does in an inflationary gap, the federal government may choose to increase taxes or reduce government spending. **Contractionary fiscal policy** is an increase in taxes or a reduction in government spending that is meant to lower aggregate demand. This is typically done in response to an inflationary gap or in order to decrease inflation in stagflation. This chapter examines the ways in which expansionary or contractionary fiscal policy work to return the economy back to full employment. This chapter also outlines supply side economics.

Bridge to nowhere

Expansionary Fiscal Policy

Recall that in Keynes' model, a recessionary gap is caused by aggregate demand being too low. According to Keynes, high levels of unemployment and low levels of output are the result of inadequate demand for goods and services in the economy. The Keynesian policy prescription to a recessionary gap is to engage in fiscal stimulus in the form of increased government spending and/or a reduction in taxation.

For example, if the government increases spending by building roads or bridges, then greater employment in construction results along with greater levels of government spending. This increase in government directed economic activity translates into higher levels of real GDP. Keynes' belief in fiscal stimulus spending was so great that he stated that the object of the increase in government spending was irrelevant. He noted that if the government hired ditch diggers to dig a ditch and then hired more workers to fill in the ditches, the economy would still be stimulated.

On paper, real GDP would be increased by the amount of money the government spent on ditch diggers and ditch fillers. According to the expenditure approach, GDP is a function of consumption, investment, government spending, and net exports. Any increase in government spending, regardless of where it was spent, would therefore increase real GDP. Of course, a ditch dug and then refilled leaves the world with no actual new wealth. How, then, is the economy made better off from stimulus spending?

Assume that the ditch digger earns $100 in income in return for his labor. The initial increase in government spending is $100. The ditch digger now has an extra $100 of income in his pocket. An increase in income to a consumer could go one of three places: to pay taxes, to increase savings, or to increase consumption.

The **marginal propensity to consume (MPC)** is the percentage of new income that a consumer spends. The MPC is found by dividing a consumer's change in consumption by their change in income. If the average American consumer spends 80% of all new income they receive, then the MPC for the US economy is said to be .8. If the ditch digger is representative of the average American, then an extra $100 of income will translate into an additional $80 worth of consumption. This increase in consumption also serves to increase aggregate demand. If the ditch digger spends his $80 at the bakery, then the baker now has an extra $80 of income. If the baker then spends 80% of his new income at the butcher shop, then his $64 of new consumption will also cause aggregate demand to increase. Table 9.1 describes the changes in spending that follow from the initial increase in spending of $100 (assuming an MPC of .8).

TABLE 9.1	THE RESULT TO THE ECONOMY OF AN INCREASE OF $100 IN GOVERNMENT SPENDING
New spending	**Resulting cumulative change in spending**
$100	$100
$80	$180 ($100 plus resulting $80)
$64	$244 ($180 plus resulting $64)
.	.
.	. total change in spending that results
.	.
0	$500

The total amount that real GDP is expected to increase as a result of increased government spending in the Keynesian model is determined by taking the initial increase in government spending and multiplying it by the **spending multiplier**.

$$\text{THE SPENDING MULTIPLIER} = \frac{1}{(1-MPC)}$$

If the MPC in the economy is .8 then the spending multiplier is 5. The spending multiplier is created by an infinite series. As each consumer increases spending by a percentage of a positive number, spending keeps increasing at smaller and smaller amounts for infinity.

In order to determine the appropriate amount of government stimulus needed to solve a recessionary gap, an economic advisor would need the following information: the full employment level of real GDP, the current level

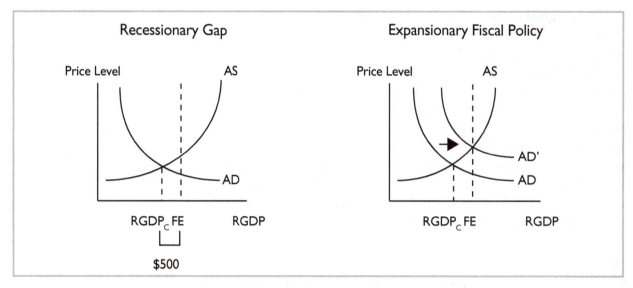

Figure 9.1
EXPANSIONARY FISCAL POLICY USED IN A RECESSIONARY GAP

of real GDP, and the marginal propensity to consume for an economy. The full employment level of real GDP requires a theoretical guess. The second piece of information, the current level of real GDP, is impossible to know given the lag in collecting economic data, but it can be approximated by looking at the most recent GDP data. The final piece of information, the marginal propensity to consume, is also impossible to know. By collecting historical spending data, economists can create an estimate of past MPC levels in the US economy. However, because consumers make choices for themselves, there is no way to know what their MPC is until after they have already spent their money. Consumer confidence and consumer uncertainty can play key roles in changing people's MPC over time. The MPC may also depend upon whose income is increased. Some economists theorize that poor people's MPC is higher than wealthier people's MPC, and therefore an increase in the income of poorer people will create a larger spending multiplier than would be created by the same increase in the income of wealthier people.

In the United States, Congress and the President control fiscal policy. If one believes as Keynes did that politicians are able to know where the economy is, where it should be, and what the spending multiplier is, then the appropriate size of fiscal stimulus spending is relatively easy to determine.

In Figure 9.1, the economy is facing a $500 GDP gap. This is the distance between the current level of real GDP and full employment real GDP. If the MPC in the economy is .8, then the appropriate amount of stimulus spending to bring the economy back to full employment is $100 = (500/5).

CHANGE IN REAL GDP = INITIAL CHANGE IN GOVERNMENT SPENDING × SPENDING MULTIPLIER

$500 = CHANGE IN G × 5

So, government spending would need to change by $100 to increase real GDP by $500, given a spending multiplier of 5. This formula only holds if the aggregate supply curve is horizontal (as Keynes saw it during recessionary gaps).

If an increase in aggregate demand occurs on the flat portion of the aggregate supply curve, then the increase in aggregate demand equals the increase in real GDP. If, however, the increase in aggregate demand occurs on the upward sloping portion of the aggregate supply curve, then the resulting higher prices faced by consumers will offset some of the potential gains in real GDP. Consumers will spend more money, but some of their increased spending will be to accommodate higher prices of existing products. When the aggregate supply curve is vertical, any increase in aggregate demand results only in higher prices with no change occurring in real GDP.

Figure 9.2   THE SAME SIZED INCREASE IN AGGREGATE DEMAND UNDER THREE SCENARIOS

In 2009, Congress and President Obama passed a $787 billion stimulus bill. That's a very specific number. Why not $750 or $800 billion? To be sure, some economists argued for less stimulus spending while others argued for more. The reason for the public disagreement between economists is that each economist was forced to make their own assumptions about where the economy was, where it was supposed to be, and how large the spending multiplier would be. Furthermore, some economists disagreed with the entire Keynesian approach and preferred to let the economy self-correct.

Work by Robert Barro found that the spending multiplier for this stimulus program was .8. For every dollar that was spent by the government, GDP only increased by eighty cents.[1] Because fiscal policy deals with so many unknowns, users of fiscal policy run the risks of not doing enough or doing too much fiscal policy and as a result either not solving the existing problem or creating new ones.

Instead of increasing government spending to stimulate an economy, the government could reduce the tax burden or increase transfer payments. As consumers are allowed to keep a larger percentage of their income, or are given more income, they have more money with which to consume and save. According to Keynes, however, a dollar reduction in taxes or increase in transfer payments does less than a dollar increase in government spending to increase GDP.

---

[1] "Stimulus Spending Doesn't Work" *The Wall Street Journal* September 30, 2009.

Assume that a baker receives a $100 tax cut or transfer payment. If his MPC is .8, he will consume $80 worth of new goods and services so GDP will increase by $80. Much like the spending multiplier, a change in taxation is magnified by the **tax multiplier**.

$$\text{THE TAX MULTIPLIER} = 1 - \frac{1}{(1-MPC)}$$

If the spending multiplier is 5, then the tax multiplier is one less and negative, or -4. The tax multiplier is negative because an increase in taxes slows down the economy, while a reduction in taxes speeds it up. A decrease in taxes increases spending, and vice versa. The difference in magnitude is due to the absence of the first round of government spending. If the government buys $100 worth of cakes, then cakes have been produced. If the government merely gives the baker $100 in tax cuts, no extra cake is made. The rounds of spending for a $100 tax cut with an MPC of .8 are given below.

TABLE 9.2	THE EFFECT OF A $100 TAX CUT OR TRANSFER PAYMENT ON THE ECONOMY	
New spending		**Total change in spending**
$80		$80
$64		$144
. ↓		. ↓ total change in spending that results
$0		$400

CHANGE IN RGDP = INITIAL CHANGE IN TAXES × TAX MULTIPLIER

THE CHANGE IN RGDP = 100 × (-4).

So, with an MPC of .8, RGDP changes by $400 as a result of a $100 tax cut, assuming the economy is operating on the horizontal portion of aggregate supply.

Because Keynes felt that dollar per dollar changes in government spending were more powerful than changes in taxes, most Keynesians prefer to increase government spending rather than cut taxes. According to empirical work done by many prominent economists, however, the opposite appears to be true.[2] The tax multiplier has been empirically found to be larger than the spending multiplier. This means that economists who are concerned with the size of the

[2] Greg Mankiw. "Spending and Tax Multipliers" Greg Mankiw's Blog. December 11, 2008. http://gregmankiw.blogspot.com/2008/12/spending-and-tax-multipliers.html

national debt should prefer tax cuts to increases in government spending during recessionary gaps in order to speed up the economy the most for the least future cost.

In addition to the empirical questions of whether tax cuts or increases in government spending stimulate the economy better, political and ethical considerations abound revolving around changes in taxation and government spending. Politicians who represent constituents with little or no tax burden but who receive government support payments may be more in favor of higher levels of government spending or transfer payments than they are lowering their non-constituent's taxes. Politicians who represent constituents with high tax burdens but who receive few government support payments may be more inclined to support tax breaks.

Contractionary Fiscal Policy

When the economy is overheating and inflation is on the rise, contractionary fiscal policy serves as the Keynesian approach. A decrease in government spending would cause aggregate demand to fall, as would an increase in taxes that leave consumers with less money to spend. The idea, as Figure 9.3 illustrates, is to actively slow down the economy by reducing aggregate demand until it intersects aggregate supply back at full employment.

Contractionary fiscal policy faces many of the same hurdles as expansionary fiscal policy.

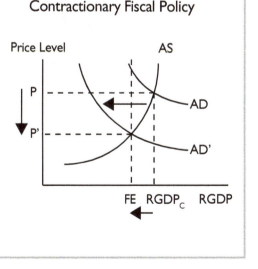

Figure 9.3
CONTRACTIONARY FISCAL POLICY

In order for its use to be successful, policy makers must know what the current level of real GDP is, what the desired level of real GDP is, and what the marginal propensity to consume will be from a potential tax or spending change. Assuming that these are all known (most likely an unrealistic assumption), then determining the amount of needed fiscal policy for an inflationary gap is similar to determining it for a recessionary gap. Once the size of the inflationary gap is determined, the spending, transfer payment, or tax multiplier can be applied to determine the optimal amount of fiscal contraction.

There is, however, an additional hurdle faced by the use of contractionary fiscal policy. Its use is usually politically unpopular. Most voters do not appreciate having their taxes increased. Nor do they like it when government programs or transfer payments that they themselves benefit from are reduced. The ironic component of this is that as the previous chapter illustrates, allowing the economy to self correct in this situation causes inflation to worsen. This is the situation in which intervention is arguably most needed and yet least likely to occur politically.

Just as empirical research has been done on fiscal stimulus packages, work has also been done analyzing **austerity** (contractionary) **packages**.[3] Research indicates that the most economically successful packages are the ones where the reduction in government spending is roughly three times the size of the tax increases. Research indicates that cutting taxes is more efficient than increasing government spending at stimulating an economy, and cutting government spending rather than raising taxes is better for long run job creation. The theme from the research is that the private sector does a better job than the public sector at using resources to create wealth over time. Taxes that distort economic incentives away from private sector wealth creation slow down the long run economic growth of an economy.

Fiscal Policy During Stagflation

While the economy is operating below full employment during stagflation, it is not a given that politicians following the Keynesian approach would necessarily advocate for an increase in government spending or a reduction in taxes. Doing so, like in a recessionary gap, would work to increase aggregate demand until it intersects aggregate supply back at full employment. This would increase RGDP, but would also lead to much higher inflation since it would occur on the steeper portion of the aggregate supply curve.

If politicians were more concerned with fighting inflation than fighting unemployment, then the correct Keynesian response to stagflation would be higher taxes or lower government spending. This would cause the aggregate demand curve to shift leftward. The result would be lower inflation but at the cost of significantly higher levels of unemployment.

---

[3] "Canada's Budget Triumph" David R. Henderson. Working Paper No 10–53, August 2010. Mercatus Center. http://mercatus.org/sites/default/files/publication/Canada%27s%20Budget%20Triumph.WP_.pdf

The use of Keynesian fiscal policy during periods of stagflation places policy makers between a rock and a hard place. Since a shift in aggregate demand creates a tradeoff between unemployment and inflation, they can only solve one problem by making the other problem much worse. It was a situation of stagflation in the 1980's that prompted President Ronald Reagan to propose policies that were directed at shifting aggregate demand rather than aggregate supply. We now turn to an examination of automatic stabilizers and supply side policies.

Automatic Stabilizers

Some taxing and spending policies put in place in the past act as automatic stabilizers for the economy. An **automatic stabilizer** is something that helps the economy return to full employment without explicit government action. Examples include unemployment insurance, welfare, and the personal income tax.

During a recession, unemployment is higher than normal. Without changing government policies, more people qualify for unemployment insurance and welfare, while income tax collections fall due to lower income levels. This automatic increase in transfer payments and decrease in taxes works to help keep aggregate demand from falling further. During an inflationary gap, fewer people collect unemployment insurance and welfare due to the fact that more people have jobs. They also pay more in income taxes. These actions work to keep aggregate demand from increasing further.

Typically, the unemployed in the US can qualify for up to six months of unemployment insurance benefits. During recessions, however, there is increased political pressure to extend those transfer payments. President George H.W. Bush refused to extend unemployment benefits during the 1991 recession and failed to get re-elected. President George W. Bush extended unemployment benefits to a year during the 2001 recession. President Barack Obama increased unemployment insurance to almost two years during the 2009 recession. While increasing unemployment insurance is meant to stimulate aggregate demand, it also reduces aggregate supply as workers take longer to re-enter the workforce. Thus, like everything else, the benefits must be weighed against the costs when determining whether or not to extend unemployment benefits.

Supply Side Economics

The US economy experienced severe stagflation in the late 1970's and early 1980's. This decrease in aggregate supply was caused by a dramatic increase in the price of oil. President Reagan's economic team, led by Arthur Laffer, attempted to develop a set of economic policies to shift the aggregate supply curve rightward. While the economy's self-correcting mechanism would eventually shift aggregate supply rightward, these policies attempted to not only bring the economy back to full employment, but also increase long term economic growth. This set of policies became known as **supply side economics** for its attempt to increase aggregate supply.

Supply side economics refers to any attempt by policy makers to increase the productive capacity of the economy. The supply side economic policies implemented by the Reagan administration have been coined **Reaganomics**. The main features of Reaganomics included deregulation and reductions in marginal income tax rates, savings tax rates, corporate income tax rates, and capital gains tax rates.

Deregulation

A reduction in government regulations reduces the cost of production. Fewer government regulations free up firms' resources to be used for production rather than to ensure compliance with government regulations. As the cost of burdensome government regulations falls, aggregate supply increases.

Lower Taxes on Income

Lower income tax rates should also work to increase aggregate supply. When Reagan took office, the top marginal federal income tax bracket in the US was 70%. The top rate had actually been even higher under Presidents Roosevelt, Truman, and Eisenhower. President Kennedy proposed cutting the top income tax bracket from 91% to 70%. His famous justification for doing so was that "a rising tide lifts all boats." This meant that if entrepreneurs were discouraged from working when nearly all of their income was confiscated, perhaps letting them keep more of their income would incentivize them to work harder, producing wealth that is enjoyed by everyone. By increasing labor supply, lower marginal tax rates should work to shift the aggregate supply curve rightward.

Art Laffer supposed that even 70% marginal tax rates worked as a disincentive for people to work. He created the **Laffer curve** to illustrate the relationship between marginal tax rates and tax revenue. At a 0% tax rate, the government would not generate any tax revenue. As tax rates increase, so, too, does tax revenue—to a point. While the higher tax rates mean a larger percentage of earned income becomes revenue for the federal government, it also means a larger disincentive for work. So, at low tax rates, tax revenues increase with the rate. After that, increases in marginal tax rates actually resulted in lower tax revenue as the reduced incentive to work overtakes the higher revenue stream. At a 100% tax rate people would not voluntarily work and report their income, because it would be confiscated in its entirety. Figure 9.4 illustrates the Laffer Curve.

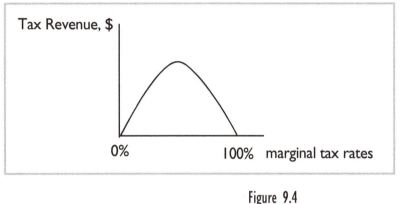

Figure 9.4
THE LAFFER CURVE

High marginal tax rates encourage people to hide income from the government or not earn income in the first place. While the shape of the Laffer Curve is not controversial amongst economists, there is much disagreement about where the revenue maximizing tax rate is. People who describe themselves as supply side economists typically assign a lower estimate of the revenue maximizing tax rate than do economists who do not consider themselves to be supply side economists. A survey of economists by the *Washington Post* places the range between 20% and 70%.[4] Under President Reagan, the top rate was reduced from 70% to 28%. In reality, the short term revenue maximizing tax rate is higher than the long term revenue maximizing tax rate, as it take time for people to respond to economic incentives.

If tax rates are reduced and the marginal tax rate is above the revenue maximizing point, then a reduction in tax rates will generate increased tax revenue. This idea was lampooned by candidate George H.W. Bush during the 1980 Republican primary as "voodoo economics." Later, he served as President Reagan's vice president. Still, when he became president, George H.W. Bush increased many of the same tax rates that President Reagan had lowered.

Nobel Prize winning economist Edward Prescott has shown that changes in marginal tax rates have indeed led to a divergence in the number of hours worked by the average American relative to the average European in the last half of a century.[5] He finds that in the early 1970's, the average German and Frenchman worked five percent more hours per year than the average American. At the same time, the average British worker worked ten percent more hours and the average Japanese worker worked twenty-seven percent more than the average American worker. Then, marginal tax rates fell in the US as they rose in Europe. By the mid 1990's, the average American worked 26% more hours than the average German or Frenchman. They worked 23% more hours than the average Japanese worker and 33% more than the average Britain.

---

[4] "Where does the Laffer curve bend?" Dylan Matthews August 9, 2010.
http://voices.washingtonpost.com/ezra-klein/2010/08/where_does_the_laffer_curve_be.html

[5] "Why Do Americans Work So Much More Than Europeans?" *Federal Reserve Bank of Minneapolis Quarterly Review* Vol. 28, No. 1. July 2004, 2–13.
http://www.minneapolisfed.org/research/QR/QR2811.pdf

Lowering Taxes on Savings

Lowering taxes on savings also works to increase aggregate supply. A reduction in taxes on savings increases the rate of return on savings. In theory, this makes savings more lucrative and should cause consumers to spend less and save more. This increase in savings makes it easier for firms to invest in new capital. By increasing the amount of capital in the economy, aggregate supply increases.

Lower Capital Gains Taxes

Likewise, a reduction in the capital gains tax increases the profitability of individuals saving money by placing it in appreciating assets, like shares of stock. Since saving money in government bonds generates tax free income, any reduction in the capital gains tax increases the relative profitability of providing capital to private sector production over government debt. Lowering the capital gains tax also frees up investment funds for firms owning appreciating capital. The long run capital gains tax rate fell from 39.875% in the mid 1970's to 20% in the early 1980's.

Lowering Corporate Income Tax Rates

An additional supply side policy is the lowering of corporate income tax rates. When President Reagan took office the top corporate income tax rate in the economy was 46%. When he left office it was 34%. As corporation's tax rates were lowered, the rate of return on corporations' capital and labor increased. Firms were able to hold onto more of their own profit which they could reinvest in new capital or use to hire new workers. An increase in capital and labor increases the productive capacity of the economy.

Issues With Supply Side Economics

While Reaganomics had been billed as a set of policies to solve stagflation by shifting aggregate supply, its effect on the economy was not as clear cut. To the extent that reductions in the capital gains and corporate income taxes increased investment in the economy, investment initially increased aggregate demand more than aggregate supply. Capital, only once it has been built, increases the productive capacity of the economy. Therefore, the principle benefit of Reaganomics was that it helped the economy experience faster growth in the decade following its implementation rather than in the months immediately thereafter.

Likewise, a reduction in the marginal income tax rate took time to impact the economy. Workers do not shift occupations or career fields instantaneously in response to new tax incentives. Worker training and education take time. Even following deregulation, firms require time to adjust before changing their business practices.

Reductions in taxes on savings did not yield the desired increase in the US savings rate. In fact, the US savings rate fell. As Americans saw their existing retirement savings grow more quickly, they started placing less money in their retirement plans.

One often placed criticism against Reaganomics is the fact that the national debt tripled during President Reagan's term. Some mistakenly suggest that so many tax reductions left government coffers empty. In reality, tax revenues increased from $517 billion in 1980 to $909.3 billion in 1988, even with large reductions in multiple tax rates. The increase in the national debt in the 1980's can largely be attributed to the massive increase in government spending during that decade. While tax revenues grew, government spending grew much faster. Government spending rose from $591 billion in 1980 to $1,065 billion in 1988.

Another criticism of Reaganomics is that it increased income inequality. The term "trickle- down economics" is a pejorative term that implies that Reaganomics was designed to reward the wealthy with the hope that an increase in their wellbeing would trickle down to other members of the economy. The idea that the purchase of a yacht by a wealthy businessman would generate jobs for middle class yacht builders is no different than that of the Keynesian spending multiplier. Economic activity is generated beyond those specifically targeted by changes in taxes or government spending.

If the tax code is designed to allow productive people to keep more of the wealth that they create, then more wealth does get created, but income inequality also increases. Assume that there are two workers in an economy. Jack makes $10,000 a year while Jill makes $100,000. There is $90,000 worth of income inequality. Now suppose that a growing economy increases each of their incomes by 10%. Jack now makes $11,000 to Jill's $110,000. There is now $99,000 worth of income inequality. Jack and Jill are both wealthier, but income inequality has increased.

During the 1980's the rich got richer faster than the poor, so income inequality increased, but the poor did get richer. **Absolute poverty** exists if people are unable to pay for the necessities of life. Absolute poverty fell in the 1980's. **Relative poverty** exists if some people make more money than others. The phrase "the rich got richer while the poor got poorer" is only true in the 1980's if relative, rather than absolute, poverty serves as the method of comparison.

President Bill Clinton was one of many politicians who campaigned against "trickle-down" economics. The irony is that his administration effectively implemented some supply side polices of its own without using the term. President Clinton's supply side policies included creating and expanding an investment tax credit and a research and development tax credit for firms along with deficit reduction that enabled more savings to flow to private investment.

Conclusion

Thus, Keynesian fiscal policy can be used when politicians desire to smooth out business cycles. However, figuring out how much policy to use (or even the correct policy to use) is not straightforward. Further, different political views about the appropriate levels of spending and taxing (and the appropriate levels to tax different sectors of the income earners) further clouds the use of discretionary policy. And, since fiscal policies used in a recessionary gap typically lead to higher levels of national debt, there are often long-term costs to short term solutions. The next chapter looks in depth at types of and trends in government spending and taxes before turning to an examination of the national debt in Chapter 11.

Key Terms

Absolute poverty

Austerity package

Automatic stabilizers

Contractionary fiscal policy

Expansionary fiscal policy

Fiscal stimulus

Laffer Curve

Marginal propensity to consume

Reaganomics

Relative poverty

Spending multiplier

Supply side economics

Tax multiplier

Questions for Review

1. a. What are fiscal policy options for a recessionary gap?

   b. According to Keynes, what is the appropriate fiscal policy to employ during an inflationary gap? Why?

   c. Why is the use of fiscal policy complicated if the economy is experiencing stagflation?

2. List two examples of automatic stabilizers and how they help keep aggregate demand near full employment.

3. If the federal government hires 10 thousand workers to count blades of grass on Capitol Hill, what would happen to GDP? Has wealth been created? Why or why not?

4. Which political party tends to favor lower levels of federal taxation? Higher levels of government spending? Why do you think that is the case?

5. Suppose the economy is experiencing a GDP shortfall of $10 trillion due to a recessionary gap and the MPC is suspected to be 0.9. What would be the desired amount of a tax change if this type of fiscal policy is used? What would be the desired amount of a government spending change if this type of fiscal policy is used? Demonstrate this graphically.

6. Suppose that the economy is experiencing a GDP excess of $8 billion and the MPC is suspected to be 0.75. What would be the desired amount of a tax change if this type of fiscal policy is used? What would be the desired amount of a government spending change if this type of fiscal policy is used? Demonstrate this graphically.

7. Suppose that the MPC is suspected to be 0.8 and simultaneously the federal government lowers taxes by $1 million and lowers government spending by $1 million. What is the overall impact on the macroequilibrium if the economy started out at full employment? Demonstrate this graphically.

8. Draw the Laffer Curve. What does the Laffer Curve imply?

Chapter 10

Government Spending and Taxing

© W. Scott McGill/Shutterstock.com

Government Spending

In order to understand how the government might increase or decrease spending over time, it is important to learn the process determining how the government spends money. The US government's budget year goes from October 1ˢᵗ until September 30ᵗʰ. This spending can be divided into two main categories: discretionary and mandatory spending. This section examines the differences between discretionary and mandatory spending, trends in each, and the intricacies of the Social Security and Medicare budgetary shortfalls facing the United States.

Discretionary spending is money that is authorized to be spent by Congress with the passage of an appropriations act. Fiscal policy utilizes discretionary spending changes to influence the economy. Congress is required to pass appropriations bills each year to fund discretionary spending. When they fail to do so, they must either pass continuing resolutions to temporarily fund government operations or engage in a **government shutdown**. A government shutdown is where the government ceases to spend money due to a lack of legal authority to do so.

Mandatory spending is money that is required to be spent according to current law. When Congress and the President create **entitlements**, they set up rules regarding who qualifies for federal money rather than stating how much money those programs will have. An entitlement is a legal guarantee to benefits. Rather than vote each year on how much money to spend on Social Security, a formula determines Social Security spending. In this way, mandatory spending is often referred to as being programmatic or automatic spending. Congress and the President can at any point pass new laws to change how the entitlement spending is handed out, but are under no legal obligation to do so.

Table 10.1 lists government spending as a percentage of GDP during selected years. In the last forty years, there have only been two presidents who have overseen a decrease in the size of the federal government as a percentage of the economy: President Reagan and President Clinton.[1] President Clinton famously remarked in his 1996 State of the Union Address, "The era of big government is over." However, by 2009 the relative size of government spending was at its largest post WWII amount at 24.4% of GDP. Even as the government spent a smaller percentage of US GDP in 2010, the level was still higher than at any year since 1983. These federal outlays include government spending and transfer payments.

TABLE 10.1	FEDERAL OUTLAYS AS A % OF GDP[2]		
1972	19.6	2000	18.4
1980	21.7	2008	20.9
1988	21.3	2010	23.8
1992	22.1	2018	20.3

---

[1] Source: Congressional Budget Office.

[2] Richard Nixon began his second term in 1972. Jimmy Carter began his term in 1976. Ronald Reagan began his two terms in 1980. George H.W. Bush began his term in 1988. Bill Clinton began his two terms in 1992. George W. Bush began his two terms in 2000. Barack Obama began his two terms in 2008. Donald Trump began his presidency in 2016.

Mandatory Spending

In 2018, mandatory spending made up 68% of federal government outlays. The five largest programs that fall under mandatory spending include Social Security, Medicare, Welfare, Medicaid, and pensions. **Social Security** is a federally managed retirement system for US workers. **Medicare** covers health care expenditures for the elderly. **Welfare** (including Temporary Aid to Needy Families and food stamps, among other programs) provides assistance to those in poverty. **Medicaid** covers health care expenditures for low income people. The pension's portion of entitlement spending refers to pension payments made to former federal government employees.

The elderly receive a larger portion of entitlement spending than the poor. Even wealthy retirees can collect Social Security and Medicare benefits. In this way, entitlement spending is more a reflection of organized political lobbying than of physical need. The elderly also receive much more entitlement spending than do young people, perhaps because the elderly can vote while those under age 18 are not allowed to do so. Table 10.2 illustrates the distribution of entitlement spending.

TABLE 10.2	2018 UNITED STATES ENTITLEMENT SPENDING IN BILLIONS OF DOLLARS[3]
Social Security	$982
Medicare	$704
Medicaid	$389
Welfare	$285
Pensions	$163
Other	$153
Veterans	$101

Source: Congressional Budget Office

The nature of the federal government has changed greatly over the last half century. Entitlement spending has grown from being 28% of federal outlays in 1965 to accounting for 68% of federal outlays in 2018. The primary function of the federal government (as defined by its spending) has become income redistribution to the elderly and the poor. In 2018, the federal government spent more on Social Security than on national defense, even with troops in Iraq and Afghanistan. As life expectancy in the US has increased, entitlement programs initially intended to help people at the very end of their lives are now being used by the average elderly person for over a decade.

---

[3] Ibid.

The 2003 extension of Medicare to cover prescription drugs is an example of entitlement reform that has resulted in more spending. As entitlement spending increases to a larger percentage of the economy, this leads to more government control of the economy unless there is a comparable sized decrease in discretionary spending. The Welfare Reform Act of 1996 dramatically reduced welfare entitlement eligibility. This helped to account for the large decrease in mandatory spending as a percentage of GDP under President Clinton. Table 10.3 illustrates the historical trend in mandatory spending.

TABLE 10.3	US MANDATORY SPENDING AS A PERCENTAGE OF GDP[4]		
1976	9.5%	2000	9.4%
1980	9.4%	2008	10.8%
1988	8.7%	2010	12.9%
1992	10.1%	2018	13.1%

In 2010, mandatory spending almost equaled tax revenues. That is, even if discretionary spending were reduced to zero, the federal government would almost run a budget deficit based on mandatory spending alone. As the percentage of its spending devoted to entitlements increases, the federal government reduces its ability to engage in Keynesian fiscal policy.

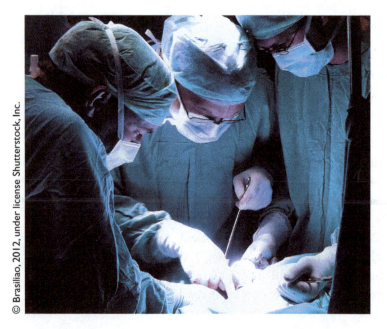

Social Security and Medicare

What makes entitlement spending so large? Social Security and Medicare are the two largest entitlement programs in the US. Both of these programs are aimed at helping the elderly. The Social Security Act that created the program was signed into law by President Franklin Delano Roosevelt in 1935. Social security taxes were collected for the first time in 1937 with benefits starting in 1940. Since its inception as a worker retirement system, Social Security benefits have been expanded to include survivors' benefits to a deceased worker's spouse and children (1939), disability benefits

---

[4] Ibid.

(1956), and an automatic cost of living increase (1972). President Lyndon B. Johnson signed Medicare into law in 1965.

At its beginning, the Social Security retirement age was set at age 65, which also happened to be the average life expectancy in the US at the time. In this way, Social Security was originally designed to help those who "unexpectedly" lived longer than average and therefore hadn't saved enough to fund their own consumption. The retirement age is now 67 years, but life expectancy is over 78 years in the US. This means that the average American can expect to receive over a decade of Social Security payments and Medicare benefits.

An increase in life expectancy is generally viewed as a good thing. However, the increased number of entitlement beneficiaries has placed a strain on the fiscal sustainability of both Social Security and Medicare. In 1945, there were 42 workers per retiree. Today there are less than three workers per retiree. What accounts for this shift? As young people have stayed in school longer to achieve higher levels of education, they have delayed their entrance to the labor force. As educated workers have been able to quickly earn wealth, they have also been able to retire at younger ages. Finally, the increase in life expectancy, combined with the demographic bubble known as the baby boom, has contributed to a change in the ratio. A large number of boomers went from being workers to retirees.

When the federal government created Social Security in the 1930's, they had the choice of how to design the retirement system. Their choices included a fully funded pension plan, a partially funded pension plan, or a pay as you go pension plan. A fully funded pension plan would have required workers to fund their own retirement. In a fully funded pension, enough money is put away during workers earning years to actuarially cover their promised benefits. Private employers who offer defined benefit pensions are legally required to fully fund their plan. Social Security, though a defined benefit pension, is not fully funded.

A pay as you go pension plan (pyramid scheme) has current workers pay retirement benefits to current retirees. Such a plan works well if each generation is substantially larger than the previous one so that the number of workers per retiree doesn't decrease rapidly. Social Security began as a pay as you go pension, but policy makers realized that the baby boom generation would place undue strain on the system if, as workers, they were only required to fund current retiree's benefits. As a result, by 2010, the **Social Security Trust Fund** contained $2.6 trillion in assets. These assets reflect that baby boomers partially funded their own retirement.

The assets in the Social Security Trust Fund are US government bonds. That is, as the Social Security system ran budget surpluses, the federal government took all of that money and replaced it with IOU's. Therefore the trust fund merely contains a promise that the government will pay future benefits out of future tax revenues. In this way, Social Security once again became a pay as you go pension plan. Even so, the Social Security 2018 Trustee Report indicated that the disability and old age trust fund will be completely exhausted by 2033. The report projected the 75-year actuarial deficit for the trust funds to total 2.84% of the taxable payroll. The 2018 Medicare Trustee's Report indicates that the Medicare Trust Fund will be completely exhausted by 2026. Medicare Part A has a 75-year actuarial deficit equal to 0.82 percent of taxable payroll.

Exhaustion of trust funds means that both Social Security and Medicare are on paths to become completely pay as you go plans. The problem is that, as entitlements, benefits for these programs are fixed at rates that cannot be supported by the current payroll tax rates. Table 10.4 illustrates changes to the payroll tax that have been made to extend the life of the programs. At first, new revenues came from higher tax rates. Then higher tax rates were accompanied by higher earnings limits. An earnings limit is the amount of money a person can make beyond which they pay no Social Security Tax. Since 1990 the payroll tax rate has remained constant while the maximum taxable earnings have increased. However, in 2013 a Medicare surcharge of .9% was added to single income earners with incomes over $200,000 or married couples with combined incomes over $250,000.

Social Security and Medicare have uncertain futures. One of three (or a combination thereof) scenarios will come to pass. First, if there is no reform to either benefits or payroll taxes, then benefits that exceed the amount collected

TABLE 10.4	HISTORICAL SOCIAL SECURITY AND MEDICARE TAX RATES				
Year	Combined Employer-Employee Tax Rate	Maximum Taxable Earnings	Year	Combined Employer-Employee Tax Rate	Maximum Taxable Earnings
1937	2%	$3,000	1973	11.7%	$10,800
1950	3%	$3,000	1978	12.1%	$17,700
1954	4%	$3,600	1979	12.26%	$22,900
1957	4.5%	$4,200	1981	13.3%	$29,700
1959	5%	$4,800	1982	13.4%	$32,400
1960	6%	$4,800	1984	14.0%	$37,800
1962	6.25%	$4,800	1985	14.1%	$39,600
1963	7.25%	$4,800	1986	14.3%	$42,000
1966	8.4%	$6,600	1988	15.02%	$45,000
1967	8.8%	$6,600	1990	15.3%	$51,300
1969	9.6%	$7,800	2010	15.3%	$106,800
1971	10.4%	$7,800	2018	15.3%	$132,900

by the payroll tax will have to come from other federal tax revenues such as the income tax. This would require a corresponding decrease in other entitlement or discretionary spending.

Secondly, Congress and the President could raise payroll tax revenues by either increasing payroll tax rates or increasing the maximum earnings limit for Social Security. Medicare already faces no such limit on earnings. As noted in Table 10.4, increased taxes have been the primary mode of entitlement adjustment in the past. A removal of the cap on Social Security earnings would immediately increase the marginal tax rate of wealthy self-employed income earners by 15.3 percentage points. On top of the 37% personal income tax they already pay, the payroll tax would place their marginal tax burden over 50%, even before they pay state and local taxes.

Thirdly, Congress and the President could reduce benefits. They could raise the retirement age to reduce the number of retirees. They could change the Social Security payment formula to reduce benefits to each retiree or change the way the cost of living increase is calculated for benefits. Another option is to means test benefits. In this way only poorer elderly individuals would get Social Security checks or receive health care assistance. As the current benefit schedule already redistributes income from wealthier to poorer retirees, this would increase the progressivity of the program.

A reduction in Medicare benefits could entail a lowering of reimbursement costs to health care providers. Significant decreases may result in less access to health care, particularly by the elderly in rural areas. Increases in patient copayments or out of pocket maximums could also save Medicare money. But, bureaucrats could end up determining which medical procedures are approved and their corresponding waiting times.

To fix the future social security shortfall, President George W. Bush advocated letting people place a portion of their payroll tax into a private account that they could invest in the stock market to earn a potentially higher rate of return. Any such movement to go from a pay as you go system to one that becomes partially or fully funded would require major benefit or tax changes. As current workers' money is diverted to their own retirement accounts, money no longer exists to pay benefits to current retirees.

Turning Social Security into a fully funded pension plan could require that a generation of taxpayers would be willing to fund the retirements of their parents plus their own. It isn't likely that any generation will voluntarily do that. Instead, a conversion to a fully funded pension plan could require that the government borrow enough money to cover current pension payments. The burden of the higher national debt could then be shared by generations to come. However, there are certainly obstacles to taking on more debt as is discussed in the next chapter. Policymakers not only have to figure out how to fix this shortfall caused by mandatory spending, they have to decide which future projects to fund via discretionary spending.

© StudioNewmarket, 2012, under license Shutterstock, Inc.

Discretionary Spending

Only under Presidents Reagan and Clinton did nondefense domestic discretionary spending fall as a percentage of GDP. This spending includes items such as the court system, domestic law enforcement, infrastructure, education, agriculture, energy, and national parks. In 2009 and 2010, the stimulus package spending led nondefense domestic discretionary spending to levels not seen since the early 1980's. Table 10.5 illustrates this in its historical context.

One example of discretionary spending is spending on farm subsidies. Table 10.6 notes that corn farmers receive more support from taxpayers than any other agricultural commodity. Seventy-four percent of farm subsidies go to the richest 10% of farmers. Agricultural subsidies enrich corporate farmers who have been able to effectively lobby their Congressional representatives for money. The Federal Agriculture Improvement and Reform Act of 1996 phased out agricultural subsidies by 2000, only to have Congress and President Bush bring them back with the Farm Security and Rural Investment Act of 2002.

TABLE 10.5	US NONDEFENSE DOMESTIC DISCRETIONARY SPENDING AS A PERCENTAGE OF GDP[5]		
1976	4.8%	2000	3.1%
1980	5.1%	2008	3.5%
1988	3.4%	2010	4.5%
1992	3.6%	2018	3.2%

TABLE 10.6	FARM SUBSIDIES 1995–2010 IN BILLIONS OF DOLLARS[6]		
Corn	$84	Rice	$13
Wheat	$36	Sorghum	$6.6
Cotton	$33	Dairy	$5.3
Soybeans	$28	Livestock	$4.0

---

[5] Ibid.

[6] Environmental Working Groups's 2014 Farm Subsidy Database, http://farm.ewg.org/.

Defense spending, as a percentage of GDP, trended downward from the early 1970s until 1980, as the US ended its intervention in Vietnam. Under President Reagan, defense spending rose in an effort to bring the Cold War to an end. The **Cold War** was an unofficial war between the US and the Soviet Union which began in 1946 and came to an end with the fall of the Soviet Union in 1991.

© Oleg Zabielin , 2012, under license Shutterstock, Inc.

Following the end of the Cold War, the US was able to benefit from the peace dividend; as resources were freed up due to the absence of a military conflict, they were diverted to meet other needs and wants for society. The US response to the September 11th attacks in 2001 brought with it an increase in military spending as the US invaded Afghanistan and Iraq. These trends are reflected in Table 10.7.

Relative to other advanced industrialized economies, the US spends a much larger percentage of its economy on national defense. Canada, for instance, spends less than one third as much as the US on national defense as a percentage of GDP. Germany and Japan, who are in part protected by US military bases located in their countries, are able to free up resources to be used satisfying nonmilitary needs and desires.

TABLE 10.7	US DEFENSE SPENDING AS A PERCENTAGE OF GDP[7]		
1976	5.0%	2000	2.9%
1980	4.8%	2008	4.2%
1988	5.6%	2010	4.7%
1992	4.7%	2018	3.1%

TABLE 10.8	2017 INTERNATIONAL DEFENSE SPENDING AS A PERCENTAGE OF GDP[8]		
US	3.1%	Canada	1.3%
UK	1.8%	Germany	1.2%
China	1.9%	Japan	0.9%

[7] Source: Congressional Budget Office.

[8] Source: Stockholm International Peace Research Institute 2018 Fact Sheet

Discretionary spending undertaken by the federal government does not have to reflect national priorities. An **earmark** is spending that directs approved funds to be spent on specific projects that affect a specific area but that have no benefit to rest of the nation. A Congresswoman may want a bridge to be built in her district. If she is able to sit on the committee that originates the spending bill, she may be able to add her earmark to the bill. She could also add her earmark by engaging in **logrolling**. Logrolling is vote trading. She may agree to vote for spending that one of her colleagues likes but she has no benefit for her constituents, in exchange for a vote for her earmark. In this way, many urban congresspersons over the years have voted for farm subsidies in exchange for more urban spending.

When Congress wishes to engage in fiscal policy the 'devil is in the details' as to where and on what the spending is spent. Government roads and bridges are named after powerful congresspersons for a reason. They have been able to use their seniority on committees to direct spending to their district or state. While spending has been discussed in this chapter, spending is largely dependent upon revenue. The next section examines the sources of tax revenue for the US federal government and compares its tax rates with those of other nations.

Taxes

"No taxation without representation" was a popular phrase used by American revolutionaries to generate anti-British sentiment in support of the American Revolution. The revolutionaries believed that British Parliament should not have the power to directly tax American colonists since colonists lacked representation in Parliament. However, American colonists only paid a fraction of the taxes that other British subjects paid.

TABLE 10.9	INDEX OF PER CAPITA TAX BURDENS IN 1765 (GREAT BRITAIN = 100)[9]
Great Britain	100
Ireland	26
Pennsylvania	4
Maryland	4
Massachusetts	4
New York	3
Connecticut	2
Virginia	2

---

[9] Source: Gerald A. Gunderson, *A New Economic History of America* (New York: McGraw-Hill, 1976): 98.

In 1932, US federal tax revenues as a percentage of GDP were 2.8%. By 1944, they had risen to 20.9%. President Franklin Delano Roosevelt oversaw a dramatic shift in the size and scope of the US government, as New Deal spending was accompanied by New Deal tax increases. While government programs must be paid for with tax revenue, taxation itself plays an important role in the economy. This section lays out the current US tax code, compares state tax rates, places the US tax code in an international comparison, and examines the code's efficiency and fairness.

The Current Federal Tax Structure

The amount of revenue generated by the federal government is dependent upon both the tax code and the health of the US economy. As the economy grows, so too does the number of taxable economic transactions. Tax revenues, then, are variable over the course of the business cycle.

Examining tax revenues as a percentage of GDP over the last forty years reveals that the presidents who oversaw an increase in tax revenues as a percentage of GDP were all Democrats. However not all democratic presidents have had tax revenues rise. Presidents Carter and Clinton saw tax revenues as a percentage of GDP increase, while Presidents Ford, Reagan, and both Presidents Bush (all Republicans) saw tax revenue as a percentage of GDP fall during their tenure. In spite of this trend, tax revenues as a percentage of GDP fell rapidly during the beginning of President Obama's presidency. President Obama extended the Bush tax cuts while also cutting the payroll tax for 2011. Combined with a slowing economy, US government revenues as a percentage of GDP were lower in 2011 than any year since 1943. They have rebounded since 2011 with a growing economy and a tax increase. Table 10.10 outlines historical federal tax revenues.

The modern income tax came into being with the passage of the 16th Amendment to the US Constitution in 1913. Before then, it was unconstitutional for the federal government to tax income. Today, the two largest sources of tax revenue for the US government are the personal income tax and the payroll tax. The first applies to all forms of income, while the latter applies only to wage labor. Corporate taxes and other excise taxes, such as the national gas tax, account for only small portion of federal tax revenues. Table 10.11 highlights the sources of the federal tax revenue of 2018.

TABLE 10.10	FEDERAL TAX REVENUES AS A PERCENTAGE OF GDP[10]		
1976	16.6%	2000	19.1%
1980	18.5%	2008	17.1%
1988	17.6%	2010	14.6%
1992	17%	2018	16.4%

TABLE 10.11	2018 FEDERAL REVENUSE BY SOURCE (IN BILLIONS)[11]
Personal Income Tax	$1,684
Payroll Tax	$1,171
Corporate Income Tax	$205
Other	$270

The payroll tax (FICA) is a tax paid by employers and employees based on their wages. An employer must pay 7.65% of their worker's income to the federal government. Each employee must also pay 7.65% of their income, for a total of 15.3%. The payroll tax applies to all wage income earned up to $132,900 in 2018. Wage income earned above that level is subject only to the Medicare portion of the payroll tax (2.9% split between the employer and employee plus .9% on single incomes over $200,000 or married incomes over $250,000.)

Table 10.12 lays out the federal income tax brackets for 2013. A **marginal tax rate** is the percentage of a new dollar in economic activity that must be paid to the government. Tax brackets represent marginal tax rates. Married households pay a tax rate of 10% on their first $19,050 of annual taxable income, whether they earn $20,000 or $2 billion a year. Married couples earning more than $19,050 pay 12% on all income past $19,050 and up to $77,400 earned. For those with taxable income greater than $77,400, 22% of this added income up to the next cutoff of $165,000 is paid to the federal government, and so forth. In this way, taxpayers in the top tax bracket do not pay 37% of their entire income in federal income taxes, but instead pay according to each tax bracket up until they exceed the cutoff. Then they pay 37% of all additional dollars earned past the cutoff.

---

[10] Source: Congressional Budget Office.

[11] Ibid.

TABLE 10.12	2018 FEDERAL INCOME TAX BRACKETS[12]	
Marginal Tax Rate	**Married Couples Filing Jointly Adjusted Gross Income**	**Single Filers Adjusted Gross Income**
10%	Up to $19,050	Up to $9,525
12%	$19,051 to $77,400	$9,526 to $38,700
22%	$77,401 to $165,000	$38,701 to $82,500
24%	$165,001 to $315,000	$82,501 to $157,500
32%	$315,001 to $400,000	$157,501 to $200,000
35%	$400,001 to $600,000	$200,001 to $500,000
37%	over $600,000	over $500,000

The **average tax rate** is the total taxes paid divided by the income. The average income tax rate is lower than the marginal income tax rate for two reasons. First, most people's first dollar of income is taxed at a lower marginal rate than their last dollar of income. Second, not all income is taxable. This is due to deductions and exemptions that serve to complicate the tax code.

A **deduction** is an amount that can be deducted from taxable income. Money given to charities, interest paid on a home loan, or state and local property tax payments are just a few examples of deductions that exist in the tax code. A person who gives half of their income away to charity has their taxable income fall by 50%, and so only pays taxes on the remaining half. The 10% tax bracket then kicks in on the first taxable dollars of income. Since the average tax rate is determined by actual income, the average tax rate in this case will be much lower than the marginal tax rate. Those who don't choose to itemize their deductions could have opted for a $12,000 standard deduction in 2018 if they were single or a $24,000 deduction if they were married filing jointly.

Once tax liability is determined, tax credits can be applied to reduce the amount taxpayers must pay. The **earned income tax credit** pays low income earners based on their income and family size. The 2018 **child tax credit** was $2,000 per child under the age of 17. In this way, many Americans face no federal income liability and instead get checks from the government. The bottom 50% of income tax earners in 2015 only paid 2.83% of the nation's income taxes. Table 10.13 illustrates the share of income taxes paid by various percentages of the population. It also demonstrates the progressive nature of the US federal income tax.

[12] Source: Internal Revenue Service.

TABLE 10.13	INCOME TAXES PAID BY VARIOUS GROUPS, 2015[13]	
All Taxpayers	**Group's Share of Adjusted Gross Income**	**Group's Share of Income Taxes**
100%	100.00%	100.00%
Top 1%	20.65%	39.84%
Top 5%	36.07%	59.58%
Top 10%	47.36%	70.59%
Top 25%	68.9%	86.62%
Top 50%	88.72%	97.17%
Bottom 50%	11.285%	2.83%

Cross Country Comparison of Tax Rates

With regard to income taxes, the United States is neither at the top, nor at the bottom when their top federal and local income tax rates are compared to other countries. Table 10.14 Sweden, Denmark, Japan, Greece, and France all impose a marginal tax rate on income earners of over 50%. Conversely, many Eastern European countries' top tax rates are less than half of that.

Ireland was able to attract large amounts of corporate investment due to its low corporate income tax rate. It has inspired other countries to lower their corporate income tax rates in order to remain competitive in attracting global capital. When Canada began to lower its corporate income tax rate they began to attract US companies to relocate their headquarters north of the border. In 2018, the US responded by lowering its corporate income tax rate from 39.6% to 21%.

TABLE 10.14	TOP MARGINAL PERSONAL INCOME TAX RATES[14]				
Sweden	55.8%	Canada	50%	Poland	21.7%
Denmark	55.8%	Germany	46.3%	Slovak Republic	20.1%
Japan	55.0%	UK	46.0%	Czech Republic	19.7%
Greece	53.9%	US	44.4%	Estonia	15%
France	53.5%	Mexico	33.0%	Hungary	10.9%

---

[13] Ibid.

[14] Source: OECD Table 1.7 Top statutory personal income tax rate, 2017.

TABLE 10.15	CENTRAL GOVERNMENT CORPORATE TAX RATES[15]		
Country	**Tax Rate**	**Country**	**Tax Rate**
France	34.43%	Germany	15.83%
Mexico	30.00%	Canada	15.00%
Portugal	30.00%	Ireland	12.50%
Australia	30.00%	Hungary	9.00%
US	21.00%	Switzerland	8.50%

The single largest difference between the US tax code and most of the industrialized world is the absence in the US of a broad based national sales tax or **value added tax (VAT)**. A value added tax is a sales tax applied to every transfer of a good based on the increased worth of that good since it was last exchanged. Many European countries have double digit VAT's. A sales tax, or VAT, can apply to all income earners. Therefore, the **tax base** for a VAT is larger than for an income tax. A tax base is the number of people who pay the tax. The larger the tax base, the lower the marginal rates must be to achieve the same level of revenue. The almost total reliance on income taxes by the US government leaves them subject to downturns in tax revenues during recessions and periods of high unemployment.

A Comparison of US State Tax Rates

State governments primarily rely on tax revenue from income and sales taxes. While some states also impose property taxes, local governments collect the majority of all property taxes paid. Eight US states have no state income tax, while two: California and Hawaii, have double digit income tax rates. High income earners, because they often have a choice of where to live in the US, can move to reduce or eliminate their state income tax burden. States compete for taxpayers by offering bundles of government spending and taxation that appeal to citizens. People can choose to sort themselves among political jurisdictions in order to find their preferred taxing and spending levels. This process of voting with one's feet is called the **Tiebout Effect**. Table 10.16 lays out the nine lowest and highest state income tax rates.

Five US states don't have statewide sales taxes, while the top sales tax rate belongs to Tennessee at 9.47%. Oregon, though it has the nation's highest income tax, has no sales tax. Their neighboring state, Washington, has no income tax. People who work in Washington but purchase goods in Oregon can avoid

TABLE 10.16	TOP AND BOTTOM 2018 INCOME TAX RATES FOR US STATES[16]		
Alaska	0%	New York	8.82%
Florida	0%	Vermont	8.95%
Nevada	0%	New Jersey	8.97%
New Hampshire	0% (5% on interest and dividend income)	Iowa	8.98%
South Dakota	0%	Minnesota	9.85%
Texas	0%	Oregon	9.90%
Washington	0%	Hawaii	11.00%
Wyoming	0%	California	13.30%

TABLE 10.17	TOP AND BOTTOM 2018 STATE SALES TAX RATES FOR US STATES[17]		
Alaska	0%	Alabama	9.14%
Delaware	0%	Washington	9.17%
Montana	0%	Arkansas	9.43%
New Hampshire	0%	Louisiana	9.45%
Oregon	0%	Tennessee	9.47%

both income and sales taxes. Table 10.17 illustrates the highest and lowest state sales tax rates.

Tax Efficiency and Fairness

An efficient tax system raises revenue without causing a significant disruption in economic activity. A perfectly efficient tax would be one that costlessly collects tax revenue while not causing any economic actor to change their behavior. Because the amount of land on earth (or in a country) is constant, a land tax would be able to generate tax revenue without the destruction of land. However, costs of collection would still exist. Property taxes generally tax both land and the improvements to the land. By taxing improvements, property taxes can dissuade people from making improvements to land.

---

[16] Source: State Individual Income Tax Rates and Brackets for 2018, Tax Foundation.

[17] Source: Combined State & Local Sales Tax Rates, Tax Foundation.

[18] McCulloch v. Maryland (1819).

As the US Supreme Court once held, "The power to tax is the power to destroy".[18] A high sales tax rate can cause people to engage in less consumption, both because consumers then have less money to spend and because the relative return to savings increases. Consumers can also choose to buy goods and services where they face a lower sales tax, or in the black market where no taxes are collected. Many states have tried to tax internet sales in an attempt to keep their citizens from avoiding state sales taxes. Because sales taxes are already collected by most states, there would be little administrative burden in collecting a national sales tax.

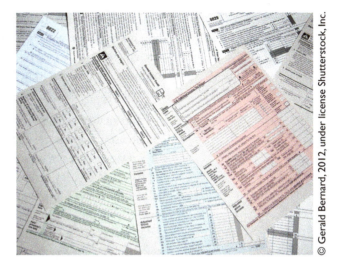

© Gerald Bernard, 2012, under license Shutterstock, Inc.

When it comes to personal and corporate income taxes, the marginal tax rate serves as a disincentive to increase earnings. As marginal tax rates increase, the opportunity cost of leisure increases and people may choose to substitute leisure for work, on the margin. An efficient income tax code would have low marginal tax rates and few, if any, deductions or exemptions. As it currently stands, the numerous personal and corporate tax loopholes work to push marginal tax rates higher and discourage economic activity. A simplified tax code would also serve to lower the compliance costs associated with filing income taxes. The current complexity of the tax code causes millions of Americans to pay professional tax preparers to help them file their tax forms. This added cost of compliance means that people pay compliance costs that the government cannot recoup. People could keep more of their money and the government could generate more revenue by reducing the complexity of the tax code.

A tax can either be progressive, proportional, or regressive. A **progressive tax** is one where the average tax rate paid increases with income earned. A **proportional tax** is one where the average tax rate paid stays the same as income increases. A **regressive tax** is one where the average tax rate paid decreases as income increases. With its multiple tax brackets and many deductions and exemptions, the US income tax is highly progressive. The payroll tax is proportional up to the earnings limit on Social Security taxes. Sales taxes, if they are applied to all goods and services, tend to be regressive. Lower income individuals tend to spend a larger percentage of their income on goods and services than do higher income individuals. As a result, lower income individuals tend to pay a larger percentage of their income in sales taxes.

The question of which type of tax system is most *fair* depends on one's own ethical considerations and is often disputed between the two major political parties in the United States. Overall, the US tax system is progressive, but the debate over how progressive it should be has no foreseeable end in sight. Often the choice of tax code involves tradeoffs. A broad based sales tax is the most efficient revenue raiser but is also regressive. A steeply progressive personal or corporate income tax rate is very inefficient because it lowers economic activity and is costly to collect, but is seen by some as being more fair.

The answer to the efficiency vs. fairness tax debate comes down to whether people are more concerned about absolute or relative poverty. As described in the previous chapter, **absolute poverty** means that people are unable to afford the basic necessities of life. **Relative poverty** is a measure of income inequality reflecting that some people can afford to buy less than others. An efficient tax code allows the economy to grow faster than it would under an inefficient tax code. This economic growth creates benefits for people of all incomes. There is less absolute poverty in the US than in Honduras because of faster economic growth over time. Still, this reduction in absolute poverty could cause an increase in relative poverty which some people find undesirable.

Key Terms

Absolute poverty

Average tax rate

Child tax credit

Cold War

Deduction

Discretionary spending

Earmark

Earned income tax credit (EITC)

Entitlement

Government shutdown

Logrolling

Mandatory spending

Marginal tax rate

Medicaid

Medicare

Progressive tax

Proportional tax

Regressive tax

Relative poverty

Social Security

Social Security Trust Fund

Tax base

Tiebout Effect

Value added tax (VAT)

Welfare

Questions for Review

1. How does mandatory spending differ from discretionary spending? Give examples of both types of spending

2. What has happened to government outlays as a percentage of GDP over time? Why?

3. What type of pension system is Social Security? What problems does Social Security currently face? What are possible reforms and which of these do you prefer?

4. Does Medicare need to be reformed? What are the possible Medicare reforms? Which do you prefer? Why?

5. What is a progressive tax? A proportional tax? A regressive tax? Give examples of taxes in each category. Which is most efficient? The most fair? Why?

6. What percentage of personal income taxes does the top 25% of income earners pay?

7. Which US states have no income tax? No sales tax? What are the advantages and disadvantages of type of tax?

8. How do US personal and corporate income tax rates compare to those of other industrialized countries? What are the pros and cons of the United States not having a national sales tax or VAT?

The National Debt

"I'll gladly pay you Tuesday for a hamburger today."

— J. Wellington Wimpy

"Neither a borrower nor a lender be,
For loan oft loses both itself and friend,
And borrowing dulls the edge of husbandry."

—William Shakespeare[1]

© zimmytws/Shutterstock.com

[1] Hamlet Act 1, scene 3, 45–77.

The prior chapter discusses spending and revenue collection for the US federal government. But what happens when current revenues are insufficient to cover desired expenditures? Governments are able to spend now and pay later, as long as someone is willing to loan them money. Consumers, businesses, and governments all have access to, and can compete for, loanable funds made available through financial institutions. Whether or not debt is used productively determines if consumers, businesses, or governments make themselves better or worse off as a result of borrowing.

For example, debt can be used as tool to finance long term investment. Businesses can take on debt to finance new factories or equipment. Consumers can take on debt to finance the purchase of new homes or a college education. In these cases, the benefits from the accumulated capital accrue over many years. These multiyear benefits might not be possible if businesses or consumers had to pay for large capital purchases up front. However, if a business borrows money to finance capital for which there is little demand or use, then the service of that debt will take away scarce resources. If a consumer uses their credit card to finance current consumption, then they will be forced to service very high interest payments while forgoing future consumption.

Debt is growth enabling only if the proceeds from the debt are used to increase future earnings enough to exceed interest payments on the debt. Another use for debt is consumption smoothing. If people know they will be wealthier in the future and want to spread their consumption more evenly over time, they can use debt to consume more today at the cost of consuming less tomorrow. For example, a student in medical school may choose to consume beyond her current budget because she knows that her incomes will increase once she graduates. When it comes to government debt, it is important to understand why a government takes on debt in order to determine the optimal level of public debt. This chapter examines government debt, where it comes from, whether it is growth enhancing or detracting, and the path of future government debt.

The US National Debt

The United States government is the largest debtor in the world. As of February 28, 2019, the US national debt stood at $22.1 trillion, roughly $67,000 for each American. Of the $22.1 trillion, $16.2 is owed to the public, while the remainder is in **intergovernmental holdings**. The Social Security Trust Fund and other government entities own government bonds. Collectively debt held by government agencies is known as intergovernmental debt. As government agencies cash in their bonds to meet spending commitments, the government will either have to generate more tax revenues, cut discretionary government spending, or borrow the money from the public.

© Elena Yakusheva , 2012, under license Shutterstock, Inc.

Pension funds, mutual funds, banks, insurance companies, local governments, and individuals can all own government bonds. The federal government pays interest on its bonds, which is tax free income for the bondholders. To the extent that the US debt is owed to US citizens, repayment of the debt merely involves the transfer of income from US taxpayers to US bondholders, with the money staying in the US economy. However, interest payments and repayments of bonds owned by foreigners results in a loss of money for the US economy.

Of the $16.2 trillion in debt owned by the public, roughly $6.2 trillion is owed to foreign entities. The government of China and Japan have each loaned the US more than $1 trillion. Foreign debt carries important foreign policy implications. Secretary of State Hillary Clinton noted in 2010 that "We cannot sustain this level of deficit financing and debt without losing our influence, without being constrained in the tough decisions we have to make".[2]

The United States was an indebted country at its birth. While fighting the American Revolution, the Continental Congress borrowed money, principally from the French, to fund the war effort. When the US Constitution became ratified, $75 million in war debt became the property of the new federal government. In order to pay down this debt, the federal government ran budget surpluses and had paid off $30 million worth of the debt by 1812, when the US returned to war with Great Britain. Between 1816 and 1835 the federal government paid off its entire debt. President Andrew Jackson started rebating taxes to states and left a nominal national debt balance of $34,000 in 1835.

Throughout most of its history, the US government has borrowed money to engage in war and then has run budget surpluses to pay down on that debt. This was true for the American Revolution, The War of 1812, The Mexican-American War, The US Civil War, and WWI. Because the benefits of peace presumably accrue to future generations, future generations are asked to help pay for current wars. Still, the American ethos was one that disliked government debt, so repayment of the national debt typically followed the end of wars. That was true until the late 1950's as illustrated in Table 11.1.

[2] Andrew Quinn, Reuters May 27, 2010.
http://www.reuters.com/article/2010/05/27/security-obama-clinton-idUSN2714967820100527?type=marketsNews

TABLE 11.1   HISTORICAL US NATIONAL DEBT

Year	Debt	Year	Debt	Year	Debt
1791	$75 million	1849	$63 million	1919	$27.9 billion
1812	$45 million	1857	$29 million	1930	$16.2 billion
1816	$127 million	1866	$2.8 billion	1946	$269 billion
1835	$34 thousand	1893	$1.5 billion	1951	$255 billion

TABLE 11.2   RECENT DEBT HISTORY

Year	Debt	Year	Debt
1976	$620 billion	2000	$5.7 trillion
1980	$908 billion	2008	$10.2 trillion
1988	$2.6 trillion	2016	$19.6 trillion
1992	$4.1 trillion	2019 (February)	$22.1 trillion

The national debt has grown every year since 1958. The US has engaged in military conflicts since then including, but not limited to: the Vietnam War, the Cold War, and the War on Terror. The principle of borrowing to finance wars with repayment to follow the war's conclusion is only fiscally sustainable if the economy experiences long stretches of peace. With the war on terror reaching no obvious conclusion, borrowing to finance the war is akin to borrowing for consumption rather than for investment. Indeed, Adam Smith argued that if countries were prohibited from running budget deficits in times of war, there would be fewer wars.[3]

Table 11.2 illustrates the pattern of debt increase over the last 40 years. Almost seventy-five percent of the US's national debt has accrued since 2000. In the next section, we examine the burden of government debt on the economy.

The Burden of Government Debt

Large amounts of public debt can be harmful for multiple reasons. The higher the debt, the greater the annual interest payments are on the debt. These payments restrict the use of government revenues to fund other government initiatives. Discretionary spending and entitlements have to fight over ever smaller government revenues in a world of rising debt.

---

[3] Smith, Adam, *An Inquiry into the Nature and Causes of the Wealth of Nations.* Edwin Cannan, ed. 1904.

As the government borrows increasingly larger amounts of money, the price of borrowed money, the interest rate, increases and firms and individuals who want loans are forced to compete for a smaller pool of savings. Government borrowing decreases private investment, as it drives up interest rates and decreases funds available for private companies. Larger debts also increase the likelihood of default, causing savers to demand a higher rate of return on their loans. These higher interest rates discourage private investment and therefore slow down long term economic growth. This process is referred to as **crowding out**.

The opposite occurs when governments pay down their debt. When the federal government ran budget surpluses following the US Civil War, the government used these surpluses to pay down debt. This allowed money to be made available for private investment, and private investment soared. This process is referred to as **crowding in**.

Government debt is inherently redistributive in nature. The government chooses to allocate resources based on its preferences rather than the preferences of individual decision makers. Debt also redistributes wealth from future generations, unless citizens privately save more to compensate for increased public debt. Japan's large public debt is less burdensome on their economy because most of their debt is held by Japanese citizens. Repayment of debt is likewise redistributive. It redistributes income from future workers to bondholders. By raising marginal tax rates on future workers, said workers will likely adjust to these higher marginal rates by providing less work to the economy, thereby causing slower growth rates.

Thus, government debt redistributes income from taxpayers to bondholders and from future generations to present generations. Further, government borrowing limits future government spending, raises interest rates, and consequently crowds out private investment and restricts economic growth. On the other hand, government borrowing can be used to finance infrastructure improvements or the preservation of freedoms or other investments that lead to increased productivity. So when are increases in government debt beneficial to the economy and when do the costs outnumber the benefits? To better answer this important question, one must fully understand the burden of government debt.

The best measure to determine the burden of government debt on an economy is the debt/GDP ratio. The debt/GDP ratio describes an economy's debt with respect to its ability to pay it back. If a government borrows to fund growth enhancing projects, the added government debt will lower the debt/GDP ratio over time. If the debt is growth inhibiting, the added debt increases the debt/GDP ratio over time and is a sign that government borrowing is being used to finance current consumption. Seventy-five million dollars was a lot of debt for the revolutionaries in the 1700's, but would not be terribly burdensome for a $22 trillion economy. By 1945, the debt/GDP ratio had risen to 121.2%. Even without paying down on the debt after 1958, economic growth exceeded deficit

TABLE 11.3	2018 DEBT AND DEFICITS				
Country	**Debt/GDP[4]**	**Deficit/GDP[5]**	**Country**	**Debt/GDP[4]**	**Deficit/GDP[5]**
Japan	238.2%	3.2%	Australia	40.5%	0.6%
Greece	188.1%	0.1%	South Korea	40.4%	1.1% (surplus)
Italy	130.3%	1.9%	Switzerland	40.15%	0.9% (surplus)
Portugal	120.8%	0.7%	Sweden	37.9%	0.8% (surplus)
Singapore	112.9%	0.4% (surplus)	Norway	36.4%	7.0% (surplus)
US	106.1%	3.8%	Taiwan	34.4%	0.6%
Belgium	101.2%	1.0%	New Zealand	30.4%	2.0% (surplus)
Spain	97.2%	2.7%	Luxembourg	22.8%	1.3% (surplus)
UK	87.4%	1.3%	Estonia	8.8%	0.4%
Ireland	66.6%	0.1%	Hong Kong	0.05%	2.0% (surplus)

spending, so the debt/GDP ratio fell to 62.5% by 1981. As of 2018, the US debt/GDP ratio had increased to 106%, as Table 11.3 illustrates.

Controversial research by Reinhart and Rogoff[6] (studying debt and economic growth data from 44 countries over 200 years) suggests that countries with a higher debt/GDP ratio have had the lowest average rate of economic growth. Not only does the fiscal imbalance entail an intergenerational transfer of wealth, it also impoverishes future generations by slowing down their trajectory of economic growth. Put another way, countries with high debt/GDP ratios end up taking money from future generations to give it to the current relatively wealthier generation.

Table 11.3 lists advanced countries with the lowest and highest debt/GDP ratios. These are the countries that are doing the best and worst jobs of paying for current consumption with their current revenues. Although there is great variation in the amount of public sector involvement in the countries listed, countries in the right-hand column have all kept their spending more in line with the revenues they collect. Economies that fall over the 100% threshold: Japan, Greece, Italy, Portugal, US, Belgium, and Singapore owe more in debt than their entire economy produces in a year's time. These countries are in a serious need of budget reform to lower their debt/GDP ratio. Many of the most indebted countries continue to run the largest budget deficits. It is this path of continued borrowing that led Standard and Poor's to downgrade the United States' bond rating in August, 2011.

---

[4] Source: IMF October 2018 Economic Outlook.

[5] *The Economist Magazine.* February 2019.

[6] Reinart, C.M., and K. S. Rogoff, 2010, "Growth in a Time of Debt," American Economic Review, vol. 100(2), pages 573–78.

Debt and Unfunded Liabilities for US States

Government debt in the US is not confined to the federal government. Table 11.4 illustrates the states in the best and worst fiscal condition. The five states with the best fiscal condition are Nebraska, South Dakota, Tennessee, Florida, and Oklahoma. The overall fiscal condition includes both state debt and unfunded state pension liabilities. The five states in the worst fiscal condition are Illinois, Connecticut, New Jersey, Massachusetts, and Kentucky.

The failure of some states to live within their means will put tremendous strain on their future ability to provide public services to their state constituents over time. Both people and capital are fairly mobile between states. Thus, it is difficult for states to dramatically raise taxes to fund debt without motivating income earners to move to other states. Because people are more likely to move across states than across countries, the federal government has more power to increase tax rates than do individual states.

TABLE 11.4	2018 FISCAL CONDITION RANK[7]		
Rank	**State**	**Rank**	**State**
1.	Nebraska	46.	Kentucky
2.	South Dakota	47.	Massachusetts
3.	Tennessee	48.	New Jersey
4.	Florida	49.	Connecticut
5.	Oklahoma	50.	Illinois

Unfunded Liabilities and National Governments

With the US national debt over $22.1 trillion, the 2018 unfunded liability in Medicare and Social Security was roughly $50.2 trillion.[8] That amounts to over $150,000 per person. Seventy-four percent of the US unfunded liability comes from Medicare. Left unchecked, the US federal government is on a collision course

---

[7] Source: 2018 Mercatus Center State Fiscal Rankings

[8] 2018 Social Security and Medicare Trustees Report

with fiscal disaster. Piling on more current consumption without paying for it simply is not possible without seriously jeopardizing the future standard of living for all Americans.

The US federal government is not the only developed country with unfunded liabilities. Even in 2003, Europe's unfunded pension liabilities were already beginning to pile up, as Table 11.5 illustrates. Yesterday's unfunded liabilities add to tomorrow's debt. Greece, Spain, Portugal, and Italy were among the countries where the European debt crisis intensified in 2010 and 2011. Their unfunded pension liabilities of 2003 transformed into high levels of debt in a very short time frame. In contrast, countries such as Japan, Norway, Netherlands, and Canada lead the way in funding their pension liabilities with fully funded public systems.

TABLE 11.5	UNFUNDED PENSION LIABILITIES AS A PERCENTAGE OF GDP, 2003[9]		
Greece	807%	Finland	379%
Spain	717%	Italy	352%
France	407%	Denmark	317%
Portugal	396%	Austria	292%
Belgium	395%	Sweden	264%

Conclusion

In summary, debt is not always harmful to the debtor. If the debt is used to finance investments that increase future earnings by more than the interest payments on that debt, then debt can be growth enhancing. If debt is used to increase current consumption, then it will be growth diminishing. An increase in a country's debt/GDP ratio over time indicates that their public debt is primarily being used to finance current consumption at the cost of future consumption. As noted in Chapter 10, the vast majority of US federal spending is on entitlement programs, which are consumptive in nature. The United States is borrowing in an attempt to increase current consumption at the expense of future generations. Unless the US government meaningfully addresses entitlement and tax reform, the US national debt will continue to grow and will inhibit future economic growth.

---

[9] Source: ABN AMRO 2003.

Key Terms

Crowding in   Crowding out   Intergovernmental holdings

Questions for Review

1. How large is the US national debt?

2. What measure of national debt is most important? Why?

3. How do US debt levels compare to other countries?

4. Where did the US national debt come from?

5. Why are high debt levels problematic for future economic growth? What role does crowding out play? Is debt always harmful to the economy? Explain.

6. Which states have the least amount of debt? The most?

7. Which states have the least amount of unfunded pension liability? The most?

8. Which countries are most likely to default? Why?

9. Which countries have the lowest debt burdens?

10. How is government debt redistributive in nature?

Chapter 12

Monetary Policy

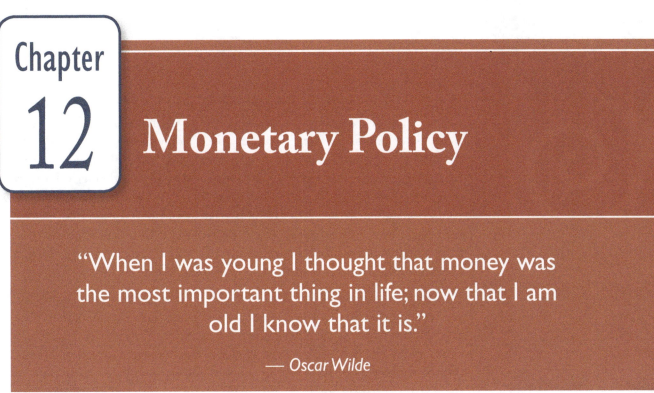

"When I was young I thought that money was the most important thing in life; now that I am old I know that it is."

— *Oscar Wilde*

"I traded a video game for three beans."

Many classic fairy tales claim that the accumulation of money allows people to live happily ever after. The widow and her son Jack in the story *Jack and the Beanstalk*[1] were very poor. Jack was sent by his mother to the market to trade their cow for food. Instead, Jack traded the cow for magic beans, which meant that Jack and his mother had to go to bed hungry. Later in the story, when Jack steals gold from a giant, he and his mother are able to live happily ever after. Neither Jack nor his mother intended to eat the gold, and yet the mere presence of gold meant that their lives would be comfortable. In a different children's story, all of Hansel and Gretel's worries were likewise over when they returned back to their father with the wicked witch's jewels.[2]

Money might not be able to buy you love, but it can buy you a smart TV. This chapter examines what an economy looks like without money, describes what constitutes money, and illustrates how money has evolved over time. It also examines the role that banks play in monetary creation and destruction. Finally, it discusses how a central bank can conduct monetary policy in an attempt to stabilize the macroeconomy.

Money

Money is a human invention, and as such has not always existed. People existed and engaged in economic transactions long before money came into being. Economies without money are called **barter economies**. In a barter economy, people engage in economic transactions by trading goods and services directly for each other. In order for a voluntary economic transaction to occur, both parties involved in the exchange need to value the other's offerings more than their own. This act of both parties wanting what the other party is offering is known as a **double coincidence of wants**.

An economics professor would likely have a hard time generating wealth in a barter economy. What she has to offer to the market is a series of lectures regarding the interworking of an economy. If she desired pizza for dinner, not only would the economics professor need to find a pizzeria, she would have to find a pizzeria that wanted to trade pizza for an economics lecture. Likewise a shepherd would have to trade with people who wanted sheep, wool, or mutton. Wealth creating economic exchanges face high transaction costs in a barter economy. These high transaction costs discourage wealth creation. As a result, barter economies have had poor records of wealth creation. Monetary economies can overcome some of these transaction costs with the use of money.

---

[1] Benjamin Tabart. *The History of Jack and the Bean-Stalk* (1807).

[2] The Brothers Grimm. *Hansel and Gretel* (1812).

Three Functions of Money

A **monetary economy** is an economy where goods and services are exchanged for money. Money serves three major functions in an economy. Money serves as a medium of exchange, a store of value, and a unit of account. If everyone wants a common asset, then that asset substitutes for the double coincidence of wants. If party A likes money and party B also likes money, then exchanges can occur without barter. Put another way, bartering still occurs, but that barter is between a good or service and money. By serving as a **medium of exchange**, money acts as the grease in the wheels of an economy. A shortage of money makes transactions difficult to complete. A surplus of money means than even more of it is required for any given transaction.

© Yellowj, 2012, under license Shutterstock, Inc.

Some people produce goods or services that create temporary wealth. A farmer who grows a tomato only creates wealth if that tomato is sold, traded, or consumed before it becomes rotten. By selling the tomato for money, the farmer is able to store his wealth in order to purchase goods or services in the future. Money only serves as a good **store of value** if the quantity of money does not increase relative to the quantity of available goods and services in the economy. If the tomato farmer sells his tomato for a ruby and tomorrow a new ruby mine is discovered that increases the number of rubies in existence, then any given ruby will be less scarce, and thus, less valuable.

When people go to the store, they like to see how much each of the items cost that they are considering buying. The price of each item is presented to them in terms of that country's money. Because money is the common denominator for economic transactions, it serves as a **unit of account**. All products and prices become priced according to the common money. Note that this common money may be a form of **commodity money** which has its own intrinsic value or **fiat money** that has no value other than its usefulness as money.

Commodity Money

Throughout history, societies have identified certain items that most people were willing to accept in trade. Whether that product was useful or not to one owner, if everyone else wanted it, it served as a useful commodity money. Commodity money is money that has an inherent or intrinsic value. Historically, people have valued shiny metals and minerals. Diamonds, rubies, and gold have value because they are scarce and people tend to find them pretty.

Gold, silver, and to a lesser extent bronze, seashells, and tobacco leaves have all served as commodity money in different economies. In truth, any commodity or asset could be called money if large numbers of people wish to own it. Still, some commodities have been more popular than others when it comes to their use as money. For instance, gold has been a much more popular commodity money over time than have cows. The most practical types of commodity money are uniform, durable, easily divisible, have a high value to weight ratio, and are difficult for the average person to reproduce.

Fourteen karat gold is fourteen karat gold. It doesn't matter if Eon or Madison mined it. It has a uniform metallic characteristic. Diamonds are not uniform. Diamonds differ by carat, color, cut, and clarity. Rather than learn the four C's of diamonds, people just had to learn how to weigh gold to determine its value. While diamonds are durable and have a high value to weight ratio, they are not easily divisible. Unlike gold, you can't melt diamonds and then cool them to create the size you want.

Due to its relative scarcity, gold is a more popular commodity money than either silver or copper. Its value to weight ratio is much higher than the other two metals. For instance, on March 4, 2019, gold sold for $1,288 an ounce compared to $15.10 for an ounce of silver or $2.91 for an ounce of copper. A person looking to buy a parcel of land with a bag of precious metal was much more likely to be able to carry the necessary gold than if they had to carry the equivalent value in silver or copper. Imagine trying to carry enough pennies to buy a new Corvette!

Cows can die on their way to market, gold cannot. Porcelain china can be dropped and broken on the way to market. While gold can be dropped, you can't realistically break it such that it is of no future use. Gold too does not grow on trees, making it harder to supply more of than, say, apples. Because gold has to be located and mined from the ground in an arduous process, new gold is difficult to produce. Nevertheless, when the Spanish imported massive amounts of gold from South America to Spain in a relatively short period of time, there was massive inflation as the value of gold fell.

When the United States gained its independence from Great Britain, the US set a bimetallic standard. That is, it used both gold and silver as an officially recognized currency, with a set price for gold in terms of silver. Fifteen ounces of silver equaled one ounce of gold. Because this was an arbitrary price of gold, only gold or silver typically was used in the US. When gold was undervalued by the official rate of exchange, people sold their gold abroad in exchange for silver and only silver coins circulated. **Gresham's Law** states that bad money drives out good. When the government increased the price of gold to sixteen ounces of silver, gold became overvalued and silver fled the country as only gold coins circulated, leaving the US with a de facto gold standard. In 1900, the US government officially adopted a gold standard. Any paper money issued by the federal government had to be redeemable by gold.

In 1933, President Roosevelt declared it illegal to hoard gold or use it as money in economic transactions. All gold deposits had to be turned over to the federal government in exchange for paper currency. While the relationship between paper money and gold was linked thereafter, it was not linked at a 1 to 1 ratio. Instead, the government increased the price of gold for international exchange purposes, as they increased the domestic money supply faster than the supply of new gold. In 1971, President Nixon ended all convertibility of US currency into gold. Later, President Ford made it legal again for private individuals to own gold. Today there is no relationship at all between the amount of gold in the US and the amount of paper money in circulation. Thus, there is not currently a gold standard in the United States.

Fiat Money

While commodity money may be bulky to handle, an additional problem with commodity money is that its supply is not constant or predictable. During early American history, the colonists faced a shortage of money. They lacked the gold and silver they needed to make monetary exchanges and therefore often had to resort to barter. The gold and silver the colonists came into was quickly used to purchase goods from Great Britain. One solution to the scarcity of money is to create an artificial, or fiat money.

Fiat money has no intrinsic or inherent value. People have no use for it apart from it being used as money. The value of fiat money is derived from faith in the government that issues the money. On each United States dollar are the words, "this note is legal tender for all debts public and private." The US dollar is worth something not because you can eat it, smoke it, or stitch it into cloth, but because the United States government says it has worth. At a minimum, the federal government says that they will accept US dollars as payment for taxes, so people will be willing to trade goods and services for dollars because tax payment in said dollars keeps the government from taking one's other, more useful, assets.

The federal government has made it illegal not to accept payment in US dollars. It is illegal to demand to be paid in gold for an economic transaction offered to the public. Because the value of a fiat currency is derived from faith

that the issuing government will back up its claim as legal tender, the value of a currency is only as good as its issuing government. The value of US and Confederate dollars fluctuated daily with events of the US Civil War. Confederate dollars became worthless once the South lost. What good is a Confederate Dollar without a government to accept it as payment for taxes or enforce its use as currency? Confederate dollars ceased to have worth.

As a country increases the quantity of fiat money, more of their currency is needed to buy goods and services in the economy. When Germany printed currency following World War I to make reparations payments, the value of the German mark went from $1 = 4.2 marks in 1916 to $1 = 4.2 trillion marks by 1923. A more extreme example is the country of Zimbabwe, which printed money so quickly in 2008 and 2009, it had a 98% inflation rate *per day*. This means prices almost doubled each day. Once their currency notes reached $100 Trillion, they lopped off zeros, went back to $100 and kept printing. Apparently they thought that a quadrillion dollar bill would have been ridiculous. Zimbabwean currency also has became worthless, except as a souvenir of a country that experienced record-breaking inflation. The willingness to hold fiat money is dependent upon peoples' faith that the issuing country will not dramatically increase the supply of the currency.

The Money Supply

The money supply is the amount of money in circulation. If a government prints more fiat currency (or creates more money electronically), the money supply will go up. If it shreds (or electronically destroys) currency without replacing it, the money supply will go down. Other than physically changing the amount of money in circulation, the other way to increase the money supply is to make multiple people believe they have access to the same physical dollar. Two people each having a dollar in their pocket has the same effect as each believing they have a dollar in their checking account, even if only one dollar actually exists.

Before fiat money was commonly used in the US, gold was the commodity money of choice. Many people felt unsafe storing their gold on their person or in their house, as robbers and thieves would routinely steal gold. Goldsmiths, people who turned raw gold into jewelry and golden objects, dealt with large sums of gold. As a result, they commonly owned safes and hired watchmen to protect their gold stores. People often turned to goldsmiths to store their gold for them. In return, these depositors would receive certificates indicating that they could redeem their certificate at the goldsmith in return for their gold. As such, goldsmiths became bankers.

Goldsmiths quickly learned that it was unlikely that everyone who paid them to store their gold would demand that their gold be returned to them on the same day. Therefore, they could loan out some of the gold to other people and charge them interest. By not holding one hundred percent of deposits in their vault, goldsmiths initiated the **fractional reserve banking system**. This system allowed them to lend out part of their deposits in order to earn interest payments. Inadvertently, goldsmiths created money in the process.

The gold that goldsmiths loaned out circulated as money. So too did the certificates handed to gold depositors. Shopkeepers were willing to sell their wares for gold certificates because the certificates were redeemable for gold and easier to carry. Therefore, multiple people began believing they had access to the same gold, and the money supply increased. Over time, banks began to make so much money charging interest on loans that they often didn't charge depositors for watching their money. Some banks even paid depositors interest to attract deposits. Still, some people still pay banks to watch valuables in safe deposit boxes.

While there are many modern definitions of the money supply, the most common is **M1.** Deposits in checking accounts are counted as money because people have ready access to the money. When they look up their checking account balance online and see $1,000, they know they can purchase a good or service with a check if it costs less than that $1,000. Still, it is unlikely that their $1,000 is really in the bank. The bank loans out a majority of its deposits to earn interest, knowing that not everyone will want their money back at once. If everyone does want their money back at once, it is known as a **bank run**. If during a bank run a bank is unable to meet the demand for cash by depositors, it is legally forced to close. Popular representations of bank runs can be found in such movies as *Mary Poppins* and *It's a Wonderful Life*.

M1 = CASH + CHECKABLE DEPOSITS

Bank runs, and the subsequent banking panics they caused, plagued the US banking system until the **Federal Deposit Insurance Corporation (FDIC)** was created in 1935. The FDIC insures peoples' bank deposits up to $250,000. That is, even if a bank makes bad loans, if it is FDIC insured, depositors are guaranteed to get their money back. As a result, bank runs are no longer a problem.

Because banks can change the money supply simply by lending out money and creating the belief that multiple people have access to the same physical dollar, any attempt to manipulate the money supply must also include power over banks. The end of this chapter examines how monetary policy is conducted in the United States. But first, lets examine how a change in a bank's balance sheet can create or destroy money.

Table 12.1 represents a typical bank's balance sheet. **Assets** are things a bank owns. **Liabilities** are that which a bank owes. At any given time, a bank's assets must equal their liabilities. **Deposits** represent money placed in the bank by savers. This money is owed back to the depositors. **Stockholder equity** is the money a bank's owners' initially placed in the bank in order to gain a banking charter, along with any bank profit that has not been distributed to bank share holders. **Reserves** are money the bank has in its vault or on deposit with another bank. Loans are money lent to others that a bank has the legal right to reclaim. These loans include federal government bonds, since in order to gain a national charter, banks must loan some of their deposits to the federal government.

TABLE 12.1	THE FIRST BANK OF TUCKER		
Assets		**Liabilities**	
Reserves	$100	Deposits	$1,000
Loans	$900	Stock Holder Equity	$1,500
Bonds	$1,500		

Banks must hold on to a minimum amount of their deposits as reserves at all times. The reserve requirement is a function of the **required reserve ratio**, or the percentage of deposits that banks must legally hold in required reserves. If the required reserve ratio is .1, then banks must hold at least 10% of their deposits as **required reserves** at the close of every business day. Failure to do so will force a bank to close.

REQUIRED RESERVES = TOTAL DEPOSITS * REQUIRED RESERVE RATIO

Banks can choose to hold onto **excess reserves** in addition to their required reserves. In Table 12.1, assume that Tucker deposits $1,000 in The First Bank of Tucker. If the reserve requirement was .1, then the bank's required reserves are $100 (10% of deposits). Since the bank has $1,000 in actual deposits, they are holding $900 in excess reserves.

ACTUAL RESERVES − REQUIRED RESERVES = EXCESS RESERVES

Now assume that The First Bank of Tucker has decided to loan out all of its excess reserves. It does so by lending $900 to Colette. As it does so, now two people believe they have access to the same $900, both Colette, who has the money in her pocket, and Tucker who thinks his entire deposit is in his checking account.

If Colette deposits the money in her checking account before she spends it, then her bank's balance sheet will change as indicated in Table 12.2. Deposits will increase by $900. If the First Bank of Colette wants to make money and loan out 90% of its checkable deposits, then it will loan out $810 while keeping $90 in reserve.

TABLE 12.2

The First Bank of Colette		The First Bank of Oliver		The First Bank of Thatcher	
Assets	**Liabilities**	**Assets**	**Liabilities**	**Assets**	**Liabilities**
Reserves + $90	Deposits + $900	Reserves + $81	Deposits + $810	Reserves + $72.90	Deposits + $729
Loans + $810	Stock Holder	Loans + $729	Stock Holder	Loans + $656.10	Stock Holder
Bonds	Equity	Bonds	Equity		Equity

If that $810 loan is made to Oliver, then he will have $810 in his pocket that both Colette and Tucker believe is in their checking accounts. Now three people believe they have access to the same $810. If Oliver deposits the $810 into his bank and his bank again loans out 90% ($729) to Thatcher, then yet another person will believe they have access to the same money. As long as new borrowers place their loans in their checking accounts and hold no cash while no banks hold onto excess reserves, then the resulting increase in the money supply will equal the initial increase in excess reserves multiplied by the **money multiplier**.

$$\text{THE MONEY MULTIPLIER} = \frac{1}{\text{REQUIRED RESERVE RATIO}}$$

The money multiplier represents the infinite series of changing the money supply by ever smaller incremental amounts. The money multiplier is oversimplified, because some borrowers do hold onto cash, and banks are rarely fully loaned out. However, if banks did fully loan out their excess reserves and individuals kept their money deposited in their banking institutions, then

CHANGE IN MONEY SUPPLY = CHANGE IN EXCESS RESERVES*MONEY MULTIPLIER

In the above example, by loaning out $900, The First Bank of Tucker set in motion a chain of events that resulted in a an increase in the money supply of ($900 *(1/.1)) = $9,000.

While banks are not legally allowed to destroy legal tender, they can reduce the money supply by reducing the amount of money loaned out, thereby reducing the number of people who believe they have access to the same dollar. If The First Bank of Tucker decides that it cannot find good credits risks to loan money to, then it may decide to loan out less money. If it makes $200 in fewer loans, this sets in motion a contraction of the money supply that is greater than

$200. Again, the change in the money supply will equal the initial change in loans times the money multiplier. An initial decrease in loans by $200 would cause a decrease in the money supply by ($200 * (1/.1)) = $2,000. This assumes that the reserve requirement is .1 and that banks are fully loaned out with no one holding onto cash.

All of a bank's loans are not immediately callable. When a borrower signs a thirty year mortgage on their house, they cannot be forced to repay the entirety of their loan at a bank's whim. However, some businesses do engage in callable loans in order to get a reduction on the interest rate they are charged. A certain percentage of all banks' loans are callable so that they can react to changing market conditions. Table 12.3 illustrates the chain of events that occurs as The First Bank of Tucker calls in $200 in loans. Colette is forced to withdraw $200 from her checking account. This causes her bank to have to call in a loan from Oliver in the amount of $180. Oliver's Bank will then have to call in $162 worth of loans from Thatcher. Thatcher's bank will have to call in $145.80 in loans, and so forth and so on until the money supply falls by $2,000.

TABLE 12.3

The First Bank of Colette		The First Bank of Oliver		The First Bank of Thatcher	
Assets	**Liabilities**	**Assets**	**Liabilities**	**Assets**	**Liabilities**
Reserves: – $20	Deposits: – $200	Reserves: – $18	Deposits: – $180	Reserves: – $16.2	Deposits: – $162
Loans – $180	Stock Holder	Loans – $162	Stock Holder	Loans – $145.8	Stock Holder
Bonds	Equity	Bonds	Equity	Bonds	Equity

When the economy is growing and banks are making more loans, the money supply naturally increases. As banks make fewer loans due to a sluggish economy, the money supply naturally decreases. The causal relationship between the change in the money supply and the growth of the economy is a subject of debate between Milton Friedman and Friedrich Hayek. Friedman believes that a decrease in the money supply will cause a decrease in output, as fewer loans are made available to businesses. Hayek believes that the decrease in the money supply is caused by a lack of loans made by profit maximizing banks. There is no doubt that the money supply and short term Real GDP are correlated. The debate over monetary policy revolves around how changes in the money supply will affect short term economic growth and or long term economic growth. We now turn our attention to the Federal Reserve Bank of the United States.

The Federal Reserve

The words at the top of every US dollar proclaim "Federal Reserve Note." The **Federal Reserve**, the **central bank** of the United States, is one of the most powerful institutions in the world. Its decisions have ramifications on inflation, unemployment, interest rates, economic growth, the value of the US dollar, financial sector regulation and liquidity, the ability of the federal government to borrow money, and the stability of the global financial system. Unlike the United States Congress which has

535 representatives, policies of The Federal Reserve are controlled by a committee of twelve people in a single board room. In other words, The Federal Reserve has "Phenomenal cosmic powers! Itty bitty living space."[3]

The Federal Reserve is not the only significant central bank in the world. Nor is The Federal Reserve the oldest central bank in the world. In fact, it is not even the United States' first attempt at a central bank. It represents the US's third attempt at central banking. Perhaps the third time is the charm? We now turn our focus to the primary functions of a central bank, the history of central banking, the structure of The Federal Reserve, and the power The Federal Reserve has to manipulate the economy.

Functions of a Central Bank

Each developed country in the world has a central bank, which serves as a bank for its respective government. When governments collect tax revenues, they must store that money somewhere. As the government engages in government spending or makes transfer payments, it writes checks out of its account at the central bank. By virtue of acting as the sole bank for a central government, a central bank needs to be larger than other banks in the country in order to handle the volume of transactions needed to accommodate government activity.

A central bank also serves as a source of loanable funds for a central government. The Bank of England was formed in 1694 in part to help the English government pay for war. A central bank holds deposits of other banks, and therefore has reserves it can lend to the federal government. A central bank also typically can print money to loan to the government if need be. **Seigniorage** is revenue generated by a government from printing currency that is valued more than the cost of creating it. Rather than directly raising taxes, a government can print money for itself. However, doing so would certainly lead to inflation,

---

[3] The Genie. *Aladdin* (1992).

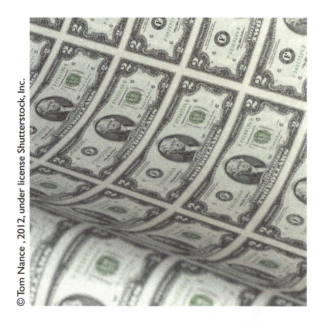

© Tom Nance , 2012, under license Shutterstock, Inc.

thereby lowering the value of the currency held by everyone else.

Most central banks, then, also control the money supply. The fact that the US dollar is merely a Federal Reserve note indicates that The Federal Reserve controls the money supply in the United States. While the Department of the Treasury's Bureau of Engraving and Printing physically prints US dollars, it is the Federal Reserve that determines the amount of money that gets created or destroyed. Paper currency routinely wears out. The average life expectancy of a US dollar is just eighteen months. By increasing or decreasing the money supply, central banks engage in **monetary policy**. Monetary policy can be used to influence inflation, unemployment, interest rates, the value of a currency, and the ability of a country to carry debt. China's Song Dynasty (960–1279) was the first central bank to use paper money to control monetary policy. Monetary policy will be examined in depth in the final section of this chapter.

In addition to serving as a bank to the central government and directing monetary policy, many central banks, including The Federal Reserve, serve as a bank for banks. That is, it serves as a place for banks to hold deposits, it provides banks services such as serving as a clearinghouse for checks, and it serves as a lender of last resort for banks during a banking crisis. Many central banks also serve as the principle regulator of private banks in the economy. Banks are regulated to ensure that depositor's assets are not embezzled or invested in risky activities. Of course, different central banks have different degrees and effectiveness of bank regulations. Some central banks, such as that in Canada, helped their country to prevent a housing bubble like that experienced in the United States by enforcing more stringent home loan practices. Alternatively, allowing banks to fail when they make "bad" loan choices would have the same effect for the long run prevention of market bubbles.

The History of Central Banking in the US

When America gained its independence from Great Britain, it faced the question of whether or not to create a central bank. American colonists had lived previously under the rule of the Bank of England. Dutch colonists had lived under The Netherlands's central bank, which was started in 1609. France created their central bank in 1800. Alexander Hamilton, America's first Secretary of the Treasury and a member of The Federalist Party, advocated for the creation of a central bank in the United States modeled after the Bank of England. The purpose of the bank was to help the US government to service its war debts and issue currency for the new country.

Congress charted **The First Bank of the United States** in 1791. It was given a twenty year charter, which had to come before Congress to be renewed at twenty year intervals. The bank was based in Philadelphia, the nation's first capitol, with eight branches in other major US cities. Eighty percent of the $10 million in bank stock was owned by private individuals while the other twenty percent was owned by the federal government. In this way, The First Bank of the United States was a private bank. It could loan out taxpayer money, even for commercial loans, charge interest, and make profit for the private owners of the bank. Its notes could be used to pay taxes to the federal government.

When the US house voted on the charter's renewal, it was voted down by one vote. The US Senate was evenly split as to whether or not to renew the charter. Vice President George Clinton cast the deciding vote to kill the bank. Critics of the bank feared foreign influence over US monetary policy. While three-fourths of the bank's privately held shares were owned by foreigners, foreigners could not directly elect bank directors. As tensions were rising between the US and Great Britain leading up to the War of 1812, the American public was suspicious of British control of the bank. Critics also complained that the bank consolidated too much power in the hands of Philadelphia bankers. While people connected to these bankers could get loans, capital was scarce in most of country. So, the United States went without a central bank from 1811 to 1816.

Without a central bank, state banks began issuing an ever larger number of bank notes. Yet, many banks began refusing to provide specie (gold or silver) for their notes. In order to create a national currency, keep state banks in check, and help to pay down war debt, Congress chartered the United States' second attempt at a central bank in 1816.

The Second Bank of the United States, like its predecessor, was given a twenty year renewable charter. Again it was based in Philadelphia, albeit with 29 offices in other major US cities. Once again, eighty percent of the banks' shares were privately owned. With $35 million in capital, The Second Bank of the United States was a very large bank. There was less than $70 million worth of currency in the entire US at the time.

President Andrew Jackson disliked The Second Bank of the United States. He saw it as a concentration of private power that was difficult for the government to control. He made ending the bank's charter the signature theme of his re-election campaign of 1832. President Jackson started pulling federal deposits out of the bank in 1832 and worked to ensure their charter was not renewed. As a result, President Jackson had to put federal revenues elsewhere. He hand-selected what became called his "pet banks" to hold onto the federal government's money. In this way the federal government had multiple bank accounts spread throughout the country. In theory, this was done to make capital more accessible to the rural population.

Consequently, the US had no central bank from 1836 until 1913. The era between 1837 and 1863 became known as the **free banking era**. States were allowed to charter their own banks, but no national banks existed. Therefore, no banks could operate across state lines, and each state was in charge of writing their own banking regulations. Each state bank issued their own bank notes, and these notes circulated as currency within a geographical range of their bank. The further the notes circulated, the more of a discount people demanded since they had to travel further to redeem the bank notes for gold or silver. By the 1960's there were over nine thousand bank notes circulating in the United States. Private banks, such as the Suffolk Bank in Boston, served as clearinghouses for state bank notes, a function once handled by The Second Bank of the United States.

In 1863, the federal government began chartering national banks. These banks could operate between states. In order to get a national bank charter, banks had to use a portion of their capital to purchase government debt. National banks only began to thrive once the federal government began to tax state bank notes. Once state banks abandoned bank notes in exchange for personal checks, their numbers began to rise. State and national banks coexisted in a dual banking system until the creation of The Federal Reserve in 1913.

During the time when there was no central bank in the US, there existed a very public political debate over monetary policy. In the absence of a central bank, the money supply changed frequently. As banks issued more or less notes and as silver flowed in from Mexico or gold from France, the money supply was anything but constant. Populist pressure to mint silver coins was brought by indebted farmers who wanted to prevent deflation and encourage inflation at the end of the nineteenth century. The book *The Wizard of Oz* is a parody of a prominent turn of the century Democratic politician named William Jennings Bryan (the cowardly lion) who wanted to expand the money supply through the printing of silver coins.

As there was no lender of last resort, bank panics, such as the ones in 1873, 1893, and 1907, put strain on the nation's banking system and on the economy. Fear that a bank could not meet the demand for specie by its depositors could cause a run on a bank. As people pulled their money all at once from a bank, few banks, even those engaged in solid lending practices, had the liquidity to give everyone their money back at once. Many sound banks were forced to close due to bank runs. Bank failures decreased people's willingness to hold bank notes or store their money in financial institutions. As a result, capital became scarcer for businesses to borrow for investment. The Banking Panic of 1907 increased interest in a central bank to serve as a lender of last resort. In 1913, Congress chartered the third attempt at a central bank, The Federal Reserve. This time the charter was not up for renewal, though any subsequent Congress could abolish it.

The Structure of the Federal Reserve

The first two attempts at a central bank in the US were criticized for placing too much power in the hands of unelected, private eastern establishment bankers with foreign ties. In an attempt to address this criticism, The Federal Reserve Act of 1913 established twelve central banks rather than one central bank. The United States was broken up into twelve districts with one Federal Reserve Bank serving as the central bank for each region. The locations of the twelve banks were chosen by Congress based upon population statistics of the early 1900's and political influence of senators from particular states. The twelve cities that contain a Federal Reserve Bank are: Atlanta, Boston, Chicago, Cleveland, Dallas, Kansas City, Minneapolis, New York, Philadelphia, Richmond, San Francisco, and St. Louis. Each Federal Reserve note (dollar) has written on it the name of the Federal Reserve Bank which issued it. Figure 12.1[4] illustrates the twelve districts. Each bank also has branches in other cities in their district.

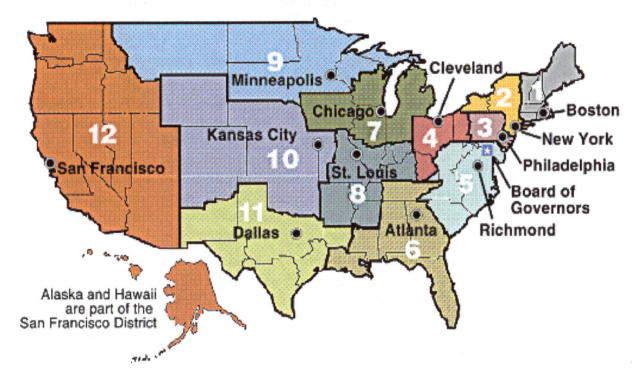

Figure 12.1

Each bank is a private corporation whose shares are owned by member banks in their district. Six of the nine bank directors are elected by the private shareholders of the bank, while the other three are government appointees. The president of each Federal Reserve Bank is elected by the board of directors of each bank and is a private sector employee. Each bank serves as a lender of last resort, a check clearinghouse, and a regulator for the member banks in its district. Unlike the first two central US banks, each Federal Reserve Bank's profits are capped at a 6% annual rate of return on their assets. Profit earned above these rates must be returned to the US Treasury.

Originally, each Federal Reserve Bank was charged with conducting monetary policy for their district. This resulted in banks engaging in different contradictory monetary policies during the Great Depression. The New York Fed

---

was busy increasing the money supply, as the Chicago Fed was busy letting it decrease. As a result, Congress formed the **Federal Open Market Committee** in 1935 to set a single monetary policy for the United States.

The Federal Open Market Committee has 12 members. It is made up of seven presidential appointees, known as the **Board of Governors,** and five Federal Reserve Bank presidents. Members of the Board of Governors are appointed by the US president and confirmed by the US Senate to serve fourteen year terms. They are located in Washington D.C. Their terms are staggered so that one position on the Board of Governors comes open every two years. Federal Reserve Governors are limited to serving a single term, though they can fill the end of someone else's unexpired term and then serve a full term of their own. It is often the case that Fed Governors leave before their term expires because they are able to make more money in the private sector.

While all twelve Federal Reserve presidents attend the Federal Open Market Committee meetings, only five get to vote on monetary policy. The President of the New York Federal Reserve always gets to vote, as it represents the district with the largest amount of bank transaction volume. The four other spots are rotated between the other eleven bank presidents. The presidents of the Chicago and Cleveland Federal Reserve Banks alternate voting membership every other year. The presidents of the other nine banks rotate voting members such that each gets to vote on monetary policy every third year.

The Federal Open Market Committee meets every six weeks to determine monetary policy, though emergency meetings can be called. The meetings are run by the Federal Reserve Chairperson. The Federal Reserve Chair is one of the Governors appointed by the President to a four year term. Current Federal Reserve Chair, Jerome Powell, was appointed by Donald Trump. He was preceded by Janet Yellen (President Obama), Ben Bernanke (President Bush), Alan Greenspan (Presidents Reagan, Bush, Clinton, and Bush), and Paul Volker (Presidents Carter and Reagan). The Federal Reserve Chair acts as the face of the Federal Reserve and testifies at least twice a year before Congress to answer questions about monetary policy. They have but one of twelve votes on the F.O.M.C. and can be outvoted. Nevertheless, monetary policy is commonly assumed to be directed by the Fed Chairperson. For instance, Fed Chairman Paul Volker was credited with bringing inflation under control in the early 1980's.

The 2008-2009 financial crisis brought heightened criticism to The Federal Reserve. The Federal Reserve made trillions of dollars of loans to US and foreign banks alike while working to keep the details of these loans from being made public.[5] Much like the public criticism that felled the first two central banks in the US, current criticism focuses on the secretive nature in which private banks are able to use public money to benefit private interests of their choosing.[6]

---

[5] "Foreign Banks Tapped Fed's Secret Lifeline Most at Crisis Peak" *Bloomberg,* April 1, 2011

[6] "Wall Street Aristocracy Got $1.2 Trillion from the Fed" *Bloomberg.* August 22, 2011.

Monetary Policy

As the previous section discusses, private banks trigger a change in the money supply as they increase or decrease the number of loans and consequently the amount of checkable deposits. Without outside intervention, a fractional reserve banking system can cause violent swings in the supply of money. Such swings in the money supply can affect inflation and output in an economy, both in the short run and the long run. In order to prevent large swings in the money supply, economists have advocated either eliminating fractional reserve banking or constructing a monetary authority charged with overseeing the money supply. This section explains what monetary policy is, describes how the Federal Reserve conducts it, outlines why many economists advocate for monetary policy, and discusses how the economy would operate in its absence.

An Economy Without a Central Bank

The United States operated between 1836 and 1913 without a central bank or monetary policy for the economy. During this time, banks engaged in fractional reserve banking, and deposits were not insured by the FDIC. While this period of time is associated with rapid economic growth and development in the US, it also contained banking panics (1837, 1857, 1873, 1884, 1890, 1893, and 1907[7]) and prolonged periods of deflation. Between 1867 and 1899 there were two years of inflation, ten years with neither inflation nor deflation, and twenty-two years of deflation.[8]

Fractional reserve banking without deposit insurance is prone to bank runs, increased failure rates of banks, and unnecessary stress on financial institutions. If fractional reserve banking was prohibited such that banks were restricted from loaning out funds in excess of those deposited, drastic swings in the money supply would be reduced dramatically. This would be the case even in the absence of a central bank. It would also work to restrict the access to credit when the economy is booming. As firms and consumers seek to borrow more for investment or consumption, they could only do so if others saved more money. This would help eliminate overconsumption and a cycle of booms and busts that result from the increases in credit access that occur with fractional banking.

The end of fractional reserve banking would also incentivize saving (through higher interest rates) and discourage credit driven consumption. The presence of private or governmentally supported bank insurance could eliminate bank runs. By ending fractional reserve banking and continuing bank insurance, the instability characteristic of the nineteenth century banking sectors could be reduced.

---

[7] Wicker, Elmus. "Banking Panics in the US: 1873–1933". EH.Net Encyclopedia, edited by Robert Whaples. September 4, 2001. URL http://eh.net/encyclopedia/article/wicker.banking.panics.us

[8] Samuel H. Williamson, "Seven Ways to Compute the Relative Value of a US Dollar Amount, 1774 to present," Measuring Worth, April 2011.

In a world with technological advance and economic growth, the natural state of the economy is one of mild gradual deflation. As products are produced more efficiently, the cost decreases are passed onto consumers. Recall the Quantity Theory of Money ($MV = PY$). If the money supply and the velocity of money are held constant over time, then an increase in RGDP (Y) will cause there to be the same amount of money chasing more goods. This will cause average prices to decline. Deflation works to discourage debt financed economic expansion. Those who take out loans must repay them with ever more expensive dollars. Advocates of a centrally controlled monetary policy often desire, and benefit from, inflation. Yet, as outlined earlier, inflation can be costly to the vast majority of society.

What Is Monetary Policy and Why Is It Often Advocated?

Monetary policy is the purposeful increase or decrease of the money supply by a central monetary authority. The Federal Reserve Act states that the purpose of monetary policy is to "promote effectively the goals of maximum employment, stable prices, and moderate long-term interest rates."[9] The goal of maximum employment was added to the act in 1977 and is referred to, in combination with the goal of stable prices, as the **dual mandate**. Before 1977, the Federal Reserve's stated mission was one of maintaining price stability. Unemployment and inflation are inversely correlated when aggregate demand changes. They are directly correlated when aggregate supply changes. Therefore, the only policies consistent with the dual mandate are policies that promote an expansion of aggregate supply.

Keynesian monetary policy works to alter aggregate demand in the economy. This means that members of the FOMC must use their own discretion as to whether they are currently more concerned about unemployment or inflation. Because inflation is generally caused by central bankers, they can affect inflation much easier than they can employment. Long run inflation is solely the result of a central monetary authority increasing the money supply at a faster rate than the economy is growing.

The strategy of Keynesian monetary policy, much like fiscal policy, is to manipulate aggregate demand to get it to return to full employment. If the economy is experiencing a recessionary gap, then the goal of monetary policy is to make investment cheaper by lowering interest rates in the economy. A monetary authority can do this by expanding the money supply. This is called **expansionary monetary policy**. As the money supply increases, loanable funds increase. This means that the price of taking out a loan (the interest rate) will fall. This lowers the opportunity cost of investment. Because investment is a component in aggregate demand, as investment increases, so, too, does aggregate demand. This process is illustrated in Figure 12.2.

---

[9] Federal Reserve Act Section 2A. Monetary Policy Objectives.

**EXPANSIONARY MONETARY POLICY: ↑ MONEY SUPPLY
=> ↑ LOANABLE FUNDS => ↓ INTEREST RATES
=> ↑ CONSUMPTION AND ↑ INVESTMENT => ↑ AD**

Figure 12.2   **EXPANSIONARY MONETARY POLICY USED IN A RECESSIONARY GAP**

If the economy is experiencing an inflationary gap, then the goal of monetary policy is to make investment more expensive by increasing interest rates in the economy. A monetary authority can do this by contracting the money supply. This is called **contractionary monetary policy**. As the money supply decreases, loanable funds decrease. This means that the price of taking out a loan (the interest rate) will increase. This increases the opportunity cost of investment. Because investment is a component in aggregate demand, as investment decreases, so, too, does aggregate demand. This process is illustrated in Figure 12.3.

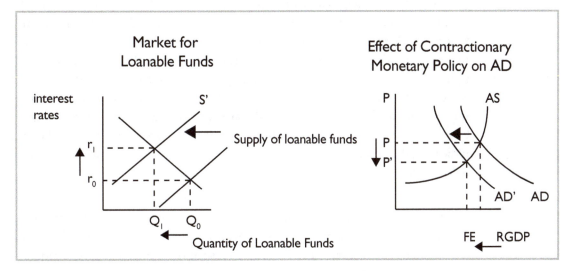

Figure 12.3   **CONTRACTIONARY MONETARY POLICY USED IN AN INFLATIONARY GAP**

CONTRACTIONARY MONETARY POLICY: ▼ MONEY SUPPLY => ▼ LOANABLE FUNDS => ▲ INTEREST RATES => ▼ CONSUMPTION AND ▼ INVESTMENT => ▼ AD

Rather than manipulating aggregate demand through changes in taxes or government spending, monetary policy's target is investment. Like fiscal policy, the use of monetary policy is complicated during stagflation. As policymakers face both high inflation and high unemployment, they can choose to do expansionary monetary policy (as they did in the 1970's) to tackle high unemployment, or do contractionary monetary policy (as they did in the early 1980's) to tackle high inflation. A central bank with the sole mandate of stable prices would use contractionary monetary policy during stagflation.

Increases in aggregate supply place downward pressure on prices. If the increase in long term economic growth is slow and steady, the economy will experience low, steady deflation. Between 1940 and 2010, the US experienced only two years of deflation and no years of price stability. Throughout the other fifty-nine years, the US experienced inflation. This inflationary trend is a product of the inflationary bias of the FOMC. In the summer of 2011, the FOMC debated setting an inflation target. Many members revealed that they wished to formally set an inflation target between 1.5% and 2%.[10] Over twenty central banks use inflation targeting to determine monetary policy. In so doing, central banks commit themselves to conducting both expansionary and contractionary monetary policy in such a way as to prevent both high inflation and deflation, potentially at the cost of ignoring the dual mandate of full employment.

How Does the Federal Reserve Conduct Monetary Policy?

When the FOMC meets to discuss monetary policy, their public announcement mainly consists of a specific interest rate targeted for the federal funds rate. **The federal funds rate** is the interest rate that banks charge each other to borrow money overnight. Each day, some banks desire to increase their reserves in order to meet their reserve requirement or increase their excess reserves. Other banks wish to loan out some of their excess reserves. While each loan is a separate transaction, the federal funds rate is the average overnight interest rate charged by private banks. When the FOMC sets an interest rate target, it is implicitly indicating that it will increase or decrease the money supply in order to have the federal funds rate hit their target.

The FOMC cannot set interest rates by decree. They must use indirect tools to influence the federal funds rate. As a result, the actual federal funds rate often varies from the Fed's target. The New York Federal Reserve reports the daily federal funds rate history.[11] The Federal Reserve also provides a history of federal

---

[10] "Fed Officials Said to Discuss Adopting Inflation Target backed by Bernanke" *Bloomberg* June 15, 2011. http://www.bloomberg.com/news/2011-06-15/fed-officials-said-to-discuss-adopting-explicit-inflation-target.html

[11] http://www.newyorkfed.org/markets/omo/dmm/fedfundsdata.cfm

TABLE 12.4	SAMPLE OF FEDERAL FUNDS RATE TARGETS 1990–2018				
July	1990	8.00%	June	2003	1.00%
September	1992	3.00%	June	2006	5.25%
February	1995	6.00%	December	2013	0–0.25%
May	2000	6.50%	December	2018	2.25–2.50%

fund targeted interest rates.[12] Table 12.4 provides the federal funds rate target from July 1990 through 2018. It reveals that US monetary policy in the twenty first century has focused on keeping interest rates at historical lows. Given that the federal funds rate target cannot be negative, the FOMC reduced the federal funds rate to its lowest possible level in 2008 and kept it there for years. Never before in US history had the federal funds rate been so low for so long.

3 Tools of Monetary Policy

The primary tool the FOMC employs to conduct monetary policy is engaging in open market operations. **Open market operations** refers to the purchase or sale of government securities. Recall that banks which belong to the Federal Reserve System must hold some of their assets in government bonds. When the Fed buys bonds, it gives cash to banks in exchange for government bonds. Since the banks had earned interest on their government bonds, the presumption is that they will then lend out this new cash from the sale of bonds in order to still earn interest. The Fed can't force banks to loan out the money, but if banks do increase loans, then the money multiplier can cause the money supply to increase by more than the initial purchase of government bonds. The money supply is increased both by increasing the amount of cash in circulation and through the issuance of more loans via the fractional reserve banking system.

© Zlatko Guzmic, 2012, under license Shutterstock, Inc.

When the Fed wishes to decrease the money supply, they can sell government bonds that they own to other banks. If these banks are fully loaned out, then they will have to call in loans in order to buy the government bonds at auction. This decrease in loans in conjunction with the fractional reserve banking system causes a contraction in the money supply greater than the initial sale

12 http://www.federalreserve.gov/monetarypolicy/openmarket.htm

of government bonds. Federal open market operations can only take place if a government has issued bonds. Governments with no debt cannot use a central bank to engage in open market transactions. In reality, the FOMC buys and sells government bonds on a daily basis in order to ensure that their federal funds target is being hit.

The FOMC could employ other, less commonly used, tools to manipulate the money supply. Serving as the lender of last resort, the Fed can loan money to member banks. The interest rate the Federal Reserve charges to these banks for overnight loans is called the **discount rate.** The discount rate serves as a penalty to banks for over-lending. If a bank cannot meet its reserve requirement they will need either to borrow money from another bank or from the Federal Reserve Bank. The higher the discount rate, the bigger the penalty banks must pay when borrowing money overnight. As the Federal Reserve raises the discount rate, banks may choose to hold onto more excess reserves in order to avoid having to pay the higher interest rate to the Fed. Therefore, an increase in the discount rate works to lower the money supply by discouraging loans. Likewise, a reduction in the discount rate encourages banks to lend more by reducing the penalty for over-lending, thereby causing the money supply to increase. However, because borrowing money from the Fed carries a stigma, few banks choose to borrow money directly from the Federal Reserve in normal times, making changes to the discount rate largely symbolic. In other words, this tool of altering the discount rate is relatively ineffective at changing the money supply because the Federal Reserve is a lender of last resort.

The Federal Reserve also controls the reserve requirement for member banks. By increasing the reserve requirement, the Fed could force banks to make fewer loans. This would cause the money supply to decrease. By lowering the required reserve ratio, the Fed would allow banks to offer more loans and increase the money supply. The Fed cannot force banks to make more loans, but they can encourage it by removing lending restrictions. In reality, the Fed rarely changes the reserve requirement because even small changes in the reserve requirement can cause large swings in the money supply. Thus, this tool is extremely powerful, but in reality is rarely used for monetary policy.

During the 2007–2008 financial crisis, the Fed created new tools to provide liquidity to the market and they began making loans to domestic and foreign commercial and investment banks. This unprecedented access to the Fed as the lender of the last resort raised many questions regarding the transparency of the Federal Reserve's business operations. These new tools include the term asset backed securities loan facility, the term deposit facility, and the decision to pay interest on bank reserves it holds. The former tool was created to provide liquidity to banks that make loans to consumers and businesses. The latter two tools were designed to help the Fed lower the money supply when the time came to curtail its monetary easing.

TABLE 12.5

Expansionary Monetary Policy Tools (Used to increase the money supply)	Contractionary Monetary Policy Tools (Used to decrease the money supply)
open market operations: buy bonds	open market operations: sell bonds
▼ discount rate	▲ discount rate
▼ required reserve ratio	▲ required reserve ratio

Monetary, or quantitative, easing is the process of a central bank creating large amounts of new money and using that money to purchase government bonds. Once the F.O.M.C. had reduced the federal funds rate as much as they could, they resorted to quantitative easing to increase the money supply. Fears that such an increase in the supply of money would translate into long run inflation caused the Fed to set up tools to ensure that they could withdraw money quickly from the economy if need be. By paying interest on reserves held by the Fed, the Fed could increase their interest rates. Doing so would discourage banks from loaning out funds, as they now could instead earn higher interest rates by depositing these funds with the fed.

As the fed intervenes in the loanable funds market to meet their federal funds target, they act as a price-fixer for interest rates. Whether an institution tries to set prices for corn, apartments, prescription drugs, or for money itself, problems arise. Chapter 13 examines this and other problems with the use of Keynesian fiscal and monetary policy.

Key Terms

Assets

Bank run

Barter economy

Board of Governors

Central bank

Commodity money

Contractionary monetary policy

Deposits

Discount rate

Double coincidence of wants

Dual mandate

Excess reserves

Expansionary monetary policy

Federal Deposit Insurance Corporation (FDIC)

Federal funds rate

Federal Open Market Committee

Federal Reserve

Fiat money

Fractional reserve banking system

Free banking era

Gresham's Law

Liabilities

M1

Medium of exchange

Monetary economy

Monetary policy

Money multiplier

Open market operations

Quantitative easing

Required reserve ratio

Required reserves

Reserves

Seigniorage

Stockholder equity

Store of value

The First Bank of the United States

The Second Bank of the United States

Unit of account

Questions for Review

1. What are the three functions of money?

2. What characteristics would an ideal commodity money have?

3. How does fiat money differ from commodity money?

4. Is the US dollar fiat or commodity money? Why?

5. What is M1? Why is the money supply more than currency in circulation?

6. What is a bank run? Why did they come to an end in the US?

7. How can private banks create or destroy money?

8. Why do barter economies find it difficult to grow?

9. How does changing the supply of commodity differ from changing the supply of fiat money? Under which type of money is hyper-inflation more likely? Why?

10. Use the following T account to answer:

The Bank of Kent			
Assets		**Liabilities**	
Reserves	$ 1,500	Deposits	$6,000
Loans	$4,500	Stock Holder Equity	$1,000
Bonds	$1,000		

   a. if the reserve requirement is .2, how many required reserves does the Bank of Kent have?

   b. by how much will the money supply increase if the Bank of Kent loans out all of its excess reserves (assuming no one holds cash and banks are fully loaned out)?

11. What are the major functions of a central bank?

12. How does the structure of The Federal Reserve differ from the first two central banks in the US?

13. Who determines monetary policy in the US? What is the structure of the Federal Open Market Committee?

14. What is the primary monetary policy tool used by the Federal Reserve?

   a. What happens to loans, the money supply, interest rates, and investment if the Fed buys bonds?

   b. What happens to loans, the money supply, interest rates, and investment if the Fed sells bonds?

15. Why has deflation virtually disappeared in the US? Is this a natural phenomenon? Why or why not?

16. Suppose that we have an Aggregate demand excess of $100 million due to an inflationary gap.

   a. Suppose the Fed wishes to change the rrr. In what direction would this need to be change?

   b. What would be the appropriate monetary policy (buy or sell bonds) if the Fed wishes to use open market operations?

   c. If the fed instead wished to change the discount rate, would these need to be increased or lowered to treat the AD shortfall?

   d. Which of the above options is most powerful? Which is most likely to be used by the federal reserve?

   e. What would be the adjustment process if neither fiscal nor monetary policy is implemented?

   f. Graph the economy starting out in an inflationary gap. Now graph monetary policy being used (Hint: which curve shifts back to fe?). What happens to price levels, unemployment, and RGDP as a result?

17. Suppose that we have an Aggregate demand shortfall of $100 million due to stagflation, and the federal reserve chooses to target lower unemployment.

   a. What three policies (and which direction of a change) could the fed consider using?

   b. What would be the adjustment process if neither fiscal nor monetary policy is implemented?

   c. Graph the economy starting out in stagflation. Now graph monetary policy being used to lower unemployment. What happens to price levels, unemployment, and RGDP as a result?

18. I decide to hold $1,000 less in currency and deposit that money into my checking account. If the required reserve ratio is currently 10%, how much ADDITIONAL money will be created from my deposit of $1,000? What is the money multiplier?

19. Suppose in the above example, the RRR were instead 25%. In that case, how much additional money would have been created?

20. What happens to interest rates, level of unemployment, RGDP, and price level if

    a. the Fed buys bonds

    b. the Fed raises the required reserve ratio

21. How might monetary policy increase the size of business cycles?

22. Why might an economy face a liquidity trap?

23. Why does contractionary monetary policy often work more quickly than expansionary monetary policy?

24. How are interest rate targets similar to price floors and price ceilings?

25. Why might independent central banks have better records of low inflation than politically controlled central banks?

26. How can fiscal policy constrain a central bank's use of monetary policy?

27. In what ways does central bank transparency help/hinder their role in the economy?

Chapter 13

Problems with Fiscal and Monetary Policy

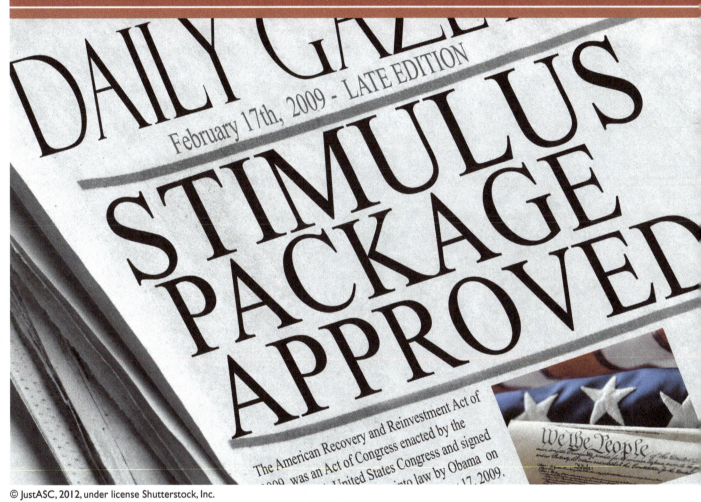

© JustASC, 2012, under license Shutterstock, Inc.

Fiscal and monetary policy do not happen in a vacuum. Advocates of fiscal or monetary policy assume either that individual actors are not engaging in actions that maximize their own self-interest (broadly defined); that in so pursuing their own self-interest they have made systematically incorrect errors that can corrected by government intervention; or, that if everyone correctly pursues their own self-interest, they reach an equilibrium that is inferior to one that could be reached by government directed collective action.

It is one thing to identify that people make forecasting mistakes and another to suggest that the government is able to predict and correct these mistakes in a systematic fashion. Put another way, real market failures should not be compared to theoretical government intervention by an all knowing, all caring government.

They should be compared to actual government actions complete with their own mistakes. If markets were perfect, we would not need governments. If governments were perfect, we would not need markets. The relevant question, then, is one of relative competence.

Policymakers also make decisions that are politically popular or unpopular. Given that the politician typically is seeking near term reelection, they have an added incentive to make decisions favored by the public. Unfortunately, the vast majority of the public doesn't understand unintended consequences of policies intending to benefit the short term. For this reason, they may push their representatives to make decisions that make them better off in the short term, even if it diminishes prospects for the long term. Groups of constituents may also encourage policymakers to make decisions based on their own self interests rather than the interests of the whole.

The Capital Building in Washington DC

Rent Seeking

Government spending is done through a political process rather than an economic one. No group of government economists sits and objectively determines the best spending projects with cost-benefit analysis. Government spending disproportionately goes to states and districts of Congressional committee chairpersons and ranking members of each political party's establishment. The receipt of government largess is often more a function of Congressional tenure than of economy boosting potential. For example, between 1995 and 2006, Senator Byrd (D-WV) brought over $1 billion in federal funds in projects to his state such as the Robert C Byrd Bridge, the Robert C Byrd Courthouse, the Robert C. Byrd statue, and the Robert C. Byrd Biotechnology Center.[1] As a ranking member of the Senate Appropriations Committee, Senator Byrd was able to direct spending to where it benefitted his interests the most.

Congressional interest in bringing government projects to their own districts is obvious. If politicians can be seen as delivering free goods, they are often viewed as successful. After all, the taxes for the spending are spread throughout the country. This concentration of benefits and dispersion of costs allows special interest groups to also hold sway over what and how much spending occurs. In his parting address as president,[2] President Eisenhower warned of the undue influence of the industrial military complex. Certain companies benefit from war and defense spending, so they will lobby leaders to spend more on the military.

---

[1] "West Virginia Loves Byrd and Pork" ABC News, Imaeyen Ibanga, September 17, 2008. http://abcnews.go.com/Politics/5050/story?id=5830414&page=1

[2] "Farewell Address to the Country" January 17, 1961.

Lobbying and donating to political campaigns are both done in order to influence government spending and the tax code. **Rent seeking** is engaging in costly nonproductive actions in search of profit. Money spent on lobbying and on political campaigns represents a cost to society in forgone output, as scarce resources are directed away from production and shifted towards motivating the system to reallocate resources. The more of a society's resources they devote to taking things from each other, the less they devote to making new wealth. While taking from party A to give something to party B may improve party B's life, it comes at the cost of party A and the economy.

© bearsky23/Shutterstock.com

Special interest groups compete with one another to gain political favor. They hire lobbyists, pay for Congressional junkets, and try to "educate" politicians about the issues. The expenses associated with lawmaker influence erode the benefit of a government perk or contract. A firm who pays a lobbyist to get a tax break will be willing to pay up to the amount they get in the tax break in order to earn the tax break.

Lobbying expenses and political donations are all required by law to be reported. As a result, individuals can see which politicians get money from special interest groups and how much. Open Secrets.org[3] provides a database for such information. For instance, the National Association of Realtors contributed over $39 million to federal politicians between 1990 and 2010. In 2010 alone, they spent an additional $17.5 million employing lobbyists. It is not uncommon to find politicians who are in charge of writing regulations for an industry to be the primary beneficiaries of political donations by firms in that industry. Senator Barney Frank (D-MA), who co-sponsored the Dodd-Frank Financial Reform Bill, received $945,771 in political donations between 1989 and 2010 from the securities and investment industry.[4] The other co-sponsor, Senator Chris Dodd (D-CT), during the same time period received $6.4 million in political donations from the securities and investment industry.[5]

By diverting resources from the production of goods and services, rent seeking slows economic growth. There are two methods that could be used to limit rent seeking. The first is to more strictly limit the amount of money people and groups can give to the political process or to restrict the access of lobbyists to politicians. However, the United States Supreme Court in Citizens United v. Federal Election Commission (2010) restricted the government's ability to limit the inflow of money into politics. They ruled that such limits on political funding violate the first amendment.

The second and more productive way to lower rent seeking is to decrease the number of special favors that the government can hand out. Simplification of

---

[3] http://www.opensecrets.org/

[4] http://www.opensecrets.org/politicians/summary.php?cid=N00000275&cycle=Career

[5] http://www.opensecrets.org/politicians/summary.php?cid=N00000581&cycle=Career

the tax code, the banning of earmarks, and elimination of entitlement programs would dramatically decrease rent seeking activity. People will not pay for favors if favors cannot be granted. However, as long as the government engages in taxing and spending policies, firms and individuals can gain by tilting the rules of the game in their favor.

Time Lags

There is no easy button to push to dispense the appropriate amount and makeup of fiscal or monetary policy. There are three specific time lags. The **recognition lag** is the time it takes to realize that a problem exists in the economy. Since macroeconomic data takes weeks or months to accrue, the economy may be experiencing a recessionary gap, inflationary gap, or stagflation before policy makers are aware that a problem exists.

While Bill Clinton campaigned for president in 1992 by advocating a fiscal stimulus package, by the time he took office in January 1993, the economy had already self-corrected. Real GDP increased by 4.3% in the fourth quarter of 1992. Because it was no longer needed, Congress, though controlled by members of the president's own party, voted against a fiscal stimulus package.

Once a problem is recognized, there exists a **policy lag**, which is the time it takes to enact a policy designed to fix the problem. When both houses of Congress are controlled by members of the same party as the president, the policy lag may be short. Politicians whose ideologies and constituents are similar are more likely to come to agreement on fiscal policy than politicians of differing ideologies or differing political parties. When differing parties control differing houses, then policy lags can be quite long.

Once a change in taxes or spending makes it out of committee in the House of Representatives, it has to be passed by the House, taken up by a committee in the Senate, and passed verbatim by the Senate. If the Senate bill differs from the House bill, the bill must go to a conference committee made up of selected House and Senate members, returned to both the House and Senate for an up or down on the same language, and sent to the President's desk to be signed into law. At that point, the President could veto the legislation, which would require a two-thirds majority in the House and Senate to override. The policy lag tends to be shorter for monetary policy. Rather than engage in partisan brinksmanship, members of the F.O.M.C. meet over a two-day period every six weeks to discuss and vote on monetary policy. Typically the policy lag is much shorter for monetary policy than it is for fiscal policy.

Once a policy is enacted, it will then face an **implementation lag**, which is the time it takes for a policy to have an impact on the economy. If an increase in government spending involves the building of a new highway, for instance, once the government decides to build the road, it must acquire right of way for the road, have firms bid on the design and construction of the road and award the bids. Then the building of the road is not instantaneous. Payments to construction workers happen over time as they provide their labor to the construction project. Each successive round of spending, as hypothesized by the spending multiplier, takes even more time to materialize. The call for "shovel ready" projects in the 2009 stimulus bill was a recognition of the fiscal challenges faced by the implementation lag. Even then, only one-third of the $787 fiscal stimulus had been spent in the year following its passage.[6]

The implementation lag, however, can be longer for monetary policy than fiscal policy. While the F.O.M.C. immediately begins targeting a new federal funds rate following a meeting, the effects of this policy are often not felt in the economy for eight months or longer. Firms cannot instantaneously invest in new plants and equipment. Once interest rates are changed, boards of directors of firms have to take time to decide how the new interest rate environment affects their short and long term investment strategy. If the change causes them to invest more or less, this too takes time to implement. To build a new factory, a firm will have to hire an architect and a construction manager, send construction specs out for bids, and physically engage in construction. The act of paying construction workers and paying for supplies could only have a multiplicative effect on the economy over time, as construction workers buy more as a result of their employment. If the construction workers believe that today's investment comes at the cost of future investment, they might spend and save according to what they believe is their permanent income. Thus, once policymakers decide the course of action, the monetary policy takes longer to affect the economy than does fiscal policy.

Together the recognition, policy, and implementation lags make it even harder to fine tune fiscal policy to bring the economy back to full employment. The economy doesn't stand still while it waits for policy makers. It is constantly changing. Conducting fiscal or monetary policy is like trying to hit a moving target through one's rear view mirror with the knowledge that pulling the trigger will release a bullet sometime tomorrow. Conducting contractionary fiscal or monetary policy is even more complicated by that fact that the general public will not always welcome such actions.

Biases of Fiscal Policymakers

While the special interest groups of today can funnel money into the political process, the next generation of citizens cannot. As a result there is an asymmetry in the lobbying process in favor of short-term targeted economic gains and against broad long-term economic growth. The buildup in state and federal debt is the direct result of discretionary fiscal policy's unwillingness to address the long-term consequences of today's policies. Governments around the world

6 "Bulk of Stimulus Spending Yet to Come" *Wall Street Journal* February 17, 2010.
http://online.wsj.com/article/SB10001424052748704804204575069772167897834.html

have systematically fallen victim to unsustainable fiscal policies precisely because politicians are more concerned with their short-term reelection than the long-term health of the economy. While many countries have tried to institute an independent central bank void of short-term political pressures, the same cannot be said of attempts to insulate fiscal policy from those same short-term special interests. As a result, global government debt levels continue to rise.

Since individuals are still in charge of most of their economic decisions, governments are incapable of knowing what is in everyone's best interest. A one size fits all government policy to affect 320 million people of varying preference and time horizons is unlikely to serve as a **Pareto improvement**. A Pareto improvement is an improvement that makes at least one person better off without making anyone worse off.

In the absence of Pareto improvements, governments are left picking winners and losers for their policies. Members of the US House of Representatives serve two-year terms and are therefore perpetually concerned with winning an upcoming election. Because their interest in getting re-elected near term may differ from the long term interests of the economy, politicians often engage in actions that benefit today's constituents (theirs) over tomorrow's (someone else's).

Fiscal policy has become increasingly concerned with income redistribution over time. The extension of unemployment benefits to 99 weeks (up from 26) during the Great Recession had nothing to do with providing public goods or building infrastructure. It was merely an income transfer from current workers to those currently unemployed or from one special interest group to another. Increased social safety net spending and income transfers made up the majority of the 2009 stimulus package.[7] Subsidizing unemployment does not stimulate production. Quite the opposite, increased transfer payments decrease the marginal incentive for people to work, and so production falls.

Furthermore, aggregate data can lead policy makers to misread economic signals that are being sent to and from individuals in an economy. If aggregate data suggest that new home construction has fallen nationwide, for instance, a national policy maker may push for tax changes to encourage new home construction. However, such policies may lead to a surplus of homes in places where individuals cannot find work. Attempts to create public policy from aggregate data often result in policies with negative unintended consequences. These consequences arise from policy makers' unwillingness or inability to discover the microeconomic foundations of individual decision-making. In addition, fiscal or monetary policies do not offer instantaneous relief. Indeed, there are several time lags that slow the impact of such policies.

Given that politicians, rather than economists, are in charge of fiscal policy, politicians' ideologies play a role in the selection of the approved policy. Ideology is a doctrine or belief that guides an individual, an institution or a social

---

[7] "Getting to $787 Billion" *Wall Street Journal* February 17, 2009. http://online.wsj.com/public/resources/documents/STIMULUS_FINAL_0217.html

movement. Stereotypically, conservative politicians in America tend to favor tax cuts during recessionary gaps and reductions in government spending during inflationary gaps. Conversely, liberal politicians in America tend to favor government spending increases during recessionary gaps and tax increases during inflationary gaps. Since the 1930s, most politicians of both above ideologies have favored the use of Keynesian fiscal policy. President Nixon famously announced "We are all Keynesians now." Libertarian politicians in the United States prefer to let the economy self-correct. Their focus on taxing and spending policies tend to favor long run structural reforms to lower the amount of government influence and interference in the economy.

Biases of Central Bankers

The FOMC, like all other economic actors, faces tradeoffs. Its dual mandate to fight both unemployment and inflation can cause conflict between the two goals. The members of the FOMC decide which problem they wish to attempt to solve. When a single President, due to resignations by members of the Board of Governors, ends up selecting the majority of Fed governors, monetary policy becomes less independent of the political system. Historically, politically influenced central banks have tended to prefer pro-inflationary policy in an attempt to lower short term unemployment. Inflation targets ensure that a central bank will increase the money supply to prevent natural deflation, but hopefully not so much as to be above their target inflation range. The bias of central bankers to avoid deflation often means that inflation targeters are more likely to miss their inflation targets to the upside rather than the downside. The result has been high inflation rates in many developing and under developed countries in South America, Central America, and Africa. Independent central banks have fared much better at maintaining price stability over time.

Independent central banks can be restrained in their use of monetary policy by politicians who issue public debt denominated in their fiat currency. Excessive amounts of public debt can slow down economic growth as a greater number of productive resources are tasked with making interest payments on existing debt. This economic slowdown would likely reduce employment and/or cause deflation. A central bank which is concerned with unemployment and deflation may feel the need to engage in expansionary monetary policy. Expansionary monetary policy works to also decrease the burden of the existing debt by causing an uptick in prices. Thus, the central bank of a heavily indebted country has an incentive to **monetize** the debt by expanding the money supply, thereby making public debt easier to repay.

Bank independency and transparency to the public can be opposing goals. Serving as a lender of last resort allows The Fed to provide liquidity to banks when they are in need of it. However, public disclosure that a bank needs help from the Fed can reduce the confidence the public has in the bank and thereby exacerbate its liquidity problem. On the other hand, the lack of transparency can allow The Fed to make loans to foreign banks despite opposition by the general public. Bank independence helps to keep politicians from inflating the currency, but also allows the bank to secretly engage in actions that politicians, and the public, may find objectionable without being held accountable for their actions. If the actions of a central bank become known to be at odds with the will of the public, a central bank may be forced to submit to political, and often inflation causing, oversight. In the end, central bank independence is a double-edged sword.

Because countries have different fiat currencies, their relative values are affected by the respective monetary and fiscal policies adopted by central banks and governments. Central banks may make their choice of monetary policy based upon a target exchange rate with other currencies. By so doing, central banks can face tradeoffs between domestic monetary policy and stated international monetary policy goals. As long as the US remained on an international gold standard, domestic monetary policy was constrained.

Inefficiencies Created When Targeting Price Stability

If monetary policy is accompanied by laws and regulations that prohibit changes in prices, economic chaos ensues. During the Great Depression, The Federal Reserve allowed the money supply to fall 33%. Such a dramatic and unexpected decrease in the money supply, accompanied by unions and minimum wage laws preventing nominal wage reductions, worked to slow the market's ability to quickly lower prices in response to the lower money supply. Artificially higher wages worked to keep the unemployment rate abnormally high for years.

Prices, even average ones, are signals. Should price stability be a legitimate goal for the Federal Reserve (or any central bank)? Consider this: should the government be in charge of creating price stability for automobiles? When the price of autos increase, should the government increase the supply of autos? When the price of autos falls, should the government buy up automobiles on the open market? After all, the government (i.e. taxpayers) owns a car company (GM) and could manipulate the equilibrium price of automobiles.

Why might the government like price stability in cars? You could argue that producers could better plan production if they knew in advance what their cars would sell for. Consumers might be able to better plan their car purchases as well. So what is the problem? By masking real prices, the government covers up information from market actors. Prices aren't arbitrary or meaningless. The price of every product is a little piece of information telling the market how to efficiently allocate resources.

Does the government know better than the market how to allocate resources in the car (or for that matter any other) industry? History tells us that centrally planned economies fail in part because planners lack information. Hayek's "man on the street"[8] is the guy with information, and he uses this information he sees from prices to make decisions to maximize his own self-interest. An ill-informed central planner setting prices will cause surpluses and shortages of products they misprice.

If the government cannot set the prices of individual goods any better than markets can, then why should we believe that a central bank can set average prices better than the market? There is an aggregation problem here. Setting one price is bad; setting two prices is bad; setting three prices is bad; setting all prices is good?

What could possibly go wrong if a central bank used activist monetary policy to achieve price stability at the cost of ignoring market signals? During the 1990's and into the 2000's, many developing economies increased their ability to export cheap consumer goods to the US and other industrialized markets. All things being equal, this placed deflationary pressure on consumer prices in the US. In absence of activist monetary policy, the US would have experienced deflation as measured by the consumer price index. What the US experienced instead was a Federal Reserve increasing the money supply to prevent deflation.

There are three major questions to examine from this experience. First, what signals were deflation trying to give the US economy? Second, what signs did the Fed give the economy instead? Third, what were the consequences of getting our signals crossed?

Pretend that the US money supply was held constant while cheap consumer goods flooded the US market. The US would have the same amount of money chasing more goods, i.e. deflation in the short term and a reduction in real GDP in the long term. In the short term, deflation causes consumers to cut back on consumption. Why buy today if stuff is cheaper tomorrow? Thus, the market's natural response to an increased trade deficit would have been an increase in domestic savings and a reduction in said trade deficit.

Being overly scared of deflation, the Fed increased the money supply, caused interest rates to plummet, and caused a positive rate of inflation. These low interest rates led to an unprecedented increase in consumer, business, and government borrowing. This borrowing increased the current demand for foreign goods, driving up the US trade deficit, and destabilizing the international economic system.

When the proper response was to increase savings rates, the Fed put up street signs that said borrow as fast as you can. In so doing, the Federal Reserve aided the creation of asset bubbles and sowed the seeds of the global financial meltdown. Had the Fed allowed the market to naturally read the deflationary signs, the financial crisis could have potentially been avoided.

The moral of the story is that average prices are just as much signals to the macroeconomy as individual prices are to the microeconomy. To think that the government or a central bank has more information than the economy on what the "right" prices are is a stretch. Capitalism works best when prices are set by markets, not central planners.

Some argue that a more effective and less biased way to conduct monetary policy is to follow a set of rules rather than using discretion. John Taylor developed the **Taylor Rule** as an attempt to direct monetary policy based upon changes in inflation rates.[9]

Interest rate targets require the central bank to know what the "appropriate" interest rate is. Price fixing requires an almost infinite amount of information, unless policy makers are content to cause shortages or surpluses in the loanable funds market. Monetarists, on the other hand, prefer to focus on money supply targets, as they believe it is primarily a change in the money supply that causes the slowdowns or expansions in the economy. Over time, by increasing the money supply by a fixed amount each year, they aim to control long run inflation which could occur from interest rate targeting. Strict adherence to a monetarist rule could cause swings in inflation, deflation, and interest rates in the short run.

Liquidity Trap and Increased Volatility

Monetary policy which seeks to centrally direct investment through time often works to increase the volatility of investment from one year to the next, thereby creating business cycles. Monetary policy makers often attempt to fight fire (business cycles) with fire (creating investment cycles). Their hope is that they can correctly predict the appropriate amount of aggregate investment that is needed in the economy at any given time. Still, individual investment decisions are only profitable if their marginal benefits exceed their marginal costs. If the Fed thinks that the economy should have more aggregate investment and this causes condo builders to build condos they will not be able to sell in Las Vegas, then the resources used in that investment are not only wasted, they become unavailable for other productive uses in the economy.

9 Taylor, John. (1993). "Discretion versus Policy rules in Practice." *Carnegie-Rochester Conference Series on Public Policy, 39.* 195-214

It turns out that the FOMC can decrease the money supply much faster than it can increase it. The FOMC, by selling government bonds, can readily get banks to call in loans and lower the money supply. Paul Volker, Fed Chairman in the early 1980's, was able to quickly reduce the money supply and subsequent inflation. However, the Fed cannot force banks to make more new loans, regardless of how many bonds it buys. Banks may choose to increase their excess reserves in response to expansionary monetary policy, which would slow the expansion of the money supply and likewise the expansion of the economy. The Federal Reserve's inability to get banks to issue new loans during an economic slowdown has often been described as the Fed "pushing on a string." John Maynard Keynes referred to monetary policy's inability to force banks to make more loans during a recession as a **liquidity trap**.

Because the Federal Reserve cannot force private banks to make more loans, it becomes difficult for the FOMC to correctly estimate the amount of monetary policy they wish to engage in. The FOMC has drawn criticism for causing business cycles by rapidly changing the federal funds rate, or keeping it artificially low or artificially high for long periods of time. The inflationary gap of 2000 quickly became the recession of 2001, as the FOMC raised the federal funds rate up to 6.5% in May of 2000. To counteract the recession, the FOMC lowered the federal funds rate down to 1.75% by December, 2001 and kept it below 2% until November 2004. The housing asset bubble ensued.

Rational Expectations

A typical assumption made by economists is that people act in their own enlightened self-interest. That is, most people do not purposefully or consciously make decisions to bring harm to themselves or their loved ones. Decisions made at a specific time and place impact decision makers over both time and space. A decision to purchase a home today impacts tomorrow's house payments. A decision to invest today impacts tomorrow's bottom line. **Rational expectations theory**, introduced by John Muth,[10] states that individuals make decisions based upon their expectation of the future. Consumption, saving, and investment all happen based upon current knowledge and expectations about the future.

Robert Lucas used rational expectation theory to suggest that government intervention in the economy is ineffective.[11] Any action taken openly by the government will cause decision makers to change their future expectations and

---

[10] "Rational Expectations and the Theory of Price Movements" *Econometrica* 29, no. 6 (1961): 315-335.

[11] *Models of Business Cycles.* Oxford: Basil Blackwell, 1987.

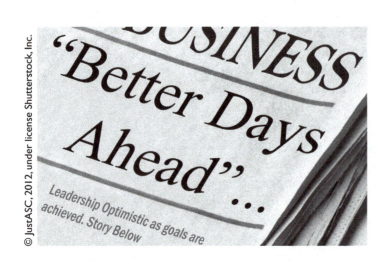

act accordingly. If the government borrows money to engage in stimulus spending, then individuals and firms know that the resulting higher debt will require higher taxes in the future. If consumers make their current consumption decisions based on their expectation of lifetime wealth (as proposed by Milton Friedman)[12], then increased government spending would not increase current consumption. In fact, current consumption would decrease so that consumers had enough money to meet their future tax burden. Likewise, businesses would curtail investment in the face of higher future taxes. The resulting decrease in consumption and investment would offset the increase in government spending.

According to the idea of **Ricardian equivalence** put forth by Robert Barro, an increase in debt has the same effect on the economy as an increase in current taxes to pay for increases in government spending. His analysis uses rational expectation theory to show that increased debt to rational observers means higher future taxes. Rather than a large public debt being seen as a sign of an intergenerational transfer of wealth, Barro assumes that private individuals will respond to higher public debt levels with an increase in their private savings for transfer to future generations. Rational expectations theory and Ricardian equivalence fall apart if people do not care about the economic fate of future generations. Likewise, if current generations assume that future generations will be wealthier than current generations, people looking to smooth consumption over generations may deliberately choose to burden future generations with debt in order to increase current consumption.

Ricardian equivalence also negates the spending multiplier. The application of a spending multiplier to a change in government spending assumes that people believe that new spending is free. The spending multiplier promises a free lunch by boosting spending beyond the original government expenditure. In reality, there is no such thing as a free lunch. Tradeoffs exist in a world of scarce resources. Increased government spending crowds out private investment and private consumption.

Under rational expectation theory, the only way that an increase in government spending would cause an increase in GDP is if that government spending provided for the optimal production of a **public good** that, due to the **free-rider problem** would not have occurred without collective government action. A pure public good has two qualities. The benefits of the good are non-excludable and

[12] 1957. *A Theory of the Consumption Function.* Princeton: Princeton University Press.

consumption of the good is non-rival. A good is **non-excludable** if there is no way to prevent those who do not pay for the good (free-riders) from consuming it. A good is **non-rival** if one person's consumption of the good or service does not prevent or limit another person's consumption. Left to the private market, pure public goods may be under invested in because people can still benefit from them without having to help pay for them. National defense, police, and the court system are often viewed as public goods. The problem with using only public good provision in order to enact fiscal policy is that the optimal amount of public goods provided is not always countercyclical.

Monetary policy, by its nature, attempts to fool people into believing that they are richer or poorer than they actually are. If wealth were actually created by printing fiat currency, Zimbabwe would be the richest country in the world and post WWI Germany would have had a thriving economy. The simple fact is that if a central bank increases the money supply, there are more dollars chasing the same number of goods. There are more dollars, but each dollar is worth less. Likewise, if a government burns fiat currency, no wealth is lost. It is just redistributed from the owners of the burned currency to the owners of the remaining fiat currency.

Just as in the case of fiscal policy, monetary policy works by making people feel more or less wealthy, even if real wealth hasn't changed. If the Federal Reserve can increase the money supply without people realizing it, then people may temporarily feel wealthier. However, as more dollars start chasing after the same number of goods, sellers will increase their prices accordingly. Recall the Quantity Theory of Money, $MV=PY$. An unexpected increase in the money supply could temporarily boost RGDP, but will not increase long run RGDP. Instead, it will cause inflation. If people know that the Fed is increasing the money supply, they will rationally adapt their behavior by quickly raising prices. This will reduce any possible impact of monetary policy on short run RGDP. Since monetary policy goals, (such as the targeted federal funds rate or amount of quantitative easing), are publicly announced, effective monetary policy relies on the hope that people are not paying attention to or do not understand the long run consequences of these actions.

The lower interest rates accompanying expansionary monetary policy are meant to encourage current investment. While current investment is cheaper that it would otherwise be, it comes at a cost. Low interest rates discourage savings. Long-term economic growth is a function of a country's ability to save and invest. While foreign savings can be turned into domestic investment, the profits of that investment will flow abroad to the savers. Since investment in new capital is a long run consideration due to the long lifespan of new capital, the decision to move investment forward often comes at the cost of less investment later.

Individuals can and do react to changes in government policies over time. An increase in the marginal tax rate might net positive revenues in the short run, but negative revenues in the long run, as people adjust their labor and entrepreneurial activities accordingly. As long as consumers and firms are allowed to pursue their own interests, the **law of unintended consequences** will remain in effect. This law suggests that for any government policy enacted, the number of unintended consequences will exceed the intended consequences. Failure to account for the unintended consequences that result from policy actions causes policy makers to overestimate the value of their policies. The true cost of government policies includes the costs of both the intended and unintended consequences.

In summary, fiscal policy and monetary policy are, at best, imperfect tools used by imperfect people. They are not tools that can actually bring about Pareto improvements. As such, policymakers pick winners and losers. Fiscal and monetary policies are related. We now turn out attention in Chapter 14 to understand exchange rates so that in Chapter 15 we can explore public policy in a global economy.

Key Terms

Free-rider problem

Implementation lag

Law of unintended consequences

Liquidity trap

Monetize

Non-excludable

Non-rival

Pareto improvement

Policy lag

Public good

Rational expectations theory

Recognition lag

Rent seeking

Ricardian equivalence

Taylor Rule

Questions for Review

1. Is the government all-knowing? Why or why not? How does their knowledge, or lack there-of, impact the use of fiscal policy?

2. Is the government all caring? Why or why not? Who is the government supposed to care for? Why? Who do politicians generally show care for? Why?

3. Is the government all powerful? Why or why not? Where are the government's powers best directed?

4. Which industries gave the most to the 2016 presidential candidates? (Use www.opensecrets.org to answer this question).

5. Which industries gave the most to the 2016 congressional candidates? (Use www.opensecrets.org to answer this question).

6. Where do the politicians who support your district/state get money from? (Use www.opensecrets.org to answer this question).

7. What can be done to decrease the amount of rent-seeking in society? Why is it important?

8. What are the three lags and how do they affect the use of public policy?

<table>
<tr><td>

Chapter
14

</td><td>

Exchange Rates

</td></tr>
</table>

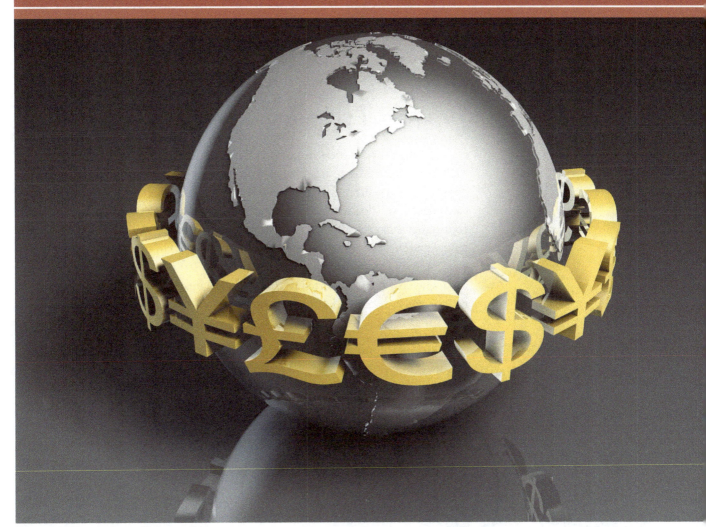

© kentoh, 2012, under license Shutterstock, Inc.

How Much Is a Dollar Worth?

That may seem like a silly question. A dollar is worth a $1, four quarters, ten dimes, twenty nickels, or one hundred pennies. However, the purchasing power of the dollar can, and does, change over time. Products once sold at the dime store are now sold at Dollar Tree or Five Below. The previous chapters have examined how monetary and fiscal policy can increase or decrease the purchasing power of a dollar relative to domestically produced goods and services.

Still, the US economy is an integrated part of the world economy. Consumers buy products made in other countries. They also vacation abroad. Producers sell products abroad that are produced domestically and purchase inputs from abroad to be used in domestic production. While the dollar serves as a medium of exchange, a store of value, and unit of account for goods and services within the US, other countries have different currencies that do the same for goods and services exchanged in their countries. Just as the value of the dollar can change relative to domestic goods and services, it can also change relative to the value of other currencies. This chapter examines international exchange with multiple currencies and the European Union's transition to a common currency.

Floating Exchange Rates

An **exchange rate** is the price of one currency in terms of another. A **floating exchange rate** is where the value of a currency is determined by the supply and demand of that currency in the international money market. Most major world currencies have floating exchange rates. The value of the US dollar fluctuates continuously against other major world currencies such as the yen (Japan's currency) and the euro (The European Union's currency) as people voluntarily trade one currency for another. For example, if I buy a Volvo produced in Germany, then when my car is imported to the United States, the importer exchanges dollars for euros. Table 14.1 illustrates how the value of the US dollar has changed over time.

Currency appreciation occurs when one currency can buy more of another currency. Between March 5, 2000 and March 5, 2019, the US dollar appreciated vs. the Argentine peso, the Japanese yen, and the Mexican peso. A dollar could buy almost forty times as many Argentine pesos in 2019 than it could in 2000. That means that goods and services denominated in Argentine pesos became cheaper for American consumers and producers to purchase (if Argentine prices stayed constant—which they did not). It also meant that goods and services denominated in US dollars became more expensive for people in Argentina to buy. If domestic prices in Argentina rose forty times faster than US prices between 2000 and 2019, then a single US dollar could buy forty times as many Argentine pesos, but no greater number of Argentine goods and services.

In a floating exchange rate regime, as one currency appreciates against another, the second currency is said to depreciate against the first. **Currency depreciation** occurs when one currency can buy less of another currency. Between March 5, 2000 and March 5, 2019, the US dollar depreciated vs. the euro, the

TABLE 14.1	CURRENCY UNITS PER $[1]		
Country	March 5, 2019	March 5, 2010	March 5, 2000
Japan	111.99	90.32	107.6
China	6.71	6.83	8.15
Britain	.76	.66	.63
Canada	1.34	1.03	1.45
Euro area	.89	.73	1.04
Switzerland	1.00	1.08	1.66
Australia	1.41	1.1	1.65
Argentina	39.83	3.86	1.00
Saudi Arabia	3.75	3.75	3.75
Mexico	19.28	12.66	9.3

Canadian dollar, The Australian dollar, the Chinese renminbi, the British pound, and the Swiss franc. As a result, it became more expensive for people holding US dollars to buy goods and services from these countries, while it became cheaper for people holding these currencies to buy goods and services denominated in US dollars (assuming no change in relative prices).

The value of the US dollar vs. the Saudi riyal was the same on March 5, 2019 as it was on March 5, 2000. The Saudi riyal did not fluctuate in value relative to the US dollar during this time, because it does not have a floating exchange rate. The Australian dollar is on a floating exchange rate and its value changed constantly between these two dates. At its highest point in this time period, the US dollar bought 2.06 Australian dollars. At its weakest point the US dollar only bought .91 Australian dollars.

Which is better, a stronger or a weaker dollar? It depends. A strong dollar is good for people who are net importers or people who own assets denominated in US dollars. If a person holds the majority of their wealth in their home in the US, or in the US stock and bond markets, then a stronger dollar increases their wealth relative to people in other countries around the world. People who store all of their wealth in a single currency open themselves up to major swings in their wealth over time. Businesses that purchase inputs from abroad face a decreased cost of production when the value of the dollar increases.

A weak dollar is good for people who are net exporters or who store their wealth in assets denominated in foreign currency. US farmers and manufactures looking to sell their products abroad find that foreign consumers can more readily afford their products when the value of the US declines. This, in turn, drives

[1] Source: *The Economist* http://www.economist.com/node/21525955

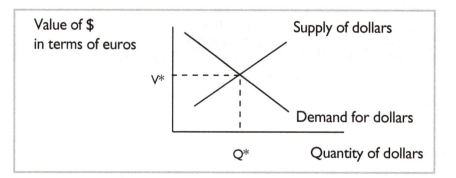

Figure 14.1
**DOLLAR TO EURO
EXCHANGE
MARKET**

up the demand for their products. People who store their wealth in foreign currencies can, when the value of the dollar falls, convert their savings back into dollars. By so doing, they can purchase more dollar denominated assets than they could do when the value of the dollar was stronger.

The relative supply and demand of the dollar to the international money market determines the value of a dollar at any given time. In reality, the dollar can appreciate vs. one currency while it depreciates vs. another on the very same day. This is because there is not just one currency market but many. The US dollar is traded against each floating currency in its own market, just as each foreign currency is traded one on one with all other floating currencies. Figure 14.1 illustrates the demand and supply of the US dollar vs. the euro. The value of the US dollar fluctuates against the euro based on changes in the supply or demand of the US dollar in the dollar/euro market.

Things That Cause the Demand for the US Dollar to Change

Why would people suddenly, or over time, want to buy more or fewer US dollars on the international market? To begin with, there could be a change in the demand for US goods and services. If foreigners decide that they want to buy more American made jeans or American grown wheat, they first must buy US dollars and then they can use dollars to purchase those products. Farmer Ron growing wheat in Minnesota is not looking to get paid in euros for his wheat. He wants to get paid in US dollars. An increase in the demand for American made goods and services by individuals and businesses abroad, including foreigners vacationing in the US, will cause the demand for the US dollar to increase, thereby causing the dollar to appreciate. A decrease in the demand for US made goods and services by individuals or businesses abroad will cause the demand for the US dollar to decrease, thereby causing the dollar to depreciate.

A change in demand for US financial assets, such as stocks listed on the New York Stock Exchange (NYSE) or US government bonds, will also cause the demand for the US dollars to change. If people who hold foreign currencies decide that they wish to buy a share of General Electric (GE) on the NYSE, they must first buy US dollars and then purchase stock with those dollars. US stocks are not sold in exchange for euros. Likewise, when the US government

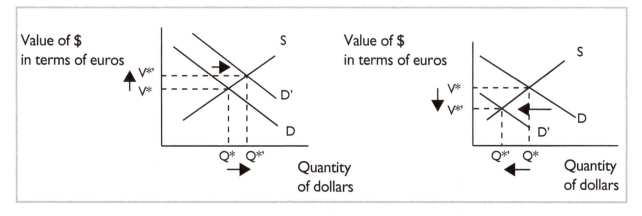

Figure 14.2   DOLLAR – EURO EXCHANGE MARKET WITH INCREASED AND DECREASED DEMAND FOR THE DOLLAR[2]

runs a budget deficit and needs to borrow money, they need to borrow dollars, not euros. Therefore, foreigners and Americans who buy US government bonds must use US dollars. This increases the demand for US dollars.

A change in the demand for US hard assets will cause the demand for the US dollar to change. If foreign persons or businesses start buying US real estate, they must pay for their purchases in US dollars. The same thing is true for any dollar denominated asset such as a business or patent. An increase in the demand for Florida vacation homes by foreigners will cause the demand for the dollar to increase, thereby causing the dollar to appreciate. A decrease in the demand by foreigners for US real estate will lower the demand for the dollar, thereby causing the dollar to depreciate.

Finally, people in other countries may prefer to use US dollars to engage in economic transactions between themselves. They may choose to do so if they lack confidence that their domestic currency will serve as a good store of value. Citizens of countries with high inflation rates in their domestic currency may seek to engage in transactions using a more stable currency. Two-thirds of all US dollars in circulation are in circulation outside of the United States. This is a

[2] D represents the initial demand for US dollars, while D' represents the new demand for US dollars. S represents the supply of US dollars to the dollar/euro exchange market.

sign that many people around the world value the US dollar as a medium of exchange, a store of value, and a unit of account. When confidence in foreign currencies fall, the demand for the US dollar increases. This causes the US dollar to appreciate. When foreign currencies gain people's confidence, then the demand for US dollars falls, causing the dollar to depreciate. Taken together, these four factors work to change the demand for the dollar on a daily basis. If the demand for dollars increases, then the value of the $ will appreciate. If the demand for dollars decrease, then the value of the $ will depreciate.

Things That Cause the Supply of the US Dollar to Change

In order to buy more of one currency, one must, by definition, supply more of another currency to the market. Therefore, the things that cause the demand for a currency to change also affect the supply of a foreign currency. Conversely, the things that cause the supply of the US dollar to change are the same as those that cause the demand for foreign currencies to change.

The supply of dollars to the international money markets will change as there are changes in the demand for foreign goods and services, the demand for foreign financial assets, the demand for foreign hard assets, and the confidence in the US dollar relative to other currencies. If people who hold dollars want to travel abroad more, consume more imports, invest more in foreign stock markets, bond markets, or real estate, or if they lose confidence in the US dollar as a safe store of wealth, they will supply more dollars to the international money market. This will cause the value of dollar to depreciate.

If however, US consumers decrease their desire to travel abroad, begin to consume fewer imports, want to invest less in foreign stock markets, bond markets, or real estate, or gain confidence in the US dollar as safe store of wealth, they will supply fewer dollars to the international money market. This will cause the value of the dollar to appreciate. Figure 14.3 illustrates an increase and a decrease in the supply of dollars to the dollar/euro exchange market. If the supply of dollars increases, then the value of the $ will depreciate. If the supply of dollars decrease, then the value of the $ will appreciate.

CHART 14.1	FACTORS WHICH ALTER THE DEMAND FOR AND SUPPLY OF US$
1.	Changes in the demand for exports/imports
2.	Changes in the demand for US financial assets and financial assets abroad
3.	Changes in the demand for US hard assets and hard assets abroad
4.	Changes in confidence in the US$ and foreign curencies as a store of value

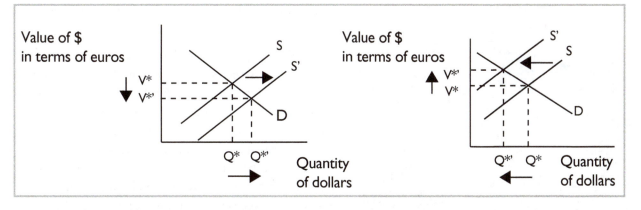

Figure 14.3   **DOLLAR – EURO EXCHANGE MARKET WITH INCREASED AND DECREASED SUPPLY OF THE DOLLAR**[3]

Changes to the Value of a Currency Over Time

A number of actions could cause the supply or demand for a currency to change on a daily basis. In the short run, the single largest factor affecting exchange rates are relative interest rate changes between two countries' currencies. Billions of dollars worth of currencies change hands on any given day. People who hold on to cash would like to earn a positive rate of return on their cash holdings. In this way, money tends to flow to currencies with higher interest rates. If country A is paying a 3% interest rate on savings accounts while country B is paying only 1%, then, all things being equal, savers will prefer to save their cash in a currency that yields them a higher interest rate. In this case it would be country A. If the central bankers in one country lower interest rates, then the value of their currency is expected to fall. That currency serves as a poorer store of wealth with a lower interest rate. Conversely, if the central bank raises interest rates, then the value of their currency is expected to increase. The decline in the value of the US dollar observed in Table 14.1 was in part due to the divergence of interest rates in the US and the rest of the world. The Federal Reserve sought to keep interest rates near zero during this time. Still, countries such as Argentina and Japan pursued rapid monetary expansion during this time, which lowered their currency's value relative to the US dollar.

In the short run, a high valued currency is a sign of higher than average interest rates within a country.

In the medium run (one to three years), changes in the relative demand for domestic vs. foreign goods and services tend to explain changes in exchange rates. As Japanese automobile sales to the US have increased over time, the value of the Japanese yen has also increased. As Americans demanded more foreign products, they supplied more dollars to the international market and demanded more yen. This caused the value of the dollar to fall vs. the yen. In the medium

---

[3] S represents the initial supply of US dollars, while S' represents the new supply of US dollars. D represents the demand of US dollars to the dollar/euro exchange market.

© nameless, 2012, under license Shutterstock, Inc.

run, a strong dollar is a sign of strong demand for US goods and services.

In the long run (more than three years), purchasing power parity is the best explanation of which direction an exchange rate is headed. **Purchasing power parity** is the concept that all goods should cost the same in every country in the long run. If a good costs more in one country than the next, and goods are allowed to move between countries at low cost with little to no trade barriers, then arbitrage will reduce or eliminate price differences. **Arbitrage** is taking advantage of price differences for profit. If a product is cheaper in Canada than in the US, then people will buy the good in Canada, transport it to the US, and resell it for a profit. This action will continue until the price of all products is the same (minus transportation or tariff costs). As this international trade happens, currencies are supplied and demanded until the exchange rate is such that prices in each country are the same.

The Economist magazine for years has published an index of purchasing power parity known as the Big Mac Index.[4] It looks at the price of McDonald's Big Macs in different countries and tries to predict whether currencies are currently undervalued or overvalued relative to the US dollar. If a currency is undervalued, it means that the currency is expected to appreciate over time vs. the dollar. If a currency is overvalued it means that the currency is expected to depreciate over time vs. the dollar.

If the current price of a Big Mac is $3 in the US and 2 euros in france, while the current exchange rate is $1 = .75 euros, then the Big Mac Index can be used to determine whether the euro is under or overvalued vs. the dollar. If instead of spending $3 on the Big Mac in the US, one were to convert the currency to euros, one could purchase 2.25 euros (3 times the exchange rate). That is more than enough euros to buy a Big Mac in france—only two were needed. In this case the US dollar is buying too many euros. The US dollar, in this case, should depreciate vs. the euro over time until the exchange rate falls to $1 = .67 euros—the relative price difference between the Big Mac in each country.

Once GDP per capita is controlled for, the Big Mac Index suggests that the US dollar was undervalued throughout the early 2000's vs. virtually every other major world currency. It was most undervalued against the Brazilian real. Brazil's head of their central bank went on the record to complain that the Federal Reserve's policy of quantitative easing and low interest rates was artificially causing the dollar to depreciate vs. the real.[5]

---

[4] Source: *The Economist.* http://www.economist.com/node/21524811

[5] 'Brazil's Meirelles: Fed's Latest move on G20 agenda' Thursday November 4, 2010. Reuters. http://www.reuters.com/article/2010/11/05/brazil-meirelles-idUSN0424672620101105

Fixed Exchange Rates

It is not random that in Table 14.1 the US dollar traded for exactly 3.75 Saudi riyals every year. Rather than letting the international currency market determine the value of a currency, a government could set by government edict the exchange rate between their currency and another. A **fixed exchange rate** is where a government artificially determines the value of its currency in terms of another currency. Until 1971, the US dollar was part of an international fixed exchange rate regime where each country's currency was pegged to the price of gold. The advantages of a fixed exchange rate include certainty, a reduction in transaction costs between trading partners, and the ability of a government to manipulate their currency to favor either importers or exporters.

Countries that engage in a lot of trade with each other may wish to provide a greater level of certainty to traders regarding the relative value of their country's currency. If a country has a long history of inflation, then a fixed exchange rate can work to insure international investors that their investment in a country will be protected from inflation by guaranteeing the exchange rate. Saudi Arabia sells a lot of oil to the US and fixes the value of its currency to the US dollar. Countries like El Salvador and Panama, rather than peg their currency to the dollar, have adopted the US dollar itself as their national currency.

The downside of having a fixed exchange rate is that an artificial price of a currency is arbitrarily set by a government. This price, by definition, will vary from the true market price of the currency. Anytime a government sets prices, one of two outcomes will occur: a surplus or a shortage. Governments, then, are forced to take further action to solve the surplus or shortage of their currency in the international market. These actions may prove to be so painful to an economy that the costs imposed by them exceed the benefits of a fixed exchange rate. The following are two examples of countries that used to have a fixed exchange rate with the US dollar but no longer do.

In the early 1990's, the Mexican government supported a fixed exchange rate between the US dollar and the Mexican peso at four pesos per dollar. Extensive Mexican budget deficits and the resulting increase in the money supply to finance them caused the Mexican peso to be overvalued relative to the US dollar. The artificially high value of the peso meant that more people wanted to trade their pesos for US dollars (which the market said were worth more) than wanted to trade dollars for pesos. The only way the Mexican government could support the artificially high value of their peso was to intervene in the international money market by buying up pesos with US dollars.

Governments who wish to support a fixed exchange rate must hold onto **foreign reserves** in order to use them when they need to increase the value of their currency. A foreign reserve is foreign currency held by a government. As the Mexican government used up their US dollar reserves to prop up the Mexican peso, the Mexican government ran out of US dollars. As they could

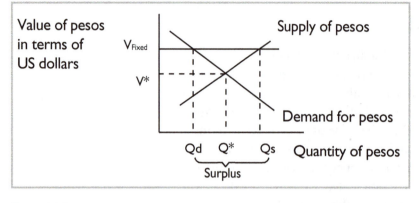

Figure 14.4
**PESO–DOLLAR
EXCHANGE
MARKET**

Figure 14.5
**PESO–DOLLAR
EXCHANGE
MARKET**

not print more US dollars, Mexico was forced to devalue the peso. A currency **devaluation** occurs when a country officially lowers the value of its currency. While the Mexican government devalued their peso by 15%, it was still overvalued. As investors feared further currency devaluation, everyone holding pesos became nervous about their use as a store of wealth. As people began to dump their pesos on the international market, the market price of pesos fell even further, making the peso even more overvalued vs. the US dollar.

Panic ensued as investors began pulling their wealth out of assets denominated in Mexican pesos. The Mexican government asked the United States to intervene. The US used US dollars to buy Mexican pesos so as to prop up the value of the peso. This action where the US government loaned dollars to the Mexican government in 1994 was known as The Mexican Bailout. By preventing the Mexican economy from imploding, the bailout helped to stabilize the Mexican economy. Mexico was able to repay their loans to the US with interest ahead of schedule. Since then, the Mexican peso has been allowed to float to prevent currency devaluation from causing further panic in the Mexican economy.

Between the mid 1990's and 2005, China had a fixed exchange rate of 8.28 yuan per US dollar. Over time, the Chinese currency became undervalued relative to the US dollar, as more people wanted to buy the yuan at that price than wanted to sell it. The Chinese government purposefully undervalued their currency in order to make their exports to the US look even cheaper. A country with an undervalued currency can either raise the official value of their currency (engage in **revaluation**) or keep it undervalued indefinitely.

A country can keep its currency undervalued by printing more currency and selling it on the world market to overcome the shortage of their currency. The downside is that expansion of the domestic money supply leads to inflation. Unlike an overvalued currency which must be devalued when a country runs out of foreign reserves, a country can keep a currency undervalued as long as it is willing to endure the ensuing domestic inflation. Yielding to pressure from Chinese citizens suffering from inflation, the Chinese government eventually somewhat abandoned their fixed exchange rate with the US dollar. While the Chinese

now claim that their currency floats with respect to the dollar, ample evidence exists to indicate that they still intervene in the currency markets to keep their currency from appreciating more strongly relative to the US dollar. While most countries have now abandoned fixed exchange rates with the US dollar, a few countries such as Saudi Arabia still actively maintain one.

Figure 14.6
YUAN–DOLLAR EXCHANGE MARKET

The **International Monetary Fund (IMF)** is an international institution with 187 member countries (including the US) that was set up following World War II to help facilitate the fixed exchange rate regime of the day. Even

as fixed exchange rate regimes have largely disappeared, the IMF still works to "foster global monetary cooperation, secure financial stability, facilitate international trade, promote high employment and sustainable economic growth, and reduce poverty around the world."[6]

Figure 14.7
YUAN–DOLLAR EXCHANGE MARKET ILLUSTRATION OF CHINA INCREASING THE SUPPLY OF THE YUAN IN ORDER TO OVERCOME THE SHORTAGE RESULTING FROM DEVALUATION

The IMF tries to serve these functions by monitoring the economic health of its members, while offering loans and technical assistance to countries in need. In this way the IMF was designed to be the lender of last resort for countries around the world. Loans from the IMF come with financial strings attached. Like any other creditor, they impose restrictions on debtor government finances to ensure that said countries are able to pay back their loans.

The European Union

Rather than adopt fixed exchange rates, countries could adopt a common currency. Because many European countries are geographically small in size, their economies rely heavily on international trade. The presence of constantly changing exchange rates throughout europe (including fixed exchange rates that were

---

[6] http://www.imf.org/external/about.htm

devalued or revalued over time) led to decreased certainty for businesses looking to engage in long-term international contracts. Consumers and businesses engaging in trade within europe faced large currency exchange expenses, as they had to obtain a new currency with each new country they did business with. These large transaction costs led to the formation of the European Union.

The **European Union** is an example of a supranational organization that employs fiscal, regulatory, and monetary rules on its member countries. The goal of the European Union was to create a single European market to lower transaction costs for people living in, travelling in, and doing business with member European countries. On its way to create a single market, the European Union has worked to harmonize regulations on goods and services to make them move more easily across borders. The European Union is a free trade zone that enables goods and services to cross international barriers without the threat of tariffs or quotas. The European Union negotiates trade agreements as a whole, because once a good or service enters a member country, it is allowed to move freely through the union.

In the single European market, capital and labor are free to move from one member country to another. If Spain experiences high levels of unemployment while Germany experiences low unemployment, then laborers are legally allowed to immigrate to Germany from Spain. French students can go to school in Italy. Greek chefs can go to work in Belgium. Polish plumbers can work in the UK. Much as a US worker can move between states, European workers are free to move among member countries. At the time of publication, the UK was negotiating terms of Brexit, in which they would leave the European Union. So by the time you read this book, they may no longer be included in the list of EU countries.

Initially, in order to enter the European Union, member countries could choose to retain their domestic currency. Denmark, Sweden, and the UK chose to do so. The other original members agreed to abandon their domestic currencies in exchange for the euro and thereby enter the European Monetary Union. Members of the European Monetary Union ceded monetary policy authority to the **European Central Bank** in Frankfort, Germany. The European Central Bank issues the **euro**. All new members to the European Union are required to adopt the euro as their official currency and enter the European Monetary Union over time.

A single currency requires a single monetary policy. The benefits of a single currency in the **European Monetary Union** include reducing the costs of engaging in trade and travel between countries. It also prevents member countries from inflating their own currencies. This gives European investors increased confidence in the long-term benefit of the euro as a store of value.

TABLE 14.2	THE EUROPEAN UNION	
"Orignal" 15 members of the EU		
Austria	Germany	Netherlands
Belgium	Greece	Portugal
Denmark*10	Ireland	Spain
Finland	Italy	Sweden*
France	Luxemburg	UK*
"New" members of the EU		
Bulgaria**11	Lithuania	Croatia**
Malta	Czech Republic**	Poland**
Cyprus	Romania**	Estonia
Slovakia	Hungary**	Slovenia
Latvia		
Candidate countries to the EU as of 2019		
Albania	Montenegro	North Macedonia
Turkey	Serbia	

* Indicates that the country did not adopt the euro as its official currency
** Indicates that the country has not yet adopted the euro as its official currency

The biggest drawback of monetary union is that countries lose sovereignty over their own monetary policy. If a country believes it is their best interest to have expansionary or contractionary monetary policy that differs from that of the European Central Bank, they are not allowed to engage in it. If the Spanish economy is struggling while the German economy is thriving, should monetary policy be made to keep inflation low in Germany or unemployment low in Spain?

Loss of monetary control prevents heavily indebted countries, such as Greece, from printing their way out of debt. Therefore a supranational currency serves as a check to keep countries from getting too far in debt. This imposed fiscal discipline helps long-term economic growth. Still, if domestic leaders ignore fiscal discipline, as they did in Greece, Italy, Portugal, and Spain, then they quickly discover that they have brought fiscal calamity to their country with no easy options for debt repayment. Lack of fiscal discipline among some euro countries has placed stress on both the European and global economies. The Greek debt crisis has served as a good example of why monetary union needs to be accompanied by fiscal rules restricting debt accumulation among members. Originally in order to join the EU, countries were supposed to keep budget deficits lower than 3% of their GDP.

Should North America have a common currency? Canada and Mexico are two of the United States' top five trading partners. Trade and travel would be easier between countries if they shared a common currency. International monetary union would also serve to help check the excessive buildup of North American governmental debt. Still, a monetary union will only work well if it is accompanied by fiscal discipline by its member countries and the free movement of goods, services, capital, and labor between member countries. Political opposition to the loss of US sovereignty over its fiscal or monetary policy has prevented much discussion of a North American monetary union, although Canadian economists once proposed the Amero as a possible North American currency. The US government does not mind a single currency as long as all monetary authority rests in the hands of the United States. In other words, if Canada and Mexico wish to adopt the US dollar as their official currency, the United States will not stop them. We now turn our attention in the final chapter to examine how the global aspects of the economy, along with exchange rates, affect the effectiveness of fiscal and monetary policies.

Key Terms

Arbitrage

Currency appreciation

Currency depreciation

Devaluation

Euro

European Central Bank

European Monetary Union

European Union

Exchange rate

Fixed exchange rate

Floating exchange rate

Foreign reserve

International Monetary Fund (IMF)

Purchasing power parity

Revaluation

Questions for Review

1. How does a floating exchange rate differ from a fixed exchange rate?

2. What are the pros and cons of a fixed exchange rate?

3. What causes the value of the dollar to change the most in the short run? Why?

4. What causes the value of the dollar to change the most in the medium run? Why?

5. What causes the value of the dollar to change the most in the long run? Why?

6. In what way is the IMF like a central bank for the world?

7. Why did the US dollar depreciate so much between 2010 and 2011?

8. If the current exchange rate is $1 = 100 yen and the price of a Big Mac is $4 in the US and 300 yen in Japan, what will happen to the value of the US dollar vs. the Japanese yen, over time? Why?

9. What happens to the value of a currency if fewer people around the globe want to buy goods and services produced within a country?

10. Who benefits from a strong dollar? Who benefits from a weak dollar? Why?

11. What are the benefits/costs of a monetary union such as the European Union?

12. Assume the price of a pound of Mexican chocolate is 4 pesos.

   a. If the exchange rate is 2 pesos per US dollar, then what is the price of the chocolate in dollars?

   b. If the value of the dollar changes to 1.5 pesos per dollar, then has the dollar appreciated or depreciated? What has happened to the value of the peso?

   c. What is the new price of the chocolate in dollars?

Public Policy in a Global Economy

© iloab, 2012, under license Shutterstock, Inc.

Domestic fiscal and monetary policies do not take place in a vacuum. This chapter explores the impact of the international sector and floating exchange rates on the use of fiscal and monetary policy. It also examines how foreign fiscal and monetary policy choices can influence the domestic economy. Three graphs that have been introduced earlier in this text: the AD/AS graph, the domestic money market, and the international money market, are used in this chapter to illustrate the interconnectedness of public policies. This chapter brings together fiscal and monetary policy with the international economy while also discussing political barriers that interrupt the international economy. Finally, this chapter concludes with a discussion of alternative fiscal and monetary rules that could be adopted in lieu of discretionary policy.

Fiscal Policy

Expansionary Fiscal Policy

Expansionary fiscal policy entails increasing government spending, reducing taxes, or a combination thereof. The purpose of any expansionary policy is to increase aggregate demand in the economy. Successful fiscal policy will increase aggregate demand (to AD' in Figure 15.1a) thereby causing more people to buy goods and services at higher prices. In order to buy more goods and services at higher prices, people will need more money. As a result, the domestic demand for money will increase. This increase in the demand for money causes interest rates to increase (from r0 to r1 in Figure 15.1b). As noted earlier in the text, an increase in interest rates will cause the international demand for the dollar to increase, as money saved in dollars now yields a higher rate of return. It will also cause fewer holders of dollars to want to dump their dollars on the international market. Combined, these factors cause the value of the dollar to increase (from vo to v1 in Figure 15.1c).

As the dollar becomes stronger, imports become cheaper and exports become harder to sell abroad. The stronger dollar yields a decrease in net exports and therefore also decreases aggregate demand. Aggregate demand falls (to AD" in Figure 15.1a) to account for the decrease in net exports put in place by expansionary fiscal policy. Thus, the expansionary power of fiscal policy is reduced by the international market. Note that an increase in the budget deficit used to finance fiscal expansion causes the trade deficit to increase. The trade and budget deficits are known as the **twin deficits** because larger budget deficits lead to larger trade deficits.

It is worth noting that the size of the shift in aggregate demand from AD' to AD" is dependent upon how engaged an economy is in the international sector. The more dependent a country is on trade, the larger this shift will be. That is, as an economy becomes more internationally oriented, fiscal policy's power

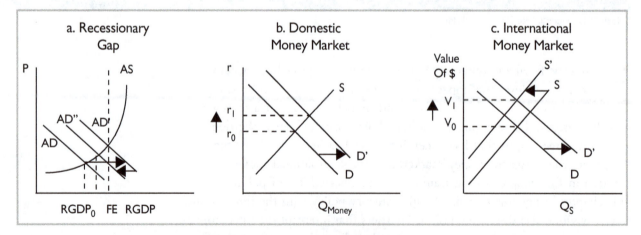

Figure 15.1   **FISCAL POLICY DURING A RECESSIONARY GAP**

weakens. In a world where the domestic economy is small relative to the world economy and fully open to it, domestic stimulus will be dissipated throughout the world while the debt derived thereof will be solely born by the country engaging in fiscal policy. If the US government lowers taxes and US consumers respond by buying Chinese imports, then production in China gets stimulated at the cost of US government debt.

Also note that as aggregate demand moves from AD' to AD", this causes an additional change in the demand for money both domestically and abroad. In truth, the policy feedback mechanism of the economy is never ending. If fiscal policy makers are able to (and they are not) correctly estimate both the impact to the economy of the initial change in aggregate demand and the resulting international effects, then they could design fiscal policy such that AD" ended at full employment.

Contractionary Fiscal Policy

Contractionary fiscal policy entails decreasing government spending, increasing taxes, or a combination thereof in order to decrease aggregate demand in the economy. Successful fiscal policy will decrease aggregate demand (to AD' in Figure 15.2a) thereby causing fewer people to buy goods and services at lower prices. As people buy fewer goods and services at lower prices, people will need less money. Therefore, the domestic demand for money will decrease as seen in Figure 15.2b. This decrease in the demand for money causes interest rates to decrease (to r1). A decrease in interest rates will cause the international demand for the dollar to decrease as money saved in dollars now yields a lower rate of return. It will also cause more holders of dollars to want to dump their dollars on the international market. Combined, these factors cause the value of the dollar to decrease (to v1).

As the dollar becomes weaker, imports become more expensive and exports become easier to sell abroad. The weaker dollar yields an increase in net exports and therefore also in aggregate demand (to AD" in Figure 15.2a). Note that a

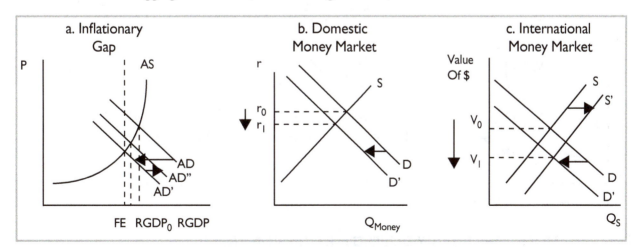

Figure 15.2 **FISCAL POLICY DURING AN INFLATIONARY GAP**

decrease in the budget deficit causes the trade deficit to decrease. Once again, as an economy becomes more internationally oriented, the impact of fiscal policy weakens. In this way, fiscal policy today has become a far less powerful tool than it once was. In 1950, imports and exports made up less than 5% of the US economy. Today imports and exports make up more than a fifth of the US economy.

Fiscal Policy in Stagflation

In the event of stagflation, policy makers can fight either inflation or unemployment, but not both. If they choose to fight inflation, the use of contractionary fiscal policy is similar to that of the inflationary gap. If they choose to fight unemployment, the use of expansionary fiscal policy is similar to that of the recessionary gap. In this way, the above graphs can be applied to stagflation, with the reminder that any attempt to solve either inflation or unemployment during stagflation will result in making the other problem significantly worse. As such, fiscal policy makers may not wish to be seen as actively making one of these problems worse.

Monetary Policy

Expansionary Monetary Policy

Monetary policy begins in the domestic money market. Expansionary monetary policy often begins when the FOMC buys government bonds. This causes banks' excess reserves to increase. If they loan out these excess reserves, the money supply will increase, as shown in Figure 15.3b. The purpose of the expansionary money supply is to get businesses to engage in investment. Successful monetary policy would cause an increase in investment, and therefore, an increase in aggregate demand as well (from AD to AD' 15.3a). In order to buy more goods

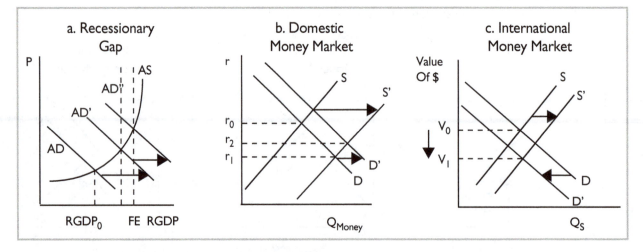

Figure 15.3 **MONETARY POLICY DURING A RECESSIONARY GAP**

and services at higher prices, people will need more money. Therefore, the domestic demand for money will increase (from D to D' 15.3b). This increase in the demand for money will not be as large as was the increase in the supply of money caused by the central bank (from S to S'). As a result, interest rates, on net, fall from r0 to r2, as shown in Figure 15.3b. A decrease in interest rates will cause the international demand for the dollar to decrease (from D to D') as money saved in dollars now yields a lower rate of return. It will also cause more holders of dollars to want to dump their dollars on the international market (from S to S'). Combined, these factors cause the value of the dollar to decrease (from v0 to v1 in 15.3c).

As the dollar becomes weaker, imports become more expensive and exports become easier to sell abroad. The weaker dollar yields an increase in net exports and therefore also an increase in aggregate demand (to AD" in Figure 15.3a). As an economy becomes more internationally oriented, monetary policy becomes a stronger tool. In this way, monetary policy has become more powerful than it was at the end of WWII when the percentage of US GDP involved in the international economy was much less than is today. If monetary policy makers are able to (and they are not) correctly estimate both the impact to the economy of the initial change in aggregate demand and the resulting international effects, then they could design monetary policy such that AD" ended at full employment.

One side effect of expansionary monetary policy is a weakening of the dollar value. As the money supply grows, more dollars are required to exchange dollars for a foreign currency. Monetary policy makers expect to boost net exports by weakening their own currency. In 2010, Secretary of the Treasury Tim Geithner publicly denied that a purpose of quantitative easing was to boost net exports in response to accusations to the contrary from emerging markets.[1] The Treasury Secretary's claim made even less sense in the face of his boss, President Obama's, stated 2010 goal of doubling exports by 2015.[2]

Contractionary Monetary Policy

Contractionary monetary policy often begins when the FOMC sells government bonds. This causes banks' excess reserves to decrease. If, as a result, they loan out fewer reserves, the money supply will decrease, as shown in Figure 15.4b. The purpose of the contractionary money supply is to get businesses to engage in less investment. Successful monetary policy would cause a decrease in investment, and therefore decreases aggregate demand as well (15.4a). As consumers buy fewer goods and services at lower prices, they will need less money. Therefore, the domestic demand for money will decrease (from D to D' 15.4b).

[1] Alan Beattie and Jonathan Wheatley. FT.com Geithner denies US bid to weaken dollar October 19, 2010. http://www.ft.com/intl/cms/s/0/1c62c304-db0c-11df-a870-00144feabdc0.html#axzz1X6tloQdx

[2] Helene Cooper. "Obama Sets Ambitious Export Goal" January 28, 2010. http://www.nytimes.com/2010/01/29/business/29trade.html

Figure 15.4   **MONETARY POLICY DURING AN INFLATIONARY GAP**

This decrease in the demand for money will not be as large as was the decrease in the supply of money caused by the central bank. As a result, interest rates, on net, increase from r_0 to r_2. An increase in interest rates will cause the international demand for the dollar to increase as money saved in dollars now yields a higher rate of return. It will also cause fewer holders of dollars to want to dump their dollars on the international market. Combined, these factors cause the value of the dollar to increase (from v0 to v 15.4c).

As the dollar becomes stronger, imports become cheaper and exports become harder to sell abroad. The stronger dollar yields a decrease in net exports and therefore also decreases aggregate demand. Aggregate demand falls to AD" in Figure 15.4a to account for the decrease in net exports put in place by contractionary monetary policy. Once again, as an economy becomes more internationally oriented, the stronger a tool monetary policy will become. Any attempt to use monetary policy to solve stagflation runs into the same problems as noted above for fiscal policy. Nevertheless, the above graphs can be used to examine the effects of both expansionary and contractionary monetary policy during stagflation.

Self-Correction

If an economy is allowed to self-correct out of a recessionary gap, then aggregate supply will shift rightward as real wages are bid down. Consumers will buy more goods and services at lower prices. The increase in consumption would lead to an increase in the demand for money while the lower prices would cause a decrease in the demand for money. The resulting demand for money would need to be an empirical matter. Theory is unable to state whether an increase or decrease in the demand for money would occur. Since the demand for money does not obviously change, interest rates, and therefore exchange rates, do not change

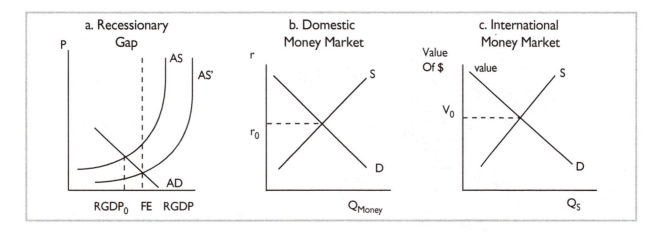

Figure 15.5   **SELF-CORRECTION DURING A RECESSIONARY GAP/STAGFLATION**

either. Therefore, the presence of the international economy has little impact on an economy's ability to self-correct. Figure 15.5 represents both what happens as the economy self-corrects from a recessionary gap or from stagflation.

If an economy is allowed to self-correct out of an inflationary gap, then aggregate supply will shift leftward as real wages are bid up. Consumers will buy fewer goods and services at higher prices. The decreased consumption would cause a decrease in the demand for money, while the increased prices would cause an increase in the demand for money. The resulting demand for money would need to be an empirical matter. Theory is unable to state whether an increase or decrease in the demand for money would occur. Since the demand for money does not obviously change, interest rates, and therefore exchange rates, do not change either. Therefore, the presence of the international economy has little impact on an economy's ability to self-correct from an inflationary gap.

Figure 15.6   **SELF-CORRECTION DURING AN INFLATIONARY GAP**

Foreign Economies' Impact on the Domestic Economy

Economic expansions and contractions are contagious across borders. All things being equal, an increase in aggregate demand in Canada will cause the value of the Canadian dollar to increase. This will decrease the relative value of the US dollar, and US exports to Canada will be cheaper for Canadians to purchase. As a result, an increase in economic growth in Canada can translate into faster economic growth in the US. The world economy is not a zero sum game. If Canada's economy grows, it does not have to come at the expense of the US economy. As people become wealthier around the world, they will be able to afford more US made products. Their purchase of US made goods and services will cause economic growth in the US.

Similarly, if a foreign country goes into recession, their consumers will have less money to purchase US goods and services. The resulting increase in the value of the dollar relative to the foreign country's currency will cause US net exports to that country to decline. In this way, a stagnant European economy can slow down US economic growth as European consumers are less able and willing to buy US made products. This is why information regarding the health of other countries' economies causes movement in US stock and bond markets. It does not take an altruist to root for a growing world economy. People who want the US economy to grow should be pleased when foreign policy makers implement long term pro-growth strategies for their own countries, as this will translate into increased economic growth in the US. With China and the European Union representing two of the top three economies in the world, the health of their economies is critically important to US economic growth.

Barriers in the International Economy

In a world without government erected economic barriers, goods, services, capital, labor, and natural resources would flow to where they are most in demand. However, the world economy is not free to self-correct. Governments erect trade barriers to prevent the free flow of goods and services over national boundaries. Barriers to immigration prevent people from crossing national borders and taking advantage of job opportunities. Investment controls stifle foreign ownership of domestic resources. Some governments also choose to fix the value of their currency to that of another country to prevent currency appreciation and depreciation.

The world does not engage in completely free trade. The US prevents free trade for numerous products such as sugar and timber. The US government also actively prevents progress in lowering worldwide trade barriers by continuing to subsidize American agriculture. Bilateral and multilateral trade deals with their many rates and exceptions often re-route trade rather than increase world trade. And, the US has slowed its approval of free trade deals with new trading partners. The existence of large and continuing trade barriers means that exports from a country may not increase as much as possible when their currency depreciates. Still, the reduction in trade barriers since WWII, largely led by the WTO, has increased the flow of goods and services across borders, thereby decreasing the power of fiscal policy while increasing the power of monetary policy.

© koya979, 2012, under license Shutterstock, Inc.

Immigration is largely an economic phenomenon. When an economy is experiencing an inflationary gap, a shortage of workers leads to inflation. If people are allowed to cross national borders freely in search of jobs, then countries whose economies are booming will benefit from an influx of workers. The influx of workers will help keep production costs lower, consumer prices down, and help people in need of money find work. When an economy enters recession, the flow of immigration into an economy slows down. Almost all countries have erected barriers to immigration, and these barriers serve to prevent the world economy from reaching equilibrium in the global labor market. The barriers also give people an economic incentive to illegally immigrate in search of jobs.

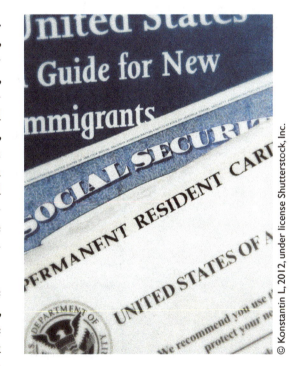

© Konstantin L, 2012, under license Shutterstock, Inc.

In this way, the global labor market did a much more efficient job of reaching global equilibrium in the 1800's, as people could more freely immigrate to places like the US and Canada. The fact that Cubans are willing to risk their lives in rafts to move from Cuba to the US or the fact that immigrants are willing to pay human smugglers to sneak them into the US is an indication that US immigration barriers actively work to prevent the US labor market from reaching equilibrium. Still, the easing of immigration restrictions within the European Union and in countries such as Australia has increased the labor mobility of millions of laborers in Europe and Southeast Asia.

Capital could be employed anywhere in the world. Yet, some governments, often for xenophobic reasons, prohibit the free inflow to and outflow of capital from their country. These restrictions prevent capital from being employed in its most efficient use. Investment controls prevent the global economy from reaching equilibrium in capital disbursement. Labor is made more productive when combined with capital, and vice versa. Regulations that prevent labor and capital reaching equilibrium reduce both short term economic adjustment and long term world wealth creation.

Fixed exchange rates, in the short run, prevent the effects of domestic fiscal and monetary policy from being transferred to the global economy. By not allowing their currency to change in value, countries on fixed exchange rates increase the relative power of fiscal policy over monetary policy. In the long run, changes in fiscal and monetary policies that cause a fixed currency to be undervalued will lead to domestic inflation. An overvalued currency will lead to a reduction in foreign reserves until they run out, thereby forcing devaluation. Currently, many countries with fixed exchange rates only fix them relative to a single foreign currency. In so doing, their currencies still float against all other world currencies, but do so based upon the fiscal and monetary policies put in place by the government to which they peg their currency. The global move to floating exchange rates away from fixed exchange rates since the early 1970's has helped to strengthen monetary policy, while weakening fiscal policy.

Public Policy Debates

The relative strength of fiscal and monetary policy over time is but one more item of concern when determining the proper policy response to periods of unemployment, inflation, and stagflation. As nothing in life is ever free, there are advantages and disadvantages to using policy to smooth business cycles. This section summaries the pros and cons of using discretionary fiscal and monetary policy to smooth business cycles rather than adopting fiscal and monetary rules designed to let the economy self-correct. It also examines how the European Union was designed to consolidate fiscal, monetary, exchange rate, trade, and immigration policy decisions to an international body and discusses the pros and cons of such a move.

Fiscal Policy Rules vs. Discretion

The use of fiscal and monetary policy depends upon the ability and willingness of policymakers to use their discretion as they attempt to influence economic outcomes. In the US, Congress and the president collectively have a large amount of discretion over decisions regarding taxes and government spending. Given the bicameral nature of Congress, along with the checks and balances imposed by the executive and judicial branches, any one chamber of Congress does not have unlimited fiscal discretion. Fiscal policy is much easier to implement in countries where a single body of parliament is able to enact fiscal policies.

Even when Congress and the president agree on fiscal policy, the US Supreme Court could rule a fiscal policy to be unconstitutional, as it routinely did in the 1930's. In 1935, the US Supreme Court ruled that the National Recovery Administration overstepped constitutionally enumerated powers. In 1936, it also ruled that the Agricultural Adjustment Act was unconstitutional. President Obama's Affordable Care Act brought constitutional battles over the legality of the individual mandate to buy health insurance.

While a government can set tax rates on things like income, sales, and property, it does not mandate a specific tax/GDP ratio. People can change their behavior in response to changed tax incentives. Often, increases in tax rates are intended to raise more tax revenue than they actually yield, as people change their behavior. Increasing marginal income tax rates to 90% might seem like it would yield more tax revenue for a government, but it likely will result in more people dropping out of the workforce or not accurately reporting their income to the government.

When an economy goes into recession, taxes derived from income naturally decrease, even without active fiscal policy. Likewise, during an inflationary gap, tax revenues increase without active fiscal policy. Policy makers who want to hold tax revenues constant are often forced to raise tax rates during a recession and lower them during an inflationary gap. Both actions tend to exacerbate the existing economic problems.

Keynes advocated that fiscal policy discretion be used to stimulate aggregate demand during a recession and depress aggregate demand during an inflationary gap. The former policy proved to be politically popular. The opposite was true of the latter. Many politicians' desires to get re-elected in the short run cause them to prefer polices that lower current unemployment. Liberal politicians like to campaign on the promise of more government programs designed to help this group or that. Conservative politicians like to campaign on decreasing their constituents' tax burdens.

In May of 2000, the economy was experiencing an inflationary gap. Federal Reserve Chairman Alan Greenspan made multiple speeches advocating contractionary fiscal policy. The two presidential candidates, George W. Bush and Al Gore, campaigned on lowering taxes and increasing government spending respectively. These were opposite of what Keynes' policies called for. Contractionary fiscal policy was not used and the Federal Reserve implemented contractionary monetary policy.

Between the early 1960's and the late 1990's the US Federal government ran over 30 years of consecutive budget deficits. Rather than use fiscal policy to smooth business cycles, it was used by politicians to reward current constituents at the expense of future taxpayers. Concern over the resulting national debt caused billionaire businessman Ross Perot to mount an independent campaign for President in 1992. In 1995, a balanced budget amendment passed the US House of Representatives but failed to reach a two-thirds majority in the US Senate by a single vote.

A **balanced budget amendment** is an example of a fiscal rule. **Fiscal rules** are laws that limit the use of discretion regarding levels of taxes and spending. A rule that forces tax revenue to equal government expenditures in every given year restricts the ability of the government to run budget deficits or budget surpluses. It effectively outlaws countercyclical fiscal policy. Changes in taxes can occur but only when accompanied by offsetting changes in government spending. The main advantage of such a rule is that it prohibits short sighted politicians from indebting future generations.

The main disadvantage of a balanced budget amendment is that it requires contractionary fiscal policy during recessionary gaps and expansionary fiscal policy during inflationary gaps. As tax revenues naturally fall during a recession while income assistance spending naturally increases, tax rates would either have to be increased or other government spending would have to be reduced. A strict balanced budget rule would impose tough political choices for politicians during times of national disasters, wars, or severe economic contractions.

Other possible fiscal rules include rules put in place regulating a maximum debt/GDP ratio, a maximum deficit/GDP ratio, a maximum government spending/GDP ratio or a maximum taxes/GDP ratio. A maximum debt/GDP rule allows budget surpluses, but limits the size of budget deficits. Germany passed a fiscal rule in 2009 that sets post 2016 budgets with a maximum budget deficit at .35% of GDP but forbids state governments from running any budget deficits. It does contain exceptions for natural disasters or severe economic crises. Since 2003, Switzerland has been forced by constitutional rule to never run a **structural budget deficit**. A structural budget deficit occurs when a government would be running a budget deficit even if their economy was operating a full employment (had no cyclical unemployment).

Monetary Policy Rules vs. Discretion

The US Federal Reserve has a large amount of discretion in its use of monetary policy. While the chair of the Federal Reserve is required to testify before Congress on a regular basis, Congress does not have control over discretionary monetary policy. To the extent that Congress can influence monetary policy, it has to amend the Fed's charter or eliminate the Fed altogether. These actions do not lend to a daily micromanagement of monetary policy. Congress has given the Federal Reserve the broad direction to provide price stability and low unemployment. The latter mandate was only added in the late 1970's.

Monetary discretion allows an independent central bank to conduct monetary policy as it sees fit. This discretion allows central banks the freedom to conduct politically unpopular monetary policy. The chief benefit of monetary policy discretion is that it lets the monetary authority use its full range of tools to encourage investment during recessions, discourage investment during inflationary gaps, and operate as a nonpolitical lender of last resort.

"Inflation is always and everywhere a monetary phenomenon."[3] The chief argument for the use of monetary rules is the tendency of central banks to cause

---

[3] Friedman, Milton. *The Counter Revolution in Monetary Theory.*, 1970.

unacceptably high rates of inflation over time by expanding the money supply faster than the economy grows. Like with fiscal policy, there is also an issue of competence. If the monetary authority lacks the knowledge of the "appropriate" money supply, then there is little reason to believe that their intervention in the money supply will aid long run growth.

Monetarists advocate a **monetary rule** that increases the money supply at a set rate each year to ensure long run price stability. If an economy is expected to grow at an average annualized rate of 3% per year, then the rule would be to increase the money supply by 3% each year. By informing every one of the expected change in the money supply, economic actors ought not be surprised by wild swings in inflation.

A major downside of monetarism is that monetary policy would be effectively outlawed. With monetarism, the monetary authority is not allowed to intervene to provide extra liquidity during a financial crisis. While prices may remain stable over time, inflation or deflation could increase or decrease in any given year, so short term price stability may be sacrificed for long term price stability. Because the central bank in a fractional reserve banking system cannot force banks to make new loans, a central bank may be limited in their ability to precisely hit their monetary rule target any given year. The missing of a stated target serves to increase uncertainty regarding monetary policy.

Other monetary rules such as The Taylor Rule provide guidance to monetary authorities on how to target interest rates based on current levels of inflation and unemployment. Such a rule seeks to direct monetary policy rather than eliminate it. The same can be said for inflation targeting, which could be an expressed goal serving to guide monetary policy.

While monetarists attempt to eliminate discretion for monetary policy, an end of fiat currency would accomplish the same task. Monetary policy discretion only arises when fiat money is introduced to the economic system. When the world used gold as the chief medium of exchange, no country could merely print more gold during recessions. The problem with the gold standard is that the supply of gold is subject to the earth's endowment of gold relative to man's ability to find it and mine it. Changes in mining technology could lead to rapid changes in the money supply.

Advocates of fiscal and monetary rules share a distrust of and distaste for discretionary policy makers. They fear that policy makers are either incompetent or corrupt. They cite years of inflation and budget deficits as evidence that discretion is not used to provide price stability or smooth business cycles. Rather, they claim that fiscal policy is used to serve the short sighted goals of current politicians and that central bankers conduct monetary policy to aid their banking friends at large national and international banks. Both sets of policy makers, by using their discretion, make the claim that they have superior knowledge regarding what an economy needs more than do the individual economic actors whose independent knowledge is aggregated through the market process.

Revisited: The Pros and Cons of Fiscal and Monetary Policy During a Recessionary Gap

When an economy faces a recessionary gap, unemployment is higher than normal while output and inflation are lower than normal. The three options for returning the economy back to full employment are fiscal policy, monetary policy, and letting the economy self-correct. Expansionary fiscal policy consists of increasing government spending or reducing taxes. Expansionary monetary policy entails the purchase of government bonds by the Federal Reserve to increase the money supply in an effort to boost investment. Self-correction relies on letting real wages fall, which lowers the cost of production and clears the surplus of labor in the economy. The first two policies seek to increase aggregate demand, while the latter increases aggregate supply.

The purpose of listing the pros and cons of fiscal policy vs. monetary policy vs. self-correction is to allow readers to make a determination, based on their own values, which policy is most appropriate. While the choice of letting the economy self-correct can be achieved through fiscal or monetary policy rules, it is theoretically, if not practically, possible for policy makers to use their discretion to not intervene in the economy. Table 15.1 lists the pros and cons of using expansionary policy versus letting the economy self-correct.

One's policy preference depends on which economic goal or goals he or she determines are most important. For instance, if a person dislikes or is hurt by unexpected inflation, they would not advocate expansionary monetary policy; whereas if they are helped by unexpected inflation, they may wish to advocate it. Politicians may like to use expansionary fiscal policy because it allows them to use their power to pick economic winners and losers. The politically connected may advocate fiscal policy if they believe they will be the primary beneficiaries of said policy. Those who believe that policy makers are incompetent, corrupt, or acting primarily in other people's interests will tend to advocate letting the economy self-correct.

The choice of recessionary policy may also depend on one's time horizon. Short sighted politicians often want to be seen as solving people's problems immediately even if by so doing they slow down long run economic growth. If increased long run economic growth is one's biggest concern then one would want to avoid increasing the national debt or transferring resources out of the private sector via expanded government spending. Temporary tax cuts that don't increase production slow down long term growth by increasing debt, while permanent reductions in marginal tax rates could incentivize more intensive resource utilization and promote long term growth. Those interested in long term economic growth would also want to avoid increasing short and long run inflation caused by implementing monetary policy. Pricing bubbles caused by inflation work to slow down long term economic growth by distorting the efficient use of resources. Letting the economy self-correct is the only policy that makes production cheaper. The chief downside is that it does so by reducing workers' real wages.

| TABLE 15.1 | PROS AND CONS OF FISCAL AND MONETARY POLICY DURING A RECESSIONARY GAP |

Fiscal Policy

Pros	Cons
1. May serve as a quick boost to aggregate demand	1. Increases the national debt
2. May lower unemployment	2. Increases interest rates which hurts long run economic growth
3. May Increase RDGP	3. Causes inflation
4. Elected politicians get to exercise their ideology (which is a con if you don't like their ideology)	4. Congress and the President could screw up fiscal policy
5. Net importers are helped by a stronger dollar	5. Time lags could slow down impact on the economy
6. Net debtors may gain from unexpected inflation	6. Net exporters are hurt by a stronger dollar
7. Does not cause long run inflation	7. Net creditors may be hurt by unexpected inflation
8. The Fed cannot screw it up	8. Fiscal policy is becoming weaker over time
9. Lower taxes gives people the incentive to work more	9. Rational expectations predicts fiscal policy will be useless
	10. Greater government spending transfers resources away from the private sector which is bad for long run economic growth

Monetary Policy

Pros	Cons
1. Does not increase the national debt	1. Increases inflation
2. Lowers unemployment	2. Increases long run inflation
3. May increases RGDP	3. The Fed can screw up monetary policy
4. Monetary policy is becoming a stronger tool	4. Net importers are hurt by a weaker dollar
5. Net exporters are helped by a weaker dollar	5. Time lags could slow down impact on the economy
6. Net debtors may gain from unexpected inflation	6. Net creditors may be hurt by unexpected inflation
7. Congress and the President cannot screw it up	7. The Fed cannot force banks to lend money
8. Politicians cannot pick economic winners and losers	8. Rational expectations predicts monetary policy will be useless
9. Makes the national debt easier to pay off	

TABLE 15.1	PROS AND CONS OF FISCAL AND MONETARY POLICY DURING A RECESSIONARY GAP (*continued*)

Self-Correction

Pros	Cons
1. Decreases unemployment	1. The economy may take time to self-correct as real wages may be sticky downwards
2. Increases RGDP	2. Unexpected deflation hurts net debtors
3. Lowers inflation	3. Workers' real wages fall potentially increasing income inequality
4. Congress and the President cannot screw it up	
5. The Fed cannot screw it up	
6. Prevents long run inflation	
7. Does not increase the national debt	
8. Politicians cannot pick economic winners and losers	
9. Unexpected deflation helps net creditors	
10. There are no time lags	

Revisited: The Pros and Cons of Fiscal and Monetary Policy During an Inflationary Gap

Policy makers again face tradeoffs when choosing their preferred policy in an inflationary gap. Contractionary fiscal policy involves increasing taxes or lowering government spending. Contractionary monetary policy involves decreasing the money supply to raise interest rates and lower investment. Table 15.2 lists the pros and cons of each policy.

Each policy will increase unemployment, since the economy is operating above full employment in an inflationary gap. The policy that most ardently attacks inflation is contractionary monetary policy. It lowers inflation in both the short run and the long run by decreasing the money supply whereas doing nothing will actually cause inflation to increase in the short run as real wages increase. By increasing interest rates, monetary policy slows down the economy as it stifles investment in new capital and consequently hurts long term economic growth.

TABLE 15.2	PROS AND CONS OF FISCAL AND MONETARY POLICY DURING AN INFLATIONARY GAP

Fiscal Policy

Pros	Cons
1. Decreases inflation	1. May increase unemployment
2. Pays down the national debt	2. May decreases RGDP
3. Reduces interest rates, which is good for capital creation	3. Does not decrease long run inflation
4. The Fed cannot screw up	4. Congress and the President could screw up
5. Net exporters are helped by a weaker dollar	5. Time lags could slow down its impact
6. Net creditors may gain from unexpected deflation	6. Requires politically unpopular actions
7. Lower government spending transfers resources away from the public sector which is good for long run economic growth	7. Higher income taxes discourage work
	8. Fiscal policy is becoming a weaker tool
	9. Rational expectations predicts that fiscal policy will be useless
	10. Net debtors may lose from unexpected deflation
	11. Net importers are hurt by a weaker dollar

Monetary Policy

Pros	Cons
1. Lowers inflation	1. May increases unemployment
2. Lowers long run inflation	2. May decrease RGDP
3. Is becoming a stronger tool over time	3. The Fed could screw up
4. Net importers are helped by a stronger dollar	4. Time lags could slow down its impact
5. Net creditors may be helped by unexpected deflation	5. Raises interest rates which slows capital accumulation
6. Congress and the President cannot screw it up	6. Doesn't pay down the national debt
7. Politicians cannot pick economic winners and losers	7. Net debtors may be hurt by a stronger dollar
8. Does not discourage work	8. Net exporters are hurt by a stronger dollar
	9. Rational expectations predicts that monetary policy will be useless
	10. Does not move resources from the government to the private sector
	11. Makes the national debt harder to pay off

TABLE 15.2	**PROS AND CONS OF FISCAL AND MONETARY POLICY DURING AN INFLATIONARY GAP** (*continued*)

Self-Correction

Pros	Cons
1. Congress and the President cannot screw up	1. Does not move resources from the government to the private sector
2. The Fed cannot screw up	2. Allows inflation to increase in the short run
3. There are no time lags	3. Decreases RGDP
4. Politicians cannot pick economic winners and losers	4. Increases unemployment
5. Does not discourage work	5. Does not pay down the national debt
6. Workers' real wages increase, potentially decreasing Income inequality	6. Does not decrease long run inflation

Contractionary fiscal policy is the only policy that uses a booming economy to pay down the national debt. If the policy entails cutting government spending, then resources are directed from the government to the private sector enhancing long run economic growth. If fiscal policy entails increasing income tax rates, then current and future workers may choose to provide less labor thereby slowing long term economic growth. If income inequality is one's major concern, then letting the economy self-correct will allow real wages to increase, thereby reducing income inequality. This is why presidential candidate Ralph Nader advocated avoiding fiscal and monetary policy during the inflationary gap of 2000. Self-correction is again often preferred by people who believe that policy makers are either incompetent or corrupt.

The pros and cons of using fiscal or monetary policy during stagflation depend upon whether policy makers target inflation or unemployment as their primary concern. Focusing on inflation reduction will generate pros and cons similar to the inflationary gap. Focusing on unemployment reduction will generate pros and cons similar to the recessionary gap. The only policy that will simultaneously fight unemployment and inflation is letting the economy self-correct. As real wages fall, both unemployment and inflation decrease. The major problem with either monetary or fiscal policy during stagflation is that it attempts to make one problem better while making another existing problem much worse.

Advocating one policy or another may depend upon the current state of the economy. If an economy is suffering from hyper-inflation, then policies designed to bring inflation under control, such as contractionary monetary policy, may be the best catalyst for long run economic growth. If an economy is struggling with a large national debt burden, then contractionary fiscal policy may be the best catalyst for long run economic growth. Adopters of fiscal or monetary rules may wish to leave room for discretion in extreme cases. For instance, a country with a large national debt burden may find it unwise to legislate a strict balanced budget rule that outlaws budget surpluses.

Conclusion

So why are some countries richer than others? Some countries pursue public policies that promote the use and expansion of available resources, encourage productivity enhancing human capital, technology, trade, and entrepreneurship, protect property rights, and prevent fiscal and monetary policy from causing large public debts and inflation. Other countries focus their attention on fiscal, monetary, and regulatory polices to micromanage today's output mix allowing rent-seekers to leverage their government connections for their personal benefit at the cost of long term economic growth via government favors or redistributive handouts. They fail to define and protect property rights or encourage the use and expansion of available resources, productivity enhancing human capital, technology, trade, and entrepreneurship.

Keynesian fiscal and monetary policy is inherently focused on the short run economic goals of controlling unemployment, inflation, and current economic growth. After all, Keynes noted that "In the long run, we are all dead." Use of these policies implies a level of knowledge and benevolence on the part of policy makers that is greater in theory than in practice. Obsessing with short run aggregate data can cause policy makers to sacrifice long term economic growth in an attempt to meet short run goals. F.A. Hayek claimed that, "The curious task of economics is to demonstrate to men how little they really know about what they imagine they can design."[4] The lack of effectiveness of fiscal and monetary stimulus following the 2007–2008 financial crisis casts serious doubts going forward as to the efficacy of short term discretionary fiscal and monetary policy.

In the end, US fiscal, monetary, trade, immigration, and regulatory policies will go a long way in explaining whether the US economy continues to grow in the future. Between 1973 and 2010 the US' share of global economy activity fell from 18.6% to 13.3%.[5] During this time the US moved from being a net creditor to a net debtor and from a net exporter to a net importer. The global economic hangover from excessive European and US debt guarantees that the future study of macroeconomics will be interesting.

---

[4] The Fatal Conceit.

[5] "Economic Focus" The Economist September 10, 2011.

Key Terms

Balanced budget
amendment

Fiscal rules

Monetarists

Monetary rules

Structural budget deficit

Twin deficits

Questions for Review

1. In a world with floating exchange rates and few trade barriers, expansionary fiscal policy will do what to the value of the dollar? To net exports?

2. In a world with floating exchange rates and few trade barriers, expansionary monetary policy will do what to the value of the dollar? To net exports?

3. In a world with floating exchange rates and few trade barriers, contractionary fiscal policy will do what to the value of the dollar? To net exports?

4. In a world with floating exchange rates and few trade barriers, contractionary monetary policy will do what to the value of the dollar? To net exports?

5. How are economic expansions and contractions contagious across borders?

6. What barriers exist to prohibit the international economy from reaching equilibrium? How have these barriers changed over time?

7. Should US citizens be concerned about the economic growth rate in China? Why or why not?

8. a. What are the pros and cons of fiscal rules vs. fiscal discretion?

   b. What, if any, fiscal rule would you propose? Why?

9. a. What are the pros and cons of monetary rules vs. monetary discretion?

   b. What, if any, monetary rule would you propose? Why?

10. **a.** What are the pros and cons of using fiscal policy to solve a recessionary gap?

    b. What are the pros and cons of using monetary policy to solve a recessionary gap?

    c. What are the pros and cons of letting the economy self-correct to solve a recessionary gap?

11. **a.** What are the pros and cons of using fiscal policy to solve an inflationary gap?

    b. What are the pros and cons of using monetary policy to solve an inflationary gap?

    c. What are the pros and cons of letting the economy self-correct to solve an inflationary gap?

12. What have you learned during your study of macroeconomics to make you a more productive citizen? A wealthier citizen? A happier citizen?

Glossary

Absolute advantage—a situation where one country or person can produce more output per unit of input than another country or person

Absolute poverty—describes the situation when individuals are unable to afford the basic necessities of life

Aggregate demand—the sum total of all domestic goods and services that consumers, businesses, the government, and foreign actors want to buy at any given price level

Aggregate supply—the sum total of all goods and services that domestic firms and governments are willing and able to produce at any given price level

American System—a system of high tariffs proposed by Alexander Hamilton, the first US Treasury Secretary

Arbitrage—taking advantage of price differences for profit by moving resources whose prices vary between markets until the price of the resource is the same in all markets

Assets—things that are owned

Austerity package—a law that increases taxes or lowers government spending or transfer payments

Automatic stabilizers—things that help the economy get back to full employment without explicit use of fiscal or monetary policy

Average price level—the cost of purchasing a typical market basket of goods and services, as constructed by the Bureau of Labor Statistics

Average tax rate—the percentage of one's income paid in taxes

Balance of trade—the flow of goods and services reflected by a trade surplus or a trade deficit

Balanced budget amendment—an amendment to the US constitution that would outlaw budget deficits or budget surpluses

Bank run—when a bank's depositors demand for cash exceeds a bank's ability to provide the money due to a lack of liquidity in a bank's assets

Barter economy—an economy where people engage in economic transactions by trading goods and services directly for each other

Bear—a stock market pessimist

Bear market—a sustained decline in stock market indices

Bilateral trade agreements—an agreement between two countries to lower trade barriers

Black market—where goods and services are exchanged illegally with the explicit intent of avoiding government recognition

Board of Governors—a seven member board designed to provide public input into monetary policy. The Board of Governors is appointed by the US president and confirmed by the US Senate and is based in Washington DC

Budget deficit—the situation that arises when a government spends and gives away more money than it collects in taxes and intergovernmental transfers

Budget surplus—the situation that arises when a government spends and gives away less money than it collects in taxes and intergovernmental transfers

Bull—a stock market optimist

Bull market—a sustained increase in stock market indices

Bureau of Economic Analysis—the federal government agency in charge of calculating GDP

Bureau of Labor Statistics (BLS)—an agency in the US Department of Labor that calculates unemployment and inflation rates

Business Cycle Dating Committee—the committee at the National Bureau of Economic Research that officially dates recessions

Business cycles—a cycle of increases (expansions) and decreases (contractions) in real GDP

Capital—a long lasting tool used for production, such as a machine or a factory

Capital account—the net amount of public and private international investment

Capital account deficit—when a country invests more abroad than is invested by foreigners domestically

Capital account surplus—when a country invests less abroad than is invested by foreigners domestically

Capital gains tax—a tax paid on the appreciated value of sold assets

Cash advance store—a firm that offers high interest loans to people with low credit scores

Central bank—a bank that serves as a bank to a central government and may serve as a lender of last resort, regulator of private banks, and a conductor of monetary policy

Certificate of deposit—a savings instrument that offers interest in exchange for a guarantee that the savings will not be withdrawn for a specified period of time

Checking account—a savings instrument that provides easy access to savings via checks

Child tax credit—a reduction in tax obligations based on the number of children one has

Circular Flow Model—a model that illustrates how groups of economic actors interact in the economy

Classical School of Economic Thought—a body of 18th and 19th Century economic thought that emphasized natural economic order

Cold War—an unofficial war between the United States and the Soviet Union that began in 1946 and came to an end with the fall of the Soviet Union in 1991

Collective bargaining—the negotiation process between employers and representatives of a labor union in regard to the working conditions of employees

Command economy—an economy where governments make decisions about what to produce, how to produce, and who gets the output

Commodity—an asset that is traded in a market

Commodity money—money that has an intrinsic value derived from its use as something other than as money

Comparative advantage—exists when one country or person can produce at a lower opportunity cost of production than another

Consumer price index (CPI)—an index used to measure inflation by examining the price change in a basket of goods and services consumed by a hypothetical urban worker relative to the price in a base year

Consumers—people who buy things for their personal use

Consumption— almost all purchases of consumers (note new home construction is the main exception as that is counted as investment not consumption)

Contraction—the phase of the business cycle where there is a decrease in real GDP

Contractionary fiscal policy—an increase in taxes or a decrease in government spending designed to reduce aggregate demand

Contractionary monetary policy—a decrease in the money supply by the central bank in order to reduce aggregate demand

Convergence theory—states that countries with a lower per capita GDP should grow faster than countries with a higher per capita GDP until their economies catch up

Corporate income tax—a tax paid by corporations based upon their reported profits

Cost of living adjustment (COLA)—a change in wage or transfer payment to adjust for a change in the average price level

Cost of living index—a measure of how expensive it is to meet the needs and wants of consumers

Creative destruction—economic innovation that renders existing technology, capital, human capital, or firms obsolete

Credit scores—a measure of a consumer's credit worthiness

Crowding in—where decreased government borrowing increases private investment by driving down interest rates and increasing funds available for private investment

Crowding out—where increased government borrowing limits private investment by driving up interest rates and decreasing funds available for private investment

Currency appreciation—when a currency can buy more of another currency (becomes stronger)

Currency depreciation—when a currency can buy less of another currency (becomes weaker)

Cyclical unemployment—unemployment caused by a downturn in the business cycle which leads to fewer jobs being available

Deduction—something to be subtracted from taxable income

Defined benefit pension plan—a pension plan that promises a certain payout to retirees

Defined contribution pension plan—a pension plan that only specifies the amount of money an employer contributes to the plan

Deflation—a decrease in the average price level

Deposits—money placed in banks by savers

Devaluation—a decrease in a government's official value of their currency

Discount rate—the interest rate that the Federal Reserve charges banks that borrow from the Fed

Discretionary spending—money that is authorized to be spent by Congress by the passage of an appropriations act

Disposable income—after tax income

Dividend—a share of profit distributed to shareholders

Division of labor—the specialization of people in specific jobs or tasks

Dominican Republic - Central American - US Free Trade Agreement (CAFTA)—a trade agreement between the United States, the Dominican Republic and Central American Countries

Double coincidence of wants—where both parties engaged in a trade want what the other has to offer

Dow Jones Industrial Average—an index of 30 of the largest firms publicly traded on the New York Stock Exchange

Dual mandate—the Congressional law that says the Federal Reserve should enact monetary policy in pursuit of both the goals of price stability and low unemployment

Dumping—selling goods below cost

Earmark—spending that directs approved funds to be spent on specific projects

Earned income tax credit (EITC)—a payment to low income earners based on their income and family size

Economic costs—forgone production

Economic growth— an increase in production possibilities

Economics—a social science that examines people's choices in a world of unlimited wants and scarce resources

Economies of scale—a situation where increased production leads to a decrease in average costs of producing

Embargo—outlawing all trade with a country

Emigration—the leaving of a country to live abroad

Entitlement—a legal guarantee to benefits

Entrepreneurs—people who invent new products, innovate new product lines, improve the quality of products, increase the efficiency of existing production and distribution, engage in arbitrage, take risks, or connect sellers with buyers and financiers with producers

Entrepreneurship—combining resources in a new or innovative way; risk taking

Euro—the common currency for members of the European Union

European Central Bank—based in Frankfort, Germany it conducts monetary policy for countries who have officially adopted the Euro

European Monetary Union (EMU)—an organization of countries which have adopted the Euro as their official currency

European Union (EU)—a political union of 27 European countries that employs common fiscal, regulatory, and monetary rules on its member countries located in Europe so that it can function as a single economic market utilizing a common currency, the euro

Excess capacity—high levels of unused resources; this occurs at production levels inside the production possibilities frontier

Excess reserves—cash a bank holds in excess of its required reserves

Exchange rate—the price of one currency in terms of another

Expansion—the phase of the business cycle where there is an increase in real GDP

Expansionary fiscal policy—an increase in government spending or a decrease in taxes designed to increase aggregate demand

Expansionary monetary policy—when the central bank increases the money supply in an attempt to stimulate the economy

Export—a good or service produced domestically but sold abroad

Extensive economic growth—growth in output due to an increase in inputs

Federal Deposit Insurance Corporation (FDIC)—an independent agency that insures bank deposits up to $250,000

Federal funds rate—the interest rate banks charge each other to borrow money overnight

Federal Open Market Committee—a 12 member committee that determines monetary policy and is made up by the Board of Governors and five Federal Reserve Bank presidents

Federal Reserve—The United States' central bank consisting of 12 privately owned and operated regional banks

Federalism—a system of government that splits power between a national government and competing regional governments

Fiat currency/fiat money—a currency whose value is based solely on confidence in the issuing government; this type of money has no other use than serving as money

Financial institutions—institutions that coordinate savings and investment. Examples include banks, credit unions, credit card companies, stock markets, commodity markets, bond markets, insurance companies, and pension plans

Firms—organizations created to provide goods or services for a profit

Fiscal policy—changes in the level of taxes or government spending intended to minimize economic fluctuations

Fiscal rules—laws or constitutional rules that restrict the use of discretionary fiscal policy

Fiscal stimulus—a decrease in taxes or an increase in government spending intended to increase aggregate demand; a synonym for expansionary fiscal policy

Fixed exchange rate—a government set value for one currency in terms of another

Floating exchange rate—a market determined value for one currency relative to another that is determined by the supply and demand of the two currencies in the international money market

Foreign direct investment—investment in a country made by residents or businesses of another country

Foreign reserve—a foreign currency held by a government

Foreign sector—consumers, firms, and governments that exist outside the political boundaries of a country

Foreign trade effect—the effect caused by lower domestic prices encouraging residents and foreigners to purchase more domestically produced goods and services, thereby lowering imports and increasing exports

Fractional reserve banking system—a system where banks only hold onto a portion of all bank deposits in order to loan the remainder to others

Free banking era—the period of time, 1837-1863, between the end of The Second Bank of the United States and the beginning of national banks

Free market economy—an economy where individuals make decisions about what to produce, how to produce, and who gets the output

Free-rider problem—where one who does not pay for a good or service is able to consume it

Free Trade Area of the Americas (FTAA)—a proposed regional trade agreement for the Western Hemisphere (minus Cuba)

Frictional unemployment—unemployment caused by a natural movement of people from one job to the next or from individuals just entering the labor force

Full employment—the level of employment that exists when cyclical unemployment is zero

Fully funded pension—a pension plan that sets aside an actuarially sufficient amount of money to meet future pension promises

Futures contract—a contract to exchange an asset in the future

GDP per capita—the average gross domestic product produced per person, calculated by dividing GDP by the population

Global Agreement on Tariffs and Trade (GATT)—a treaty signed by countries after WWII to lower trade barriers

Golden rule of economics—rational economic action occurs when economic actors engage in actions whose marginal benefit exceed their marginal cost

Government—an institution that creates and enforces laws

Government shutdown—when the government ceases to spend money due to a lack of legal authority to do so

Government spending—the purchase of goods or services by a government

Government sponsored bailout—the use of tax dollars to prevent a private firm from financial decline or bankruptcy

Gresham's Law—the principle that "bad money drives out good" as overvalued money will create surpluses and undervalued money will decline

Gross domestic product—the total market value of all final goods and services produced within a given country in a given year

Gross national product—the total market value of all final goods and services produced by a country's companies in a given year

Human capital—the education, skill set, experience, and knowledge that people have

Human costs—costs related to the physical, psychological, and social costs incurred by the absence of wealth creation; examples include divorce, suicide, crime, depression, hunger, or thirst

Hyperinflation—an inflation rate over 200%

Immigration—the act of moving permanently to a country by someone who formerly lived abroad

Implementation lag—the time it takes for a policy, once enacted, to have an effect on the economy

Import—a good and service produce produced abroad, but purchased domestically

Individual retirement account (IRA)—a savings instrument where initial deposits are made tax free

Industrialized countries—first world countries possessing the highest levels of per capita GDP and capital accumulation; examples include the United States, Canada, Japan, Hong Kong, Australia, New Zealand, South Korea, and most of Western Europe

Industrializing countries—emerging markets or second world countries that have lower GDP per capita than industrialized countries but higher levels than non-industrialized countries; examples include China, India, most of Eastern Europe, most of South America, much of Southeast Asia, Mexico, and Russia

Infant industries—new industries that have just been created

Inflation—an increase in the average price level

Inflationary gap—a macroeconomic equilibrium characterized by higher price levels due to aggregate demand shifting beyond full employment level RGDP

Injections—things that increase the current demand for domestic production

Institutional economics—the study of how institutions affect the evolutionary development of the economy

Intensive economic growth—growth in output due to an increase in the productivity of existing inputs

Interest—payment to savers in return for the use of their money

Interest rate effect—the effect that occurs as prices and interest rates lower, causing a decrease in the opportunity cost of investment and an increase in the incentive to invest

Intergovernmental holdings—government debt held by government agencies such as the Social Security Administration

Intergovernmental transfers—grants from one government to another, typically from a higher level of government to a regional or local government

Intermediate good—partially finished goods that go into the production of a final product

International Monetary Fund (IMF)—an international organization intended to serve as a lender of last resort for national governments

Inventory—unsold, stored, production

Investment—the purchase of new capital, equipment, and software by businesses and governments, changes in inventory of unsold products, and the purchase of new homes

Labor—time humans spend producing

Labor force—people 16 years of age and older who are either currently employed or are not working but are actively looking for a job

Labor force participation rate—the percentage of people aged 16 and older in the labor force

Labor union—a group of laborers who work together to improve working conditions

Laffer Curve—a graph that shows the relationship between marginal tax rates and tax revenue, it illustrates that the revenue maximizing marginal tax rate is below 100%

Law of demand—as prices fall, a good's quantity demanded increases

Law of increasing opportunity cost—the principle that as more of one thing produced, the opportunity cost of producing another unit increases as resources are diverted from other activities

Law of unintended consequences—actions always have effects that are unanticipated or unintended

Leakages—things that if increased, decrease the current demand for domestic production

Liabilities—that which an entity owes to another

Limited liability corporations—a firm whose owners' losses are limited to the value of their stock

Liquidity—an asset's ability to be quickly used as a medium of exchange without a significant loss of value

Liquidity trap—the situation that arises during a deep recession if expansionary monetary policy is unable to force banks to make more loans due to their lack of business confidence

Loan sharks—lenders who charge interest rates on loans above the legal limit set by usury laws

Logrolling—the trading of votes used to generate sufficient support for legislation that would not pass on its own

Long run economy—an economy over multiple business cycles

Luddites—a group of Englishmen who rebelled against the industrial revolution (and machines), believing that machines cause unemployment

M1—a common measure of money supply measured as cash + checkable deposits

Macroeconomic equilibrium—where the quantity of domestic goods and services demanded in the economy equals the quantity supplied

Macroeconomics—considers the economy as a whole to see how choices work to create or destroy wealth over time within and between countries around the world

Mandatory spending—money that is required to be spent under current law

Marginal benefit—the additional benefit incurred as the result of an action

Marginal cost—the additional cost incurred as the result of an action

Marginal propensity to consume (MPC)—the percentage of each new dollar of income that the average consumer spends

Marginal tax rate—the percentage of each new dollar in economic activity that is taxed

Medicaid—a federal program that covers health care expenditures for low-income people

Medicare—a federal program that covers health care expenditures for the elderly

Medium of exchange—a devise such as money that facilitates a transfer of a good or service

Menu costs—the added advertising cost associated with changing prices

Microeconomics—studies individual decision making in a world of scarce resources and unlimited wants

Minimum wage—an hourly wage below which employers are not allowed to pay

Misery index—the unemployment rate plus the inflation rate

Mixed economy—an economy where both individuals and governments make decisions about what to produce, how to produce, and who gets the output

Monetarists—people who advocate that monetary policy be restricted to a proscribed annual increase in the money supply

Monetary economy—an economy that uses money as the chief medium of exchange

Monetary policy—an increase or decrease in the money supply by a central bank

Monetary rules—laws or constitutional rules that restrict the use of discretionary monetary policy

Monetize—to make into legal tender

Money market account—an account that pays higher interest than savings accounts or checking accounts, but that typically limits withdrawals and are less liquid

Money multiplier—1 divided by the required reserve ratio; it represents the multiplicative power of an initial change in excess reserves on the money supply

Money supply—the amount of money in circulation

Moody's—a credit rating agency

Multilateral trade deals—a trade agreement between three or more countries

Mutual funds—a collection of professionally managed stocks, bonds, and/or commodities

NAIRU—the non-accelerating inflation rate of unemployment, also known as full employment

NASDAQ—the second largest stock exchange in the United States

NASDAQ Composite—a stock market composite index of over 3000 components traded on the NASDAQ stock exchange

Natural resource—a material source of wealth that exists in a natural state

Neo-classicalists—economists who see prices, output, and consumption as functions of supply and demand in the free market

Neo-Keynesians—economists who have attempted to synthesize the macroeconomic theories of John Maynard Keynes with neo-classical economics

Net exports—exports minus imports

New York Stock Exchange (NYSE)—the largest stock exchange in the United States

Nominal GDP—gross domestic product in current prices

Nominal interest rate—the interest rate without any adjustment for inflation

Nominal wage—the wage that appears on a labor contract and does not adjust for inflation

Non-excludable—a good or service for which there is no way to prevent those who do not pay for it (free-riders) from consuming it

Non-industrialized countries—third world countries, which are countries with the lowest capital to labor ratios and are the poorest countries in the world; these countries are disproportionately located in Africa and Central America

Non-market transactions—production that occurs but goes unreported to the government, often because the producer and consumer are one and the same; for example, cleaning your house is a non-market transaction

Non-renewable resources—natural resources that, once used, are depleted

Non-rival—a good or service for which one person's consumption of the good or service does not prevent or limit another person's consumption

Normative economics—value laden economic analysis

North American Free Trade Agreement (NAFTA)—a regional trade agreement between Canada, Mexico, and the United States that eliminates most tariffs between these countries

OPEC—Organization of Petroleum Exporting Countries, a cartel

Open market operations—the purchase or sale of government bonds by a central bank

Opportunity cost—the next best foregone alternative

Pareto improvement—an improvement that makes at least one person better off without making anyone worse off

Partnership—a firm owned by two or more named owners

Pay-as-you-go pension—a pension where current retiree benefits are paid with revenues derived from current workers

Peace dividend—a decrease in military spending that frees up resources to be used for the benefit of consumers

Peak—the highest level of RGDP reached in a business cycle following an expansion and preceding a contraction

Phillips Curve—a curve that illustrates an inverse relationship between unemployment and inflation; the Phillips Curve was disproven with the rise of stagflation in the late 1970s

Physical capital—forms of capital that are not human, such as a machine or factory

Policy lag—the time it takes policy makers to develop a set of policies to address an economic problem

Portfolio—a complete collection of assets

Positive economics—fact based economic analysis

Positive sum game—a game where players can engage in win-win scenarios, such as occurs with voluntary trade

Present value—the current value of an amount of money received in the future

Production possibility frontier (PPF)—a graphical representation of all currently obtainable production options, assuming that all resources are fully utilized

Production schedule—the different production combinations available to a country at a specific point in time

Productively efficient—all current resources are being used in the production process; all points on the PPF are productively efficient

Productively inefficient—not fully utilizing all available resources and technology for production

Productivity—the amount of output produced by a given level of inputs

Profit—revenues less expenses; the portion of the sales price of a good or service that goes to the owner(s) of the firm as a reward for their entrepreneurship

Progressive tax—a tax where the average tax rate paid increases with income earned

Property right—the legal right to own and use an asset

Proportional tax—a tax where the average tax rate paid stays the same as income increases

Protectionist—someone who advocates restrictions to trade

Public good—a good that is non-excludable and non-rival in consumption

Purchasing power—the quantity of goods and services a dollar is able to buy

Purchasing power parity (PPP)—the concept that all goods should cost the same in every country in the long run

Quantitative easing—an increase in the money supply that occurs as a central bank buys financial assets from the private sector

Quantity Theory of Money—the idea that nominal GDP must equal the amount of money spent on goods and services, or in other words that the money supply is directly related to the current price level

Quarterly—Three months

Quota—a limit on the quantity of an import

Rational expectations theory—a theory introduced by John Muth that states that individuals make decisions based upon their expectations about the future

Reaganomics—a set of economic policies passed during President Reagan's tenure which include a reduction in personal and corporate income tax rates, a reduction in tax rates on savings, a reduction in the capital gains tax rate, and deregulation

Real GDP—GDP controlling for changes in the price level

Real interest rate—the nominal interest rate minus the rate of inflation

Real wage—a nominal wage controlled for inflation or deflation, it represents the purchasing power of a nominal wage

Recession—a prolonged period of overall economic contraction, typically lasting two or more consecutive quarters

Recessionary gap—a decrease in output and prices accompanied by an increase in unemployment caused by a decrease in aggregate demand for domestic goods and services

Recognition lag—the time it takes policy makers to realize a problem exists in the economy

Regional trade agreements—a trade agreement between countries in geographical proximity

Regressive tax—a tax where the average tax rate decreases as income increases

Relative poverty—a measure of income inequality where some people can afford to buy less than others

Renewable resources—natural resources that regenerate over time

Rent—the portion of the sales price of a good or service that goes to the owners of the land used in the production process

Rent seeking—engaging in costly nonproductive actions in search of profit (e.g. lobbying)

Required reserve ratio—the minimum percentage of a bank's deposits a bank must hold in reserves in order to stay open

Required reserves—the minimum amount of cash held in a bank's vaults; required reserves= deposits * the required reserve ratio

Reserves—cash held in a bank's vault or in a bank's account at another bank

Resources—inputs into the production process that include land, natural resources, labor, human capital, capital, technology, and entrepreneurship

Retained earnings—profits earned by a firm that are held by the firm for future investment

Revaluation—an increase in a government's official value of their currency

Ricardian equivalence—the theory that in increase in public debt has the same contractionary effect on the economy as does an increase in taxes

Right to work laws—laws that make membership in unions optional for employees

Rule of 72—the number of years it takes for a sum to double in value can be found by dividing 72 by the annual growth rate

Russell 2000—a stock index of 2000 large companies' stocks traded on the New York Stock Exchange

S&P 500—a stock market index consisting of 500 companies' stocks listed on the New York Stock Exchange

Savings account—a savings instrument offered by banks that pays interest. Money placed in a savings account has less liquidity than in a checking account, but usually pays a higher interest rate

Say's Law—"Products are paid for with products" such that consumption follows production

Scarcity—a condition where there is not enough of something

Search costs—costs incurred by consumers as they try to determine the most cost efficient consumption pattern to meet their needs and wants

Seasonal unemployment—unemployment caused by a change in seasons

Seigniorage—revenue generated by a government derived from the value of the currency being created being higher than the cost of creating the currency

Share of stock—part ownership of a firm

Short run economy—an economy over one business cycle

Social Security—a federally managed retirement system for US workers

Social Security Trust Fund—government bonds purchased with surplus revenues from the Social Security tax

Sole proprietorship—a firm owned by a single named individual

Specialization—focusing on doing a specific job well

Specialized—having skills or traits that are not universally held

Spending multiplier—a tool to understand the total impact on real GDP resulting from an original change in spending; 1/(1-MPC)

Stagflation—high unemployment combined with high inflation; a simultaneous increase in unemployment and inflation caused by increased cost of production

Standard & Poor's—a credit rating agency

Stockholder equity—the principle put forward by a bank's owners and used to open a bank plus any undistributed (possibly negative) bank profit

Store of value—a way to hold onto wealth

Structural budget deficit—the amount by which a budget would be in deficit if the economy were operating at full employment

Structural unemployment—unemployment that exists when people searching for jobs lack the skills necessary to perform existing vacant jobs

Sunk costs—costs incurred in the past that are irrelevant to current rational decision-making

Supply side economics—the study of how to increase the productive capacity of an economy to boost long term consumption and the standard of living

Tariff—a tax on imports

Tax base—the number of people or transactions that apply to a specific tax

Tax multiplier—a tool used to understand the total impact on real GDP resulting from an original change in taxes; 1- ((1/(1-MPC))

Taylor Rule—a monetary rule that pegs target interest rates by examining unemployment, inflation, and economic growth

Technology—electronic forms of capital or new tools used for production

Terms of Trade—the rate at which one good or service is traded for another. The terms of trade lies between the relative opportunity cost of the two counties trading

The First Bank of the United States—The United States' first attempt at a central bank, which lasted from 1791–1811

The Second Bank of the United States—The United States' second attempt at a central bank, which that lasted from 1816–1836

Tiebout effect—the movement of people between political jurisdictions to better align the government policies they live under with their preferences

Trade deficit—the amount by which the dollar value of imports exceeds the dollar value of exports

Trade surplus—the amount by which the dollar value of exports exceeds the dollar value of imports

Transaction costs—transportation, cultural differences, government regulations, and currency exchanges

Transfer payments—government payments to people in exchange for no good or service

Trough—the lowest level of RGDP in a business cycle following a contraction and preceding an expansion

Twin deficits—the budget deficit and the trade deficit

Under-consumption theory—a theory which states that the economy, if left to itself, will experience general gluts of output where consumers are unable or unwilling to consume that which has been produced

Unemployment (Unemployed)—inability of people to find a job

Unemployment insurance—transfer payments given to recently unemployed workers who are actively looking for a new job

Unemployment rate—the percentage of the labor force that is actively looking for a job but cannot find one

Unit of account—a measure of value

Unobtainable—not able to be produced with current resources and technology

Usury—charging excessively, or illegally, high levels of interest

Value added tax (VAT)—a sales tax applied to every transfer of a good based on the increased worth of that good since it was last exchanged

Velocity of money—the number of times the average dollar changes hands in the course of a year

Wages—payment to workers in exchange for their labor

Wealth effect—the effect caused by lower prices enabling economic actors to engage in greater purchases of goods and services with the same amount of income

Welfare—a set of government programs that provide assistance to the poor

World Trade Organization (WTO)—an organization formed to implement GATT that currently has 153 members

Zero sum game—a game where one player wins at another's expense

Index